Where No One Can Hear You Scream

Murder and assault in the Wicklow Mountains

Sarah McInerney

Gill & Macmillan

For my parents, for always telling me I could.

Published by Gill & Macmillan Ltd
Hume Avenue, Park West, Dublin 12, Ireland
with associated companies throughout the world
www.gillmacmillan.ie

© Sarah McInerney 2008
978 07171 4357 3

Type design: Make Communication
Print origination by Carole Lynch
Printed and bound in the UK by CPI Mackays, Chatham, ME5 8TD

This book is typeset in Linotype Minion and Neue Helvetica.

The paper used in this book comes from the wood pulp of
managed forests. For every tree felled, at least one tree is
planted, thereby renewing natural resources.

A CIP catalogue record for this book is available
from the British Library.

5 4 3

Contents

Acknowledgements

In November 2006 I wrote an article for the *Sunday Tribune* about the numbers of murders and assaults of women in the Dublin/Wicklow Mountains. I researched the article in a couple of hours, conscious of the deadline looming at the end of the day. The names of some of the women were vaguely familiar to me. Their stories, less so.

After the piece was published, I was asked if it would be possible to expand the article into a book. Without thinking about it, really, I said yes. With the arrogance of someone looking forward to a challenge, I thought about 'cases', not people, 'chapters', not death.

But over the last year, the women and their stories have become intimately familiar to me. Through the help of their families and the Gardaí, I was graciously allowed to trespass into their lives, and trusted with the task of recounting how they were attacked or killed.

And with each new story, I was greeted with palpable, unbearable sadness.

I would now like to thank all those relations who spoke to me.

I know that it took a huge leap of faith for some families to open up, scarred as they were by cruel and thoughtless coverage in the past.

I know that for all the people who spoke to me, recounting the stories of the violence inflicted on their loved ones brought them only fresh pain. I watched with awe and respect as each relation willingly relived the devastation caused to their lives in order to allow me do justice to the memory of their loved one. I was humbled by their bravery and their dignity. I thank them for their trust.

I was also helped enormously in researching this book by many members of the Garda Síochána. I would particularly like to thank Assistant Commissioner Martin Donnellan, Detective Sergeant Tom Doyle, Detective Sergeant Joe O'Hara, Detective Sergeant Alan Bailey, Detective Superintendent John McMahon, Detective Superintendent Christy Mangan, Detective Inspector Michael Canavan (retired), Detective Inspector Tony Sourke (retired), and many other gardaí who cannot be named because of the nature of the information they imparted.

All the staff at the Garda Press Office were very helpful and assisted me in whatever way they could. Also, I would like to thank the gardaí from the Retired Garda Association who very kindly gave of their time to help me track down some of their members.

Without the help and cooperation of all these gardaí, it would have been considerably more difficult—in some cases impossible—to really tell the stories of these women. For this, I thank them.

I would also like to extend my sincere gratitude to the staff at the National Archives, particularly Gregory O'Connor and Elizabeth McEvoy, who went out of their way to help me find important documents. Because of their assistance, I was able to write extensively on a story of murder that has never really been told.

I would like to thank the staff at the Dublin County Coroner's Office and the Office of the State Pathologist for their help in accessing post-mortem results.

Also, I thank Finola Kennedy, economist and author of *Cottage to Crèche: Family Change in Ireland*, who spoke to me at length about the historical situation in Ireland in 1925, and the small, significant truths about the life of Honor Bright.

I must also extend my gratitude to RTÉ journalist Barry Cummins, who gave me some invaluable advice and help in researching this book.

Also, my sincere thanks to all the staff at Gill & Macmillan for their help, and a special thank you to my commissioning editor, Sarah Liddy, for giving me the opportunity to write this book.

To all the staff at the *Sunday Tribune*, I commend you for your fortitude in listening to me talk about 'The Book' for one whole year, and for not once asking me to stop.

I thank all of my friends who listened to my worried ramblings, of whom there are simply too many to name. Particularly, I must thank Shelly Mullaney for the coffee and the hugs. Also to Alison for the tea, Sheena for the texts, and Nikki for asking me to write a book when we were ten.

Finally, to my family. The cornerstones of my life. Thank you to Daniel McInerney for proofreading chapters and reassuring me that everything made sense. To Tim McInerney for having the amazing foresight to send me a card when I needed it most. To Ruth McInerney, for propping me up when I slumped, for making large casseroles and buying small lunchboxes, and for being the best friend I've ever had.

And to Martha McInerney, for her texts, her love and her unwavering support.

But most of all, for lighting the candle.

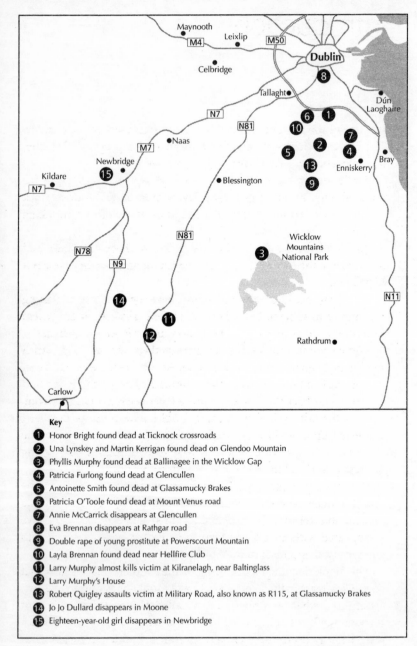

Key

1. Honor Bright found dead at Ticknock crossroads
2. Una Lynskey and Martin Kerrigan found dead on Glendoo Mountain
3. Phyllis Murphy found dead at Ballinagee in the Wicklow Gap
4. Patricia Furlong found dead at Glencullen
5. Antoinette Smith found dead at Glassamucky Brakes
6. Patricia O'Toole found dead at Mount Venus road
7. Annie McCarrick disappears at Glencullen
8. Eva Brennan disappears at Rathgar road
9. Double rape of young prostitute at Powerscourt Mountain
10. Layla Brennan found dead near Hellfire Club
11. Larry Murphy almost kills victim at Kilranelagh, near Baltinglass
12. Larry Murphy's House
13. Robert Quigley assaults victim at Military Road, also known as R115, at Glassamucky Brakes
14. Jo Jo Dullard disappears in Moone
15. Eighteen-year-old girl disappears in Newbridge

Map showing the locations of murders and assaults in the vicinity of the Dublin/Wicklow Mountains

Introduction

It is one of the most beautiful and most sinister parts of the country. The Dublin/Wicklow Mountains loom over the people of Leinster, unapologetically barren, spectacularly remote.

For centuries, the mountains have held a potent fascination for those who live in their shadow. By day, both locals and tourists flock to the rocky terrain, taking advantage of its many breathtaking charms.

But at night, the mountains are different. They are black and deserted and totally silent. They are a haven for anyone who wants not to be seen.

In recent decades the mountains have become an unwitting accomplice to some of Ireland's most violent criminals, hiding them from the world as they rape, attack and murder innocent women.

And it's not just the silence that attracts them. It's the earth, which so obligingly gives way to form a grave. As one detective pointed out, it's very easy to bury a body in the mountains. The ground is soft and pliable. It cuts back the time and effort a killer needs to hide his victim.

Over the last twenty years, many bodies have been found there, happened upon accidentally by horrified locals. In some cases, the mountains themselves have aided these discoveries, the soil having given way to reveal the remains of murdered victims.

Detectives strongly suspect that there are many more bodies to be found, hidden beneath a blanket of rough foliage, guarded by the inhospitable terrain. The remains of men and women who have disappeared without a trace, their poor beaten bodies thrown into anonymity, their graves unmarked forever.

This book documents just some of the murders and assaults that have taken place in the Dublin/Wicklow Mountains in the last century. From 1925, when a young woman called Honor Bright was shot through the heart at Ticknock, to 2006 when another young woman was viciously beaten and sexually assaulted at different locations in the mountains.

The book looks at some of the most high-profile murder cases in Irish history, as well as some horrific murders that never really hit the public radar. It notes the escalation of killings towards the end of the last century and the growing public concern that there was a serial killer on the loose in Ireland. Families of victims talk openly, bravely, about their loved ones and their loss. Detectives candidly reveal the inner workings of their investigations.

And through it all, there is one constant. The Dublin/Wicklow Mountains, looming large over the people of Leinster. Unapologetically barren. Spectacularly remote. A perfect, awful killing ground.

Chapter 1
The Murder of Honor Bright

The sun was rising over the top of the Dublin Mountains as labourer Phelix Reilly made his way to fetch the horses for work. It was just after dawn on Tuesday, 9 June 1925. A normal day for Phelix Reilly. Or it should have been.

As he came up to the Ticknock crossroads, Reilly noticed a young woman lying on the side of the road. She was smartly dressed in a dark pink blouse, a grey jacket and skirt, and a black beehive hat with a red rosette on it. She was lying on her back and her face was so peaceful that he presumed her to be asleep.

He had almost walked past the woman when he noticed that one of her black patent shoes was strewn on the ground some distance from where she lay. He walked over to her, and bent down with the intention of gently shaking her awake. It was then that he noticed a small trickle of blood running from the corner of her mouth.

His eyes travelled down to where more blood was oozing from her chest, through a neat hole in her blouse. He couldn't have known it then, but the woman had been shot through the heart, a perfect, accurate wound that had killed her instantly.

Reilly leapt back from the body, and ran the short distance to Lamb Doyle's pub to raise the alarm. Immediately the police launched an official murder inquiry and sent out an appeal for information on the identity of the victim. Soon, friends of the dead woman came forward. Some said her name was Lizzie O'Neill. Others insisted it was Lily. But most people knew her as Honor Bright.

After an initial inquiry, two obvious suspects for the murder emerged. The investigating officers from the Civic Guard gathered around a table and looked with dismay at the names of the possible killers—

one of them a member of their own police force, the other a respected doctor and police commissioner.

They then reviewed the information that had been gathered on the victim. She was a smartly dressed woman called Honor Bright, who appeared to earn her living as a 'lady of the night'.

A prostitute killed by a doctor and a policeman. For the fledgling Free State government and the newly established police force, it was the most calamitous of scenarios. Serious damage control was needed.

But any attempt to keep the news from the public failed drastically. Word spread with alarming haste, and on 2 February 1926, the Central Criminal Court opened its doors and was immediately flooded with members of the public, craning their necks to catch a glimpse of the key players in the already infamous killing. As the charges of murder were read out to a hushed courtroom, reporters scratched frantically on their notepads, recognising the scent of a sensational story.

In 1920s Ireland, when sex was wrong, doctors and policemen were revered and many people claimed that all prostitutes had left the island with the British, this case was quite simply spectacular. Thus began one of the most notorious Irish murder trials of the twentieth century.

For Honor Bright, it all began with an unplanned pregnancy. On 9 November 1920, a young unmarried woman calling herself 'Lizzie O'Neill' gave birth to a baby boy in the Coombe Maternity Hospital in Dublin. She named him Kevin Barry O'Neill, in honour of the ardent republican Kevin Barry, who had been executed by the British in Mountjoy Prison just eight days previously. There was no father's name on the birth certificate.

If Honor had still been living with her family in Co. Carlow they might have been willing to overlook her ruined reputation and she might never have found herself with a child to support on her own. As it was, the young woman had moved from her home in Craignaspidda, just outside Bagnelstown, at the age of 18. She had been living in the capital city for two years when she became pregnant.

She had settled well in Dublin, having found employment in Switzers on Grafton Street, a select clothing store that was later taken over by Brown Thomas. This was regarded as a very respectable, very sought-after job. Such an upstanding establishment, in fact, that they had no place for unmarried mothers, and after the birth of her child, Bright was forced to take to the streets to earn an income.

Even though the press was later to report that she lived at 48 Newmarket at the time of her death, records show that in the weeks before she was killed she had spent at least some of her time in a hostel for unmarried mothers at 76 Harcourt Street, a place that had earlier been used as a safe house for Michael Collins. The hostel was one of the first to be established by a man called Frank Duff, who founded the Legion of Mary to help unmarried women.

Shortly before that fateful summer evening in 1925, Duff became worried when Honor—known to her friends as either Lily or Lizzie O'Neill—had not returned to the hostel for a few nights in a row. He went around Dublin searching for her, and eventually found her swinging on the old chain fences outside the Shelbourne Hotel on St Stephen's Green. He pleaded with her to come back to the hostel, and she assured him that she would, but not immediately. In swearing to him that she would return, she said 'Honor Bright, I will', and it was this colloquial assurance of truth that is said to have led to her widely used pseudonym.

It was in the same spot, outside the Shelbourne Hotel, that a series of events unfolded on Monday, 8 June 1925 which would eventually lead to Honor Bright being shot through the heart in the Dublin Mountains.

It was one of the hottest days of the year, and that evening Honor was residing in the middle room of 48 Newmarket. She spent some time carefully preparing for her night on the town. With her bobbed chestnut hair, brown eyes, and petite five-foot four-inches frame, Honor Bright was widely regarded as a very good-looking woman. That night she chose to wear a dark pink blouse, silk flesh-coloured stockings, a slightly worn grey tweed skirt and jacket, and black patent court shoes with T-straps. She slipped a black velvet band over her hair to hold it back from her face, before covering her head with a black beehive hat with a red rosette.

In her pockets, Honor carried a few essentials for the evening—a pair of kid gloves, a hair comb, a powder puff and a box of face powder, Woodbine cigarettes and matches, and her purse. The police report was later curiously edited to show that there was also a 'Malthusian Sheath', or a condom, in her pocket. But this was not originally listed among her belongings.

Finally finished with her preparations, Honor left her lodgings accompanied by her housemate and friend, Madge Hopkins, known to most people as Bridie. At 11pm on Monday, 8 June the two women walked down the street towards St Stephen's Green.

They parted company at the corner of Bishop Street, and did not meet again until 1am, when Bridie spotted her friend near the Shelbourne Garage at St Stephen's Green. The two women wandered over to their favoured spot—the chain fences opposite the Shelbourne Hotel—and sat there together for some time, waiting for 'clients', chatting and relaxing in the balmy heat of the summer night.

Their conversation was interrupted when a little grey two-seater car pulled up noisily outside the hotel. The man in the car beckoned to them and they went over to speak to him. After a short conversation, the man said that he was going into the Shelbourne to get his friend. The women watched as he unfolded himself from the car, entered the hotel, and re-emerged with a male companion. They didn't yet realise that they had just met Dr Patrick Purcell and Superintendent Leopold J. Dillon.

For Purcell and Dillon it had already been a long, eventful day, heavily punctuated with sex and alcohol.

The two men knew each other through their work, and had had a meeting together that afternoon. During the course of their conversation, Dillon happened to mention that he planned to go to Dublin that evening to consult the City Detective Division about a case. Purcell said that he was also going to Dublin, and offered to give his friend a lift there and back. The plan was thus simply made and seemingly on the spur of the moment. The doctor and policeman travelled to the capital and, with interesting and apparently spontaneous ease, wholeheartedly launched themselves into the underworld of Dublin city.

Both men came from comfortable middle-class Anglo-Irish backgrounds, and were well regarded in their individual professions. Both later maintained that their behaviour and actions on the night of 8 June were completely out of character for them. Both were to plead guilty to soliciting prostitutes, and not guilty to murdering Honor Bright.

Dr Patrick Purcell was a well-respected family man, a father of two. By the age of 30 he had built up a good medical practice working as a GP in the small town of Blessington in County Wicklow. He also worked as a Peace Commissioner, carrying out medical duties on behalf of the police force.

His immediate superior in the police force was Superintendent Leopold J. Dillon, who was based in Dunlavin in the foothills of the Wicklow Mountains.

Dillon, who was younger than Purcell, was six foot tall, handsome and well built. He cut an imposing figure, a fact that was actually to work against him in the police investigation, as he was easily identified by witnesses who saw him with Honor Bright.

At 25, Dillon was still a bachelor. He had served time in both the British Army and the Free State Army and had then gone on to study medicine in Cork University. However, he didn't qualify as a doctor, and instead joined the Civic Guard, where he was very quickly promoted to the post of superintendent. In his relatively short career, he had already achieved a great deal and was on course for a successful career in the police force.

After the two men finished their meeting on Monday afternoon they went for a few drinks in Blessington before starting their journey to Dublin. En route to the capital city, at about 4pm, they pulled up outside the barracks at Blessington in Purcell's little grey Swift car, and approached one of the guards on duty.

Dillon asked the guard for a loan of two raincoats—a bizarre request considering the heat that summer's day. He was handed two blue nap coats and one soft fawn-coloured hat. At about five o'clock that evening, the pair called to the Railway Hotel in Naas for some more drinks, and there Dillon met a friend, from whom he requested a loan of a lounge jacket and a collar and tie. He was given a blue whipcord coat which he put on immediately, his transformation from superintendent to ordinary citizen now complete.

At about 6.30pm, the two men finally arrived in Dublin, having already consumed a substantial amount of whiskey. They went for dinner at the Bailey Restaurant, and then split up for a while, arranging to meet later at the Shelbourne Hotel. Dillon took the tram to Sandycove on business while, without any further ado, Purcell drove straight out to Donnybrook in search of prostitutes.

After a short time he picked up two women on the street and the trio went together to a pub in Donnybrook village. They stayed there for some time, before Purcell decided to move proceedings along. The three left the bar, buying a bottle of whiskey to take with them.

The doctor drove out the Stillorgan road until he found a secluded spot on the roadside. He left one woman in the car, drinking whiskey, while he took the other a short distance away to have sex. Afterwards he drove both women back to their respective residences in the city, and arranged to meet with yet another prostitute at the bottom of Grafton Street. After he had sex with her he dropped her home to Drumcondra before returning once again to the city centre.

It was 12.30am when Purcell eventually pulled up outside the Shelbourne Hotel on St Stephen's Green. He saw two women sitting on a nearby bench and—his sexual appetite still remarkably strong—he called out to them, although he later maintained that it was they who shouted to him. When they approached he told them that he was going inside the hotel to fetch his friend, and asked them to wait.

Purcell found Dillon snoozing comfortably on a chair on the upper landing of the Shelbourne. He shook him awake and brought him back outside to the Green, where Honor Bright and Bridie stood waiting.

Honor and Bridie watched the two men emerge from the hotel, one considerably taller than the other, and then followed them to where their car was parked on the Green.

Purcell immediately struck up a conversation with Bridie, and soon the pair agreed on a price for sex. They strolled away together, leaving Honor standing beside the little grey car, talking intently to Superintendent Leopold Dillon.

As they walked, Purcell and Bridie came across a group of taxi drivers who were waiting for fares outside the Shelbourne Hotel. Unprompted, Purcell struck up a conversation with the group of men. Suddenly the doctor launched into a furious tirade about how he had been robbed by one of the prostitutes that he had met earlier, and how he planned to kill her if he ever met her again.

Bridie and the group of taxi drivers listened in shocked silence as Purcell ranted about how he would recognise the girl who had stolen his money and possessions immediately, and how he wanted to murder her for her crime.

'I am after being done in tonight of eleven pounds,' said Purcell. 'What is worse, I have lost a silver cigarette case that I would not wish for twenty pounds to lose—a presentation case. Only I had this single note in my back pocket, where I keep my revolver, she would have got that too.'

On saying this, Purcell patted his hip pocket, where Bridie and the group of taxi drivers saw he had a bulky item.

'If I meet her I will do for her,' he continued. 'She wore a grey dress, had fair bobbed hair, was good-looking; I would know her, and if I don't meet her I will take out another and leave her in the country where she will not be found. My friend is a superintendent in the police. I have a Civic Guard coat on me at present. If she attempts to pass that cigarette case he will find it out. He could clear the whole Green of them with his revolver.'

In light of the fact that Honor Bright—a prostitute dressed in grey—was to be found dead the following morning, Purcell's extra-ordinary diatribe was soon to become morbidly significant.

However, on that summer's evening Bridie shrugged off the bizarre behaviour of her client and continued walking with him towards Hume Street, where the dark basements lent them some privacy.

Shortly afterwards, their business arrangement at an end, Bridie left Purcell on the Green and took a cab to Parnell Street, where she continued to socialise for several more hours, blissfully oblivious of the fate awaiting her friend.

Little is known about what happened to Honor in the hours after Bridie and Purcell walked away towards the gathered taxi drivers. For the most part, the statement Dillon later gave to police is all there is to go by.

The superintendent said that he and Honor Bright drove in Purcell's car around St Stephen's Green, at which point, he admitted, they had sex. Then he emptied out his pockets and gave her all the change he had—the royal sum of five shillings and a halfpenny.

As he began driving back around the Green, Honor Bright asked him to drop her to her house, a short distance away on Newmarket. He refused, saying that he was not the owner of the car and he couldn't keep it away from Purcell any longer.

Honor Bright stayed in the car until around 2.40am, when she spotted a taxi coming from the direction of Hume Street. She hailed it down. Dillon later fervently maintained that this was the last time he ever saw Honor Bright.

The taxi that Honor had hailed was driven by a man called Ernest Woodruffe, who knew the young woman from having seen her around the Green. When she got into the car it immediately struck him that she was upset and on edge. He asked her what was wrong.

During the court case he was never asked about her reply, or whether she gave any reason why she was upset.

Woodruffe drove along Merrion Row and then onto Adelaide Road. Just after they passed under the railway bridge at Harcourt Road, Honor asked him to stop the car. She got out and nervously peered back the way they had come. She smoked a cigarette and said that she thought they were being followed, looking anxiously down the road again before getting back into the car.

Her behaviour does not tally with Leopold Dillon's account of the night. According to Dillon, Honor seemed perfectly fine when she left him in Woodruffe's taxi. But clearly Honor was not fine. She was nervous and afraid. What had happened during her time with Dillon to cause such anxiety?

Neither the jury nor the public were ever asked this question, because they never heard about Honor's anxiety. At the inquest into her death, a barrister for Purcell objected to Woodruffe being allowed to relate his story of how the dead woman was in obvious distress just hours before her death. The barrister claimed it was hearsay. As a result, this crucial account of Honor Bright's state of mind was never aired in court.

After she finished her cigarette, Woodruffe drove Honor along Harrington Street to the corner of Clanbrassil Street, at which point she got out and paid him his fare. He turned the car around and drove back the way he had come. As he approached the corner of Harrington Street he met a car coming fast in the opposite direction. It was a small grey two-seater, similar to the one he had seen at Stephen's Green. There were two men inside. The driver was hatless, and Woodruffe believed he recognised him as Dr Patrick Purcell. The car sped past in the direction of Clanbrassil Street, where he had just left Honor, standing alone and vulnerable.

Shortly afterwards, Constable Burke, stationed at Terenure, was walking at the junction of Rathgar Avenue with Harold's Cross. It was around 3.30am when he saw a two-seater car parked on the Harold's Cross road. Two men and a woman were standing on the street, a couple of yards away from the vehicle, under an overhanging hawthorn tree. Guard Byrne saw that one of the men was about six foot tall, wearing a tight-fitting coat. The other man was somewhat shorter.

Byrne noticed that the woman was very animated and assertive and was speaking in a loud voice to the men. His antennae went up and he started walking towards them to investigate. As soon as the trio spotted him, they hurried back to the car, the tall man hopping over the side of the door in his haste. As the woman sat down between the two men, she began talking again in the same loud, assertive tone. The car sped off in the direction of Terenure before Byrne could get any closer. He didn't hear any of their conversation, nor was he close enough to positively identify any of the people he saw.

There were no more sightings that night of the grey two-seater car or the two men and their agitated companion.

At around 4.25 on the morning of 9 June, Jane Hamilton, a servant at Blessington Civic Guard Barracks, heard a motor car arriving at the station in the village. She was aware of the time because she had been tossing and turning all night, unable to sleep, and had heard the church clock chiming the hour.

A few minutes later, around 4.30am, Guard McCaffrey, stationed at Blessington Barracks, was woken by the sound of someone hammering on the outer door of the building. To his surprise, he found Dillon and Purcell standing outside, the little grey car parked behind them.

They walked into the barracks, Dillon making a passing remark that the lamps should be lighting in the dayroom. Both men asked McCaffrey to fetch them a glass of water, and Dillon asked him to get a motorcycle that was in the shed at the back of the building.

McCaffrey dutifully went to get the motorbike and when he returned, Purcell had already driven away in his car. Dillon made numerous attempts to start the motorbike, but finally admitted defeat and settled down to spend the night in the barracks.

McCaffrey went back into the dayroom to turn off the lights and lock up, and was surprised to find his own overcoat thrown on a seat. He hadn't worn the overcoat that evening, had not left it in the dayroom, and in fact hadn't even seen the coat since the previous day. Picking it up, he was further mystified to see that there were white stains on the coat and little bits of briar leaves attached to it.

At around 4.35am, Kathleen Purcell was awoken by her husband arriving home. She heard him carefully opening the study window and slipping inside the house. He prepared himself a simple supper of sandwiches and milk, before undressing and going into the bedroom. Kathleen Purcell remarked to him that 'it was a nice hour for him to be coming home'. The night had finally ended.

It was just three hours later, at 7.30am, that Phelix Reilly from Ballaley in Ticknock made his journey up the mountains to fetch the horses for work and saw Honor Bright on the road.

He thought at first she was sleeping. Then he realised she was dead. Within hours, Superintendent J. H. Reynolds had arrived at the scene.

There were not many murders in 1920—save those people killed in political warfare—and there were even fewer cases of pretty young women being murdered in remote areas of the countryside. So news quickly spread that a woman's body had been found, and within a very short time a large crowd of locals had gathered around Honor Bright's body, watching as Superintendent Reynolds and other detectives from Dublin examined the scene.

One of the first things detectives noticed was the lack of blood. A bullet wound to the chest would normally result in copious, violent bleeding. Yet there was no blood on the ground surrounding the body, and just a modest amount of blood spilling from the wound. This immediately led detectives to assume that Bright had been shot at a different location and that her body had been dumped in the mountains after she was killed. The theory tallied with the fact that no one living in the neighbourhood had reported hearing anything during the night—no gunpowder exploding, no sound of a woman screaming.

However, the discovery of a large fresh-looking hole in the road, just a few yards from the body, changed the police hypothesis. The hole was almost the size of an egg, and it led police to believe that in fact the shooting had taken place on the mountainside, and that a bullet had been discharged from a large-calibre weapon with enough force to rip through Honor Bright's body and puncture the road.

Reynolds took a detailed note of what he found on Honor's body, and his notes were accompanied by photographs taken by his sergeant. However, his deposition was later very curiously and obviously edited. In scrawled handwriting, Reynolds wrote the following on the original deposition document: 'The feet of body were about 2ft from ditch to side of road. I searched the pockets. I found in them a pair of kid gloves, a handkerchief, a purse containing one shilling and 5 pennies, also in pocket a half crown; a sixpenny bit and 7½d in coppers. A hair comb. A packet of Woodbine cigarettes. One "Players" cigarette and three cigarette butts. In the left hand of deceased was the coloured handkerchief produced. There was an end of cigarette in her costume, a scent bottle and some loose matches. A box of face cream. Photo Exhibit A. Other articles, Exhibit B.'

Some interesting changes were made to this report afterwards. The words: 'of face cream. Photo Exhibit A. Other articles' were all heavily crossed out, and new information was written in above the deleted words. The new sentence reads: 'A box containing a Malthusian Sheath was also in pocket.' (A Malthusian Sheath was an old type of condom.)

The discovery of a condom among Honor Bright's possessions was not mentioned in any of the news reports at the time, and neither was it brought up at the court case. It was quite obviously added to Reynolds's deposition after the original report was written—either by Reynolds himself or someone else entirely. What is not clear is why the change was made and whether a condom was actually found in Honor's pocket.

One explanation could be that, after the initial report was filed, the box of face cream was opened and found to contain condoms. However, Honor Bright's granddaughter believes there may have been a more cynical reason behind the edits. She points out that in 1920s Ireland a jury would have considerably less sympathy for a young dead woman who had a condom in her pocket than a dead woman without.

By Tuesday evening, Honor Bright had still not been identified, although there was talk among some locals that she might be from the city. It was hoped that the scar on her nose would help in determining her identity. Meanwhile, by the end of the first day of investigation, the Civic Guard was at a loss as to how or why she had been shot. The only thing that they had come close to determining was the time of death. They had talked to certain parties who had passed the cross-roads at one o'clock that morning, and who said there was no body on the road. The police therefore knew that the shooting had taken place sometime in the early hours of the morning, after 1am.

With the preliminary investigation of the scent complete, Honor Bright's body was carefully carried to the outhouse at Lamb Doyle's to await the arrival of the Coroner for South County Dublin, Dr J. P. Brennan, who was due the following day.

At the inquest, Dr Brennan immediately announced that, at the request of the police, proceedings were to be adjourned. He did not elaborate as to why this request had been made. It was the first clear indication that the authorities were already treating the case of Honor Bright with extreme care and caution.

The inquest was originally adjourned for a fortnight and then, at police request, for a further four weeks. Before it opened again, Dillon and Purcell had been arrested for the murder.

Just days after Honor's body was found, police had gleaned enough information from various witnesses who had been on St Stephen's Green that night to form strong suspicions about the two men.

Five days after the murder, Dillon was interviewed by the police and he signed a statement in which he admitted being in the company of Bridie and Honor on the night of Honor's death. The following day, Purcell did the same.

On 16 June, both men were interviewed again, this time in much more detail. They admitted to almost everything that witnesses had claimed had happened, but insisted that the last time they had seen Honor was when she left the Green in the taxi.

Two weeks later Dillon was officially fired from the Civic Guard before being arrested, along with Patrick Purcell, for the murder of Honor Bright.

It didn't take long for the first reports to appear in the newspapers: a doctor and a policeman had been taken into custody in relation to the murder of a prostitute. The Irish public spent a scant few moments absorbing the information. Then the entire country exploded with outrage, disgust and insatiable curiosity.

It was a massive body blow to the newly established and considerably shaky Free State of Ireland. The arrests came at a time when a notable majority of Irish people quite sincerely blamed the British for any immoral behaviour that had taken place on the streets in the past. To be faced with the reality that not only were there still 'doubtful women' in the country, but that a well-regarded doctor and a superintendent of the Civic Guard could have associated with such a woman—and perhaps even killed her—shook the Irish public to its core.

If Dillon and Purcell were convicted, they would face capital punishment. If they were killed, it would be an indisputable record of their guilt, and an embarrassing and shameful reflection on the morals of the newly formed Irish society. The Free State was already struggling to find its identity. For the police, the government, and the country as a whole, the case of Honor Bright represented a threat to the fragile society they had fought so hard to achieve.

The inquest, when it reopened, was packed. People travelled from all over Ireland to hear evidence in the National School in Sandyford, and a large number of spectators were forced to stand outside due to lack of space.

The Coroner heard from Dr Thomas L. O'Mahony, who stated that the bullet must have been fired from a distance of six to ten feet away, because there was no singeing of the clothing or the skin, and that the wound could not have been self-inflicted. Dr Jas Neary stated that there were no marks of external violence on the body. Honor's clothes were not ripped or out of place and she didn't seem to have struggled.

After examining the body, both doctors had concluded that Honor had been shot through the right breast. The bullet had penetrated straight through her heart and her left lung—accounting for the blood on her mouth—before lodging just under her left shoulder blade. The wound would have killed the young woman instantly.

The discovery that the bullet had not passed through the body and into the road behind Honor Bright brought the detective's earlier theory into question. There was now no reason to believe that Honor had been murdered in the area where she was found, and no explanation for the lack of blood around her body. However, this was never brought up in the court case.

Inspector O'Connell from the Civic Guard also gave some interesting evidence. He said that on 16 June in Blessington he was shown the blue overcoat borrowed by Patrick Purcell, the same coat that had been returned with a stain on the back, a little piece of briar in the pocket and some briar leaves stuck to the outside of the coat.

O'Connell visited the murder scene and examined the ditch towards which Honor's body had been facing. He looked closely at the briar bushes and found that some of the briar heads were fresh, and some were not.

On Thursday, 30 July 1925 a verdict of wilful murder was returned by the Coroner's jury.

The following day people flocked to Dublin District Court to watch as Dillon and Purcell were officially charged with the murder of Honor Bright. Both men were asked, on the conclusion of the evidence, if they wished to make any statement.

'I am absolutely innocent,' said Dr Purcell. His friend Dillon, standing close by, said: 'I wish to state nothing, except that I am innocent.'

Six months later, on 2 February 1926, the trial began. From early morning, queues of people gathered outside the Central Criminal Court, jostling and pushing for a better position, a better chance of gaining entry to the courthouse. Notably and unusually, there were several well-dressed ladies among the crowd.

The chief prosecutor, William Carrigan, began with a scathing opening statement that covered the main aspects of the case.

'You are dealing with a pair of moral degenerates who quitted their families and their responsibilities to spend a night of debauchery in the city of Dublin,' he declared. 'It is a hideous tale culminating . . . in the deliberate and cold-blooded murder of one of the unhappy victims of their lust.'

It was only in the pages of neurotic fiction, said Carrigan, that the jury could find a story more disgusting. The prisoners were men who had held positions of standing and responsibility in their district. Between them, said Carrigan, they murdered Honor Bright in the early morning of 9 June. He warned the jury that they would be obliged to listen to a 'protracted story of lust and crime', one of the most incredible features of which was that Dillon and Purcell had admitted everything that had happened that night except the murder itself.

He told the jury that Honor was 'one of those unhappy creatures who, not through choice, but through some cursed necessity was compelled to seek her livelihood on the streets at night'. He described how she was shot through the heart and killed instantly. 'Her death was so sudden that her features did not bear the least trace of distortion,' he said. 'Not only was her death instantaneous, but there was hardly a trace of blood.'

Having given a summary of Dillon and Purcell's activities on the night of the murder, Carrigan told the jury that they could not 'apply any decent rule of conduct to men like these'. He said he was not going to ask them to take one view rather than another. 'I simply say that by the devil's chance these men came along the road, saw this unfortunate creature in the early summer morning standing in the deserted streets and took her away,' he said. 'Having arrived at Ticknock what could they imagine happened to her? At the moment the poor girl was shot, she appeared to have stooped just as a woman would do, seized her shoe and took it off to use it as a weapon of defence when she was instantly shot. Her body was found lying with her left shoe beside her. It was the last and only chance of a defenceless and miserable woman when she saw herself in danger. You will be asked to hold without compunction that the evidence establishes a convincing case of guilt against the accused.'

The crammed courtroom was completely hushed as Carrigan finished his opening speech. The scene had been set.

Over the next few hours and days, the details of the night of 8 June were related to the stunned jury and public, as witness after witness was called forward to testify.

There were audible gasps in the court as Bridie and the taxi drivers recounted the murderous threats uttered to them by Purcell as he patted the revolver in his pocket.

When the doctor himself took to the stand he didn't try to deny most of what he had said, but insisted that it had been a drunken boast. He denied ever saying that if he got the girl who stole his possessions, he would 'do her in'.

He also said he had no revolver in his possession that day, explaining that he had left the house at ten o'clock that morning and that the only thing that he had in his hip pocket was his stethoscope, which he always carried there.

In his cross-examination Carrigan focused on this point. 'You stated that you always carried a stethoscope,' he said. 'Had you one on you the day of your arrest?' Purcell admitted he had not. 'Have you one on you now?' asked Carrigan sweetly. 'No,' said Purcell.

In his testimony the doctor insisted that it was most unusual for him to come to Dublin for an 'adventure' of the kind he had had that night. His original intention in travelling to the city was to have dinner, he said. He maintained that he and Dillon got into the car at 4am on 9 June and went straight home, and that he had not seen 'the deceased girl' after he had left her with Dillon that morning.

The question surrounding Purcell's revolver was also dealt with when Sergeant Reynolds told the court that Purcell had handed him an automatic pistol and an empty cartridge case after making his statement. The court heard that the bullet which was found in the body of Honour Bright could not have been fired from the revolver that Purcell gave the police.

Purcell's wife, Kathleen, compounded this evidence by saying that she saw the same automatic pistol in a drawer in their house at about 9pm on Monday, 8 June, which meant Purcell could not have had it with him.

However, Guard O'Sullivan from Blessington said that a few months before the murder, in January 1925, he had been to see Purcell and asked him to put in writing an application he had made for a permit to keep a revolver. While he was there, the doctor had shown him two revolvers.

Captain Edward Hornage, who lived near Blessington, also mentioned seeing Purcell in possession of two pistols. In the autumn of 1924, he said, Purcell came to his house for revolver practice and on that occasion he had two automatic pistols in his possession.

But even with evidence from two witnesses that Purcell had two guns, the second weapon was never produced in court, or compared with the bullet found in Honor Bright's body. And the seed of doubt had been sown among the jury.

The defence team took a two-pronged approach: they flatly denied that the men saw Honor Bright after she left Stephen's Green, and then spent the rest of their energies focusing on the possible guilt of the taxi driver, Ernest Woodruffe, in the crime.

The defence barrister, Joe O'Connor, blatantly suggested during his cross-examination that Woodruffe had had a sinister motive for driving around the city in the early hours of the morning, and that it was he who had driven Bright up the mountains and killed her.

The taxi driver was forced to deny this, and also to deny that he had ever been in the British Army or that he had a revolver. Pressed on this last point, he then admitted that he had bought a revolver two years previously but got frightened and handed it back the following day.

Unfortunately for him, and perhaps for the entire case, it then emerged that Woodruffe had lied in court. He had sworn that he hadn't taken his cab out on the town in the days after Honor Bright was killed. But on the day after Honor's body was found, Woodruffe had been spotted by a policeman as he was driving through the city. It didn't have any relevance to the case, but for some inexplicable reason, Woodruffe had lied about it. The defence barrister confronted him with the truth.

'What you have sworn here is not true?' asked O'Connor.

The gathered spectators collectively held their breath as Woodruffe looked miserably around the courthouse, before agreeing that he had lied.

'So you were out with your taxi on Thursday morning prowling about again?' said O'Connor, not missing the opportunity to press the point home.

William Carrigan sat tensely in his chair, watching his case take a massive blow.

For three long days, the jury listened to all the evidence. Finally, on the evening of 4 February 1926 it was time for the closing speeches. Joe O'Connor for the defence took to the floor and protested against Carrigan's previous description of the accused men as moral degenerates, before appealing to the jury with the following argument: 'Is it because they, men of education who had been medical students at one time, tiring of the dullness of village life on a warm June day, go on a spree, and fall victim to the two things that men have fallen victims to from the beginning of time—wine and women—that you are not to judge them by ordinary standards but to treat them as human vampires?' he said.

He went on to suggest that this 'girl of the town' had most likely been murdered by some sinister society that was trying to rid the city of prostitutes. With that final suggestion, the defence rested.

It was five o'clock when Carrigan stood to give his closing address. One reporter from the *Dublin Evening Mail* described the scene: 'The courthouse was packed tighter than at any time during the day. At the back of the gallery people were standing five or six deep, and it is doubtful if any of these could even hear counsel's speech, much less see him. But those who managed to gain admittance to the precincts of the court considered themselves fortunate. Outside the locked gates of the building surged a big crowd, which gave the police no little difficulty in keeping order. At every possible opportunity, they ran over to the gate and pleaded, in most cases vainly, to get in. Carrigan was presenting his case to the jury and during the hour and a quarter which he spoke, dead silence reigned.'

Carrigan gave it his all. He covered all the most pertinent and poignant aspects of the case, and ridiculed the suggestion by the defence that Bright was the victim of some political vendetta. Finally, he finished, and a restless little stir ran around all the people present before they settled down again to listen to Justice Sullivan sum up the case.

For over two hours, the judge addressed the jury. He concluded that in the eyes of the law, Honor Bright occupied the same position as the first lady in the land and it would offer her the same protection. The jury then retired from the box and the judge left the court.

For the first time that day, some of the tension seeped out of the courtroom as everyone turned to each other in relief and began discussing what had been said that afternoon. Some people began trying to make their way through the throngs of people to get outside for refreshments.

Three short minutes after leaving the court, the door of the jury box opened and the jury filed back in. People who had been queuing to leave stared in shock, before rushing back to their coveted positions. The solicitors and barristers came hurrying back, their robes and wigs still in place, and officials ran all over the place trying to inform all the relevant people while maintaining a semblance of order. Eventually, the judge sat and silence once again reigned in the court house. The tension was thick in the air as the foreman stood with the verdict in his hand.

The paper was handed to the Clerk of Peace who stood and passed his eye quickly over the jury's decision. He then announced the verdict to the court. On the charge of murdering Honor Bright, Dillon and Purcell had been found not guilty.

There was a brief, stunned silence before the judge told the men they were discharged. All hell broke loose. Purcell's father and brother rushed over and grasped him delightedly by the hand. People ran to the bottom row of the gallery so they could reach down and shake hands with both men. The doctor and policeman looked relieved and happy as they walked from the dock, free men.

Within minutes the *Dublin Evening Mail* went on sale with a 'Stop Press Edition' of the news. Every copy was eagerly snapped up. The following day every national newspaper led with the story. And then, silence. There was no more coverage, no analysis, no questions asked. The person who shot Honor Bright through the heart in the Dublin Mountains was never found. Or at least, never convicted.

Throughout the court case, no mention was ever made of Honor Bright's child, or what became of him. The fate of Kevin Barry O'Neill seemed destined to be lost in history, until two years ago an Englishwoman decided to find out who her grandmother really was. Patricia Hughes was not prepared for the story she uncovered.

'I always knew about her when I was growing up,' she told me. 'My dad had told us that she had been murdered and he told us about his foster parents. That was all he knew. I think he was probably scared to find out more. He was too frightened and upset to look into it. As a result, she was a sort of a myth in the family. We never even knew her name. We had no contact with anyone from Ireland, and we didn't even have any contact with other Irish families living here, because the first thing an Irish person asks another Irish person is where they come from, and that just brought up too many awkward questions for my father.'

Kevin Barry O'Neill himself didn't discover the truth about his mother until he was 21 years old. He spent his childhood being brought up by people he believed to be his real parents in 2 Catherine Street, two streets away from Honor Bright's home at 48 Newmarket. His name, in those days, was Kevin Magill.

It wasn't until 1942, when he was 21 years old, that Honor Bright's son discovered the truth. He wanted to enlist in the army, but to prove his age he required a birth certificate for the first time. That certificate said that he was the illegitimate son of a woman listed as 'Lizzie O'Neill' who had been killed when he was four years old. The cert also showed that Honor Bright had once lived with him in Catherine Street, but he didn't have any memory of her. 'I think he must have known a woman that was his mother, whether he knew it was her or not,' said Patricia.

Kevin Barry O'Neill died some years ago, but Patricia Hughes is now determined to find out what she can about her grandmother's life. She has done extensive research into the case, in preparation for a short book called *W. B. Yeats and the Murder of Honor Bright*, which she has published online.

In the book, Hughes suggests that Honor Bright was not a prostitute, but a 'kept woman'. In the course of her research, Hughes unearthed the deposition of Sergeant Reynolds, which had been edited to include a condom among Honor Bright's possessions. She believes this document is just one part of a myriad of inconsistencies which pointed to a deliberate attempt to sully her grandmother's name.

'I don't think she was a prostitute, I think she was a kept woman,' she told me. 'She was being funded by someone, and that is why she was well nourished and dressed well. That's also why she gave my father to foster parents, which was a very middle-class solution to her problem. The entire slant of the trial was aimed at convincing the jury that she was nothing more than a common prostitute and that she wasn't worth bothering about. For example, I didn't realise until very recently that the court was held outside normal sessions, so the judge was specially brought in during his holidays to hear the case. That cost money.'

Hughes is continuing to search for information about her grand-mother, and is currently trying to track down the details of the inquest. 'I haven't been able to find the file in any public library, and the Department of Justice have told me they don't have it. But it must be somewhere and I really do intend to find it,' she said.

Among the many new facts that she discovered in her research, Hughes also finally found a birth certificate for her grandmother, which reveals her real name.

Though she was known to her friends in Dublin as either Honor Bright or Lizzie O'Neill, her family called her Lily. This, however, still was not the name on her birth cert. She was called Lily to distinguish her from her mother, Kate, and her sister, Mary.

The true identity of the woman known as Honor Bright has been successfully hidden from history.

Her name was Mary Kate.

Chapter 2

The Murders of Una Lynskey and Martin Kerrigan

O ne death followed another. Una Lynskey and Martin Kerrigan. Both young, both abducted, both dumped unceremoniously in the exact same spot in the Dublin Mountains. In the space of just a few weeks, the lives of five families were destroyed.

The cases of Una Lynskey and Martin Kerrigan are the least well known of all the major murder investigations in the mountains. And yet the story of their lives and their deaths is tragically spectacular.

Despite a major Garda investigation, it was never determined how either of them died. Despite the fact that people were charged with murder in both cases, it was never known who dealt the killer blow in either death. Manslaughter sentences were handed down. No one was ever convicted of murder, and serious, persistent questions remained.

What of the distressed screams that were heard by numerous people on the lane where Una disappeared? What of the strange car driven by the strange man who was never found? Or the insistence of some witnesses that the men charged with Una's murder could have been nowhere near her when she disappeared?

Among the stacks of court transcripts, contradictory statements and halting confessions there is no clarity, only a muddy, potholed confusion. Taken in its entirety, the case raises many more questions than answers, the most pertinent of which is, simply, what really happened to Una Lynskey on the night she disappeared? And is it possible the truth has never been revealed?

It was 1971. The small farming community around Porterstown Lane, Co. Meath, was like any other farming district in Ireland.

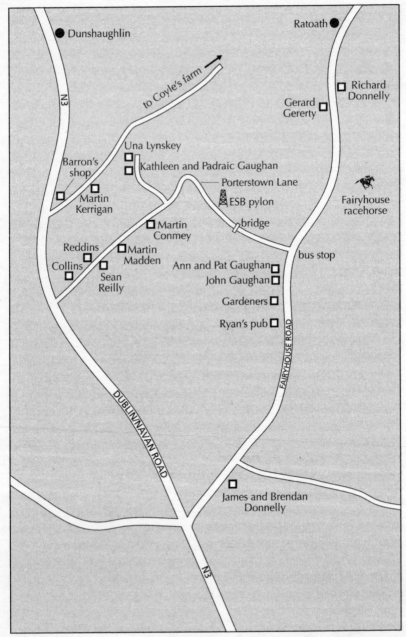

The neighbourhood of Porterstown Lane where Una Lynskey was last seen.

Everybody knew everybody, and aside from the requisite gossiping, everybody got along. If anything, the people on the lane were more closely knit than the average neighbourhood, as a large section of the community had emigrated en masse from Co. Mayo. Many of them even had the same surnames. In the wilds of an unfamiliar new county, the newcomers from the West instinctively banded together.

And so it was that Una Lynskey's family was well acquainted with Martin Kerrigan's family, and both also knew the Conmeys, the Donnellys and the Gaughans. All key players in the coming tragedy that was destined to rip their lives apart. All enveloped by a spiralling set of events that seemed to take on a life of its own.

It started on Porterstown Lane.

On a map, Porterstown Lane looks like the bottom of a triangle, linking the Dublin/Navan Road and Fairyhouse Road. The rural stretch of tarmacadam is lined on either side by hedges and fences and walls. There are no street lights. Halfway down the lane, there runs a short cul-de-sac. It was at the end of this little off-road that 19-year-old Una Lynskey lived with her family.

Born on 2 September 1952, Una was the fifth of twelve children. Her parents, Patrick and Winifred Lynskey, supported their large family by working hard on their farm. Like many of his neighbours, Patrick Lynskey was a native of Co. Mayo, having moved from Belmullet to Porterstown in 1939. Winifred, too, was a relative newcomer, but she had the comfort of having family nearby. Her brother, Anthony Gaughan, had also moved to Meath and had settled just beside the Lynskeys on the cul-de-sac. The two families were very close, and their children were the best of friends.

Like most of the young people in the neighbourhood, Una had started school when she was five, first attending the local Ratoath National School before moving to the newly built Rathbeggan School. At the age of 13 she became a boarding student in the Convent of Mercy School in Navan. She completed her Leaving Cert in 1970 and immediately set about looking for a job.

By January 1971 she had found work in the Land Commission Office on Merrion Street in Dublin city. Even though this meant a bus commute every morning and evening, Una was happy with her new job. Many young people in the community travelled to Dublin every day for work, and soon Una had established a permanent 'bus buddy' in her cousin Ann Gaughan, who lived on Fairyhouse Road at the end of Porterstown Lane.

It was also at this time that Una met her first boyfriend, Patrick Kelly. She was a bridesmaid at her sister's wedding, and he was the best man. A few weeks later, Una and Patrick went on their first date together.

For a year, the relationship was going very well. On their first Christmas together, Patrick gave Una a gold heart-shaped watch and the following Easter he gave her a signet ring inset with a red stone. He also gave her his own bracelet, engraved with his name. Una treasured the presents. The watch and ring were permanent fixtures on her hand, and when she wasn't wearing the bracelet she carried it with her in her handbag. She was besotted with Patrick Kelly the way only teenage girls can be.

Therefore, when he began talking about ending the relationship, Una was completely distraught. It was Sunday, 10 October, two days before she disappeared. Una cried throughout the night.

On Monday evening, on the journey back from Dublin to Porterstown Lane, Ann noticed that Una was very upset. 'I asked her how she got on at work and she said that she cried her eyes out all day and she couldn't work,' Ann said. 'She started crying on the bus and she said that "some of these days I'll be gone"'.

When Una spoke to Patrick the same day he relented and told her that he wouldn't end the relationship. Una then told him that she wasn't feeling well and that she wanted to go to a doctor. She had been complaining of a pain in her stomach for some time previously, but she said she didn't want to go to the local GP. Patrick said that he'd bring her to see a doctor he knew in Swords, Co. Dublin.

After a short consultation, Una emerged from the doctor's surgery with a prescription for medication and the news that there was nothing seriously wrong.

Happy to have resolved the problem, the couple went into the Harp Bar in Swords, where they had a few drinks. At 12.45am, Patrick dropped Una back to her house. He never saw her again.

The following morning, Una set off as usual to meet her cousin Ann Gaughan to get the Ratoath bus into Dublin. Ann was glad to find Una in better spirits. She seemed much more relaxed, and was uncharacteristically unbothered when they missed the first bus to the city. That evening after work, the girls met again in Store Street and got the bus home together. Their ensuing conversation was the last indication of Una's frame of mind before she died.

'She was talking normal, but did not appear to be as jolly as other evenings,' said Ann. 'Her mind seemed to be wandering or she seemed to be in a dream.'

On the journey, Una told Ann that—not unusually for a teenager—she wasn't having a good time at home, and that she'd decided not to talk to anyone when she went into the house. She said that Patrick wanted her to move into a flat in Dublin and that he intended to move out of home too. Then she confided about her visit to the doctor, and how he had told her she was run down and needed to eat certain types of foods.

The girls then started chattering excitedly about the upcoming Past Pupils Dinner Dance that was to be held in the Boyne Valley Hotel the following week. 'Una said that she would ring for the tickets that night,' said Ann. 'We also talked about going for a fit-on for new frocks we were getting made for the dance.'

Eventually the bus pulled up just outside Ann's house on Fairyhouse Road. Normally, Una and Ann's other cousin, Danny Gaughan—of the Gaughan family who lived just beside Una—would also have been on the bus. However, in a cruel stroke of fate, Danny was attending night school in Dublin that evening. This meant Una would be making the journey down the lane alone.

In her statement to gardaí, Ann estimated the time as being approximately 'seven minutes to seven'. The bus driver later said he thought it was 6.55pm. The bus conductor believed it was some time between 6.50 and 6.55pm. Four other passengers on the bus who watched Una and Ann alight all said that it was around 6.50 or 6.55pm. Only one witness, Mary Glynn, said that the bus might have been later, because she was waiting for it on its return journey to Dublin and she believed it was about ten minutes late.

The time was vitally, ridiculously important. A matter of minutes in the difference would mean that different people—different potential murderers—could have been on the lane as Una made her way home.

Unaware of the danger that lay lurking in her path, Una bid her cousin a hasty goodbye. 'We stood talking for approximately a minute,' said Ann. 'This was the shortest time ever we stood talking since we started going on the bus. The reason for this was because it was nearly the first evening that we felt the cold, and Una wasn't feeling well. When she was leaving me she put her hand on my arm and said, "I better be hurrying down, I'll see you in the morning."'

Una walked briskly down the road, and disappeared around the corner onto Porterstown Lane. If Ann Gaughan and the majority of the other witnesses were correct in their estimation of the time, it must have been around 6.56pm. Una Lynskey was never seen alive again.

It had been a very average day for Richard Donnelly, Martin Conmey and Martin Kerrigan. The three young men were good friends, and often spent their evenings together socialising or going for a few drinks in the pub.

At 23 years old, Richard Donnelly—known to everyone as Dick—was the oldest of the three men. He was also the most self-assured, renowned among his friends for his sharp, sarcastic wit and easy humour. Dick lived on Fairyhouse Road, close to Ratoath, and worked for a local farmer, Charles Coyle, a couple of miles off the Dublin/Navan Road.

At 6pm that evening, just as the CIE bus carrying Una Lynskey was pulling out from the depot in Dublin, Dick Donnelly finished his shift and drove his tractor out of the field. Behind him, his workmate Matthew Reilly followed in a second tractor. After about ten minutes, the two men reached the farmyard at Kilbrew, and Dick strolled over to his car.

At a time when only rich and important people drove big cars, Dick was very proud of his vehicle. It was a 1964 Ford Zephyr, a car distinctive for its large size, with the registration number JZE842. The Ford Zephyr was extremely similar to the Ford Zodiac. To the layman's eye, there were very few discernable differences between the two, except that the Ford Zodiac had four headlights, while the Zephyr had two. The striking similarity between the two models was later to play a huge role in the Garda investigation into Una's disappearance.

Dick's car was also remarkable for less noble reasons. It had originally been cream or primrose, but a rough paint spray had resulted in a strange honey colour which Dick himself referred to as 'amber gold'. The boot was held closed with a screw holder and the body of the car was so eaten with rust and rot that a garda later said it was in 'a dangerous condition'.

So when Dick sat behind the driver's seat after his day's work he was not surprised to find that it refused to start.

Matthew Reilly came across the yard and tried to help him get the ignition running, but it was clear the battery wasn't going to turn over without help. Reilly got behind the car and gave it a push, and finally the engine sprang into life. Calling out his thanks, Dick drove out of the farmyard. Matthew Reilly later estimated that the time was around 6.20 to 6.25pm. In his statements to the gardaí, Dick Donnelly said he thought it was around 6.30pm.

Dick drove half a mile down the road to where Martin Conmey was working in Coyle's field. It was an established habit that Dick would pick up Martin after work. At 20 years old, Martin Conmey was described by his family as a very average, happy young lad, who liked to go to dances and to the pub with his friends. Of the three men, Martin was the only one who actually lived on Porterstown Lane, a short distance from where the cul-de-sac veered up to the Lynskeys' house.

Martin had spent the day working alongside fellow labourer Raymond Coyle, pulling and loading Brussels sprouts in the field. When Dick Donnelly pulled up, the two men hadn't quite finished their work, and Dick sat in the car waiting for them to be done. Raymond Coyle later estimated that it was between 6.30 and 6.45pm when Dick arrived and left with Martin Conmey. Dick, too, said he believed it was around 6.45 or 6.50 when he and Martin left Coyle's farm.

At this point, the bus carrying Una Lynskey was only minutes away from Porterstown Lane.

Dick and Martin drove down the bog road towards where Martin Kerrigan lived, at a place known locally as 'The Bush'. The journey took around eight minutes, in Dick's estimation. Martin Kerrigan immediately came out of the house to greet his friends.

At just 19 years old, Martin—known to everybody as Marty—was the youngest of the three men. With his slight five-foot seven-inch frame, he was also the smallest. He lived with his three sisters and his father in a small farmhouse near the Dublin/Navan Road. Marty's mother had died when he was younger, and his older brother and sister had already moved away from home. His next eldest sister, Eileen, had taken over much of the running of the house.

'He was just a typical 19-year-old lad,' said Kathleen Kerrigan, Marty's younger sister. 'He was mad for motorbikes and going out to dances and having a few drinks with his friends. He had the long hair that was all in fashion at the time, you know. He was just a very normal young man, who enjoyed life.'

The men sat in the car chatting for a few minutes, discussing their plans for the evening, when Kathleen Kerrigan, who was 17 at the time, came out of the house and asked Dick if he would give her a lift down to the local shop to pick up a bale of briquettes. Kathleen later said she believed it was then around 7.05pm.

Again, the timing of this exchange was to become highly significant during the Garda investigation. If the three men were still at the Kerrigan household at 7.05pm, it would suggest that they could not have been on Porterstown Lane when Una Lynksey went missing. The clock was their alibi.

Kathleen Kerrigan had come to her estimation of the time through a few simple calculations. Like Una Lynskey, she also commuted to Dublin every day to work. Like Una, Kathleen had taken a bus home at 6pm, the only difference being that Kathleen's bus drove down the Dublin/Navan Road instead of Fairyhouse Road. Both buses generally dropped off their passengers at either end of Porterstown Lane at roughly the same time. On this evening, Kathleen Kerrigan believed she got off the bus close to her home on the Dublin/Navan Road at 6.50pm.

A local girl, Marie Mooney, who was on the bus with Kathleen Kerrigan, also told gardaí that she estimated the arrival time to be 6.50pm. Her father, Kevin Mooney, who was waiting at the bus stop to collect her, gave this time too.

After getting off the bus, Kathleen and her sister Anne went into Barron's shop for a few messages and when they emerged they met a neighbour, John Ryan, who offered to give them a lift to their house. The two sisters happily accepted the offer, and Ryan dropped them off at the small farmhouse at 'The Bush'. He told gardaí that he believed he picked the girls up between 6.55pm and 7pm.

Kathleen had been back home for a few minutes when Dick Donnelly and Martin Conmey pulled up outside and Marty went out to meet them. It was then that Kathleen realised that they needed briquettes, and she went outside to ask for a lift to the shop. She believed, at this point, it was around 7.05pm. The statements from the other witnesses seem to corroborate this.

At 7.05pm on the other side of Porterstown Lane, Ann Gaughan was settling down to her dinner, having said goodbye to Una Lynskey ten minutes previously. At this time also, a number of local people heard screams echoing through the dusk from somewhere on the lane.

Totally unaware that every minute that passed would later be meticulously documented and examined by teams of barristers, Dick told Kathleen that he had no problem bringing her to the shop. She went back into the house to get some money, and then hopped into the car alongside the three young men. They drove to Barron's shop on the Dublin/Navan Road, and Kathleen ran inside to get the briquettes.

She was served by Anastasia Barron, who said she remembered Kathleen arriving at around 7.05pm. Anastasia said Kathleen was only in the shop around three minutes. The time then, according to Anastasia Barron, would have been around 7.08pm.

But one person had a different memory of events. Sitting in a car outside was Garda Brian McKeown. He was waiting for a phone call from England to come through to the shop, and he was expecting the call before 7pm, so he had made a conscious effort to be at the shop before that time. He later described how he had driven past the Ratoath bus at 6.45pm, and said that it then took him three minutes to travel over three miles to Barron's shop, ensuring that he arrived there at 6.48pm. He said that three minutes after he arrived, he saw Dick Donnelly's car pulling up outside the car park, and watched as Kathleen Kerrigan ran inside the shop. The time, he said, was 6.51pm. Two minutes later, Kathleen emerged again, and Dick Donnelly turned his car back in the direction of the Kerrigan household. Garda McKeown said the time was 6.53pm.

This is one of the first examples of strongly conflicting evidence in the murder case of Una Lynskey. Garda McKeown, someone whose job automatically made him a reliable witness, insisted that he could not be mistaken with his times. Yet all the other witnesses gave statements that directly contradict his evidence. There is no explanation for this. It is one of the many questions that have no answer.

Dick Donnelly drove back to the Kerrigans' and Kathleen got out of the car. He then drove a short distance up the road, turned around, and headed back in the direction of Porterstown Lane. Kathleen Kerrigan, Martin Kerrigan Sr, Anne Kerrigan and Eileen Kerrigan all said in their first statements to gardaí that it was between 7.10 and 7.20 when Dick dropped Kathleen back at the house.

As the gold Ford Zephyr drove down the Dublin/Navan Road towards Porterstown Lane, Marty Kerrigan, Martin Conmey and Dick

Donnelly had cemented their fate. They were about to become prime suspects in the murder of Una Lynskey.

The lane and the surrounding area had been the centre of much activity that evening, with many locals having spotted a strange car in the area, and many people having heard cries of distress.

At 6.30pm, shortly before Una Lynskey got off the bus, Michael McIntyre, who lived just off Porterstown Lane, was driving to Ratoath to collect his brother when he came across what he believed to be a large black Ford Zephyr driving on the wrong side of the road. Michael took a good look at the errant driver. He later told gardaí he was a stout middle-aged man, about 45–50 years old, with a red face and going bald. Michael thought no more of the incident and continued his journey.

At around the same time, 23-year-old Brendan Donnelly (who was no relation to Dick Donnelly) had set out from his house on Fairyhouse Road to visit his brother.

As he drove towards Ratoath, Brendan passed a large car that he didn't recognise. 'It was either a very dark green or black in colour,' he said. 'This car was coming from the Ratoath direction. The driver I would say was small, black hair and he seemed to have sidelocks. He was between thirty and forty years of age. When we got past, I looked in my mirror and I saw the letters ZY. I could not say what number was on it.'

Brendan didn't spend too long with his brother, and got back to his house at around 6.50 or 6.53pm. On his way home, he passed the bus that was preparing to drop off Una Lynskey. He said hello to his father, James Donnelly, and went into the house and switched on the radio. A couple of minutes later, he heard his father drive out of the yard. He thought the time was '6.55pm, or maybe nearer 7pm'.

The bus stopped on Fairyhouse Road and Una set off down the lane, hurrying through the cold evening. Anyone else who was on the lane at this time suddenly became vital witnesses—and possible suspects—in an abduction and murder investigation.

At around 6.50pm, a group of young local people were getting off the Athboy bus on the Dublin/Navan Road. Among them was Paraic Gaughan, Una's cousin, who lived immediately next door to her in the little cul-de-sac. Paraic was extremely good friends with Una's two brothers, Sean and James, and spent a lot of time in the Lynskey household. His sister Kathleen had got off another bus from Dublin a few minutes earlier, and was already a few hundred yards ahead of him, hurrying towards home, eager to get out of the cold.

This left Paraic walking with three other locals, Mary Madden, and Michael and Jenny Reilly. The small group set off up Porterstown Lane and had walked about 400–500 yards when Paraic heard a soft noise behind him. He turned around and saw that a large car was almost upon them.

'It was that type of a car that it crept up on you, you'd know it wasn't one of the local lads, because their cars were noisy,' said Paraic. 'It was a lovely flashy car, dark in colour. At the time I thought it was a Zephyr but now I know it was a Zodiac. No one in the area had anything like it at the time. They were all small farmers, and it was only government people or wealthy people you'd see in a car like this. It was probably no more than ten yards away from me when I turned around so I got a good look at the driver. He was a middle-aged man, well dressed in a coat and tie and jacket. His hair seemed to be combed back off his forehead, he had a heavy mop of hair, brownish, maybe going a little grey. He looked to be a stocky man, not tall.'

Paraic watched the car drive up the lane towards where his sister Kathleen had run ahead. Kathleen was halfway home when she met a local schoolteacher, Mary Collins, who was out for a walk with her young child in a pram. As the two stopped to talk to each other, the large car passed them, going at about 50mph in the direction of Fairyhouse Road. 'I thought at the time of seeing it, it was a Zephyr or something very similar,' Kathleen later told gardaí. 'This car was long in the front and short at the back and I thought it was grey with a brown tint in it.'

Mary Collins also noted the car. She realised that it wasn't slowing down as it approached them and she quickly pulled her pram onto the grass at the side of the road. 'I'd say it was a Zephyr,' she told gardaí. 'I'd say the colour of the car was chocolate brown. I was unable to see in the windows. I was surprised as I tried to look in to see whose the car was. I think the glass in the windows must have been tinted.'

Kathleen and Mary continued talking for another two minutes, when Kathleen remarked that it was getting cold. The two women said goodbye and went their separate ways.

Just before 7pm, as Kathleen got to the turn-off for the cul-de-sac, a piercing cry cut through the silence of the night. 'It lasted for about ten seconds and it sounded as if somebody was very frightened,' she told gardaí. 'After about a minute I heard two more screams of shorter duration. [They] came from near the bridge on Porterstown Lane. The last two screams were much softer than the first one. I stopped towards the corner to look up the road and I thought of my brother Danny and Una Lynskey coming down that road. I looked in the direction that I heard the screams and I could see nothing. I may have stayed there for about five seconds. I delayed for a minute or two, waiting for Danny and Una. I arrived at my home at five past seven.'

Further down the lane, Mary Collins was approaching her own house when she too heard the cries. 'It sounded like a shout coming from a frightened person,' she said. 'I'd say about seven minutes would have elapsed from the time the brown car passed and the time I heard the shout.' Mary Collins believed it was around 7.07pm when she heard the cries.

Paraic Gaughan was still walking home when he, too, heard the screams. He instinctively looked towards the bridge, where he believed the sound to have come from, but couldn't see anything across the fields. The dusk was turning to dark.

Ethel Gardener, a local woman, was leaving her mother's house on Fairyhouse Road at around 7.05pm. 'Just as I was opening my mother's gate I heard loud screams coming from the Porterstown Lane or the fields nearby,' she told gardaí. 'The screams lasted for a good few seconds. I think there may have been three or four screams. They appeared to be made by a frightened person.'

Close by, Patrick Gaughan, Ann's father, was lowering his bucket into the well at the side of the road. 'As I was letting it down I heard a shout, which was loud, I heard a second shout, which was louder, a little time elapsed and I heard two more shouts, and they didn't last as long,' he said. 'I did not pass any remarks on the shouts as I often heard shouting in the evening with children playing down the lane.'

A few fields away, John Conroy was rounding up his cows. He believed he had reached the cow field at about 7pm, and he was just getting the animals together when he heard a girl's cry. 'It was a distressed sort of cry and lasted for about one minute,' he said. 'I had walked about twenty yards towards my home when I heard the cry again. It lasted for about a half a minute and died down gradually, note after note.'

It was around this time that James Donnelly set off to milk the cows. Unaware that screams had been heard from the Porterstown

Lane, he left his son Brendan inside listening to the radio, and drove out of the yard. He told gardaí that he believed it was about two minutes to seven when his journey took him up Fairyhouse Road in the direction of Porterstown Lane. As he approached the small junction, a large car dashed out of the lane into his path.

'It was a Zephyr or Zodiac, a dark green or black car,' he told the gardaí. 'I had to slow or I would have hit this car. I saw a girl standing up in the back with her back to the driver and I took it to be the man in the back seat was kissing her. She had shoulder-length hair and it seemed to be a little bit wavy on the bottom. I could not be definite of the colour of her hair. I saw the length of her body down to her knees and her coat did not seem to be very long, it might have been three-quarter length and it was darkish in colour. She seemed to be a light build of a girl. My impression was that the girl was overpowered with fright. This was only an afterthought.'

James Donnelly could not have known that his description of the girl was extremely similar to that of Una Lynskey. He could not have known that within an hour the entire neighbourhood would be on the lane, calling out for Una, searching in the bushes for clues to her disappearance. And yet something compelled him to look closely at the occupants of the car.

'The driver was between 45 and 50 years, reddish complexion, heavy build,' he told the gardaí. 'His hair was going light in the front and going grey at the side and back. He stopped his car when he saw me coming and he was very far out on the road. He turned around in the car, and he turned right to face me. I got a full view of his face. This man had high cheek bones, a long thin nose, ears were normal. He was wearing a grey-coloured jacket, I think he was wearing a light blue shirt. The car was an old type car but was well kept. I am not certain but I think it had four headlights on the front.'

As he passed by the entrance to the lane, James Donnelly looked in his rear-view mirror to see if the car would follow him. 'The first impression I got was that the car was turning for Ratoath and the last few seconds he turned it back towards the Navan Road,' he said. 'I went on towards Fairyhouse and there was no sign of the car in my mirror.' James Donnelly couldn't see the car driving away in the other direction either. It didn't seem to have emerged onto the main road. Did the car do a U-turn and, for some reason, return back down the lane? Another question with no answer.

At around 7.10pm, 15-year-old Sean Conmey was in the back yard of his house, milking the cows. Sean was Martin Conmey's younger brother, and as such gardaí later approached everything he said with the knowledge that he was a relation of a prime murder suspect. However, just five days after Una disappeared—before there was any indication that Martin Conmey was considered a suspect in the investigation—Sean Conmey made a very interesting statement to gardaí.

'I think it was about 7.10pm,' he said. 'From the back of the cow shed I noticed a car parked near the pylon on the Porterstown Lane. This car looked fairly new. It was black in colour and it looked to be a big car. About seven or eight minutes later I noticed somebody going around the car with a flash lamp. I cannot say if it was a man or woman as it was almost dark at the time.'

Sean didn't think anything more of the sighting until after Una disappeared. The time now was around 7.15—7.20pm. The gold Ford Zephyr containing Martin Conmey, Marty Kerrigan and Dick Donnelly turned onto Porterstown Lane.

When they reached Conmey's house, Dick stopped the car to let Martin out. Inside, Eileen Conmey, Martin's mother, had already cleared up the remnants of the family dinner. They had all finished eating at around 6.40pm, at which point Eileen had started to get another dinner ready for Martin. She put it on the range, covered with a saucepan lid to keep it warm, and then sat down on the settee beside the kitchen window.

'The lights were on in the kitchen and the curtains were drawn,' she told gardaí. 'I remember hearing the noise of the engine of a car pulling up at our gate. The engine of the car kept running. I then heard a car door banging and I recognised my son Martin's voice, and he said "I'll see ye". I heard the car pulling away and from the sound I believe the car drove away towards Fairyhouse direction. Martin then came into the kitchen and I gave him his dinner. I cannot remember looking at a clock, but I believe the time was between 7.15 and 7.20pm.'

Outside in the yard, David Conmey, Martin's father, was feeding the calves when he saw the lights of a car stopping at the gate to his house. 'I went into the house a couple of minutes after seeing the lights of this car and Martin was just after arriving in,' David told gardaí. 'He was eating his dinner. I did not check the time, but to the best of my knowledge it was between 7.15pm and 7.20pm.'

Having dropped off Martin Conmey, Dick Donnelly and Marty

Kerrigan continued up Porterstown Lane towards Fairyhouse Road. In their first statements to gardaí, made directly after Una went missing, Dick Donnelly described what happened next. 'About 150 yards above the bad bend from Conmey's I saw a car parked on its correct side facing towards me. I had to nearly stop as the car was taking up a lot of the road. I saw that this car was a Ford Zodiac Mark Four. It was of light grey colour. It was very clean and the bodywork was that of a new car. As we came up to the car, Kerrigan said "Look at the Zephyr." I said, "It's a Zodiac, there are twin headlamps on it." I had a look at the number plates and there was two noughts on it. I can remember that plain. I'm nearly sure there was a J in it. I had to drive very slowly to get past this car and I had to go up on to the bank on my left side a bit. I looked into the car and there was nobody inside the front. I didn't look into the back seat as I was watching the back of my car as I passed by. I noticed that there was papers and a brief-case on the front passenger seat. This car was completely strange to me, although I use this lane quite a lot. The nearest I can place the time I was passing the car is twenty past seven.'

Dick and Marty didn't see anyone else on the lane. They turned left on Fairyhouse Road and drove up to Dick Donnelly's house.

A local man, Gerard Gererty, was putting out milk cans on the stand outside his house on Fairyhouse Road when he saw a gold Zephyr go past. He estimated the time to be around 7.15pm. He told gardaí that while he didn't actually see who was driving the car, he remarked to himself that it was Dick Donnelly's vehicle. Dick was a neighbour, and he and his car were well known to Gererty.

When they arrived at Dick's house Marty stayed in the car as Dick went inside to have his dinner. Dick's father, mother, brother and sister-in-law were all in the house when he went in. He finished his dinner in ten minutes and then helped his brother Anthony put a headlamp unit into his car. Dick then got back into his own vehicle where Marty Kerrigan sat waiting. The two men set off again towards Porterstown Lane to collect Martin Conmey for their planned night out. Dick Donnelly believed it was around ten to eight when they drove down the lane. The Ford Zodiac was nowhere to be seen.

After collecting Martin Conmey, the men dropped by the house of another friend who lived on the lane, Christopher Ennis. He wasn't home, but they agreed to give his sister Evelyn a lift to 'The Bush'. After dropping Evelyn off, the trio picked up Martin Conmey's girlfriend in

Dunshaughlin before heading to Ryan's pub in Ratoath. They settled down for a few drinks, unaware of the huge furore that was unfolding on Porterstown Lane. Their lives would never be the same again.

It was 7.40 and Una still wasn't home. Her mother Winifred became mildly concerned and asked Una's 14-year-old brother Andrew to go out and look for her. Andrew cycled to the Gaughans' house on Fairyhouse Road. He was greeted with surprise by his uncle, Patrick Gaughan, who said that Una had set off for home almost an hour before.

Maybe Patrick suddenly remembered the screams he had heard on the lane earlier. Perhaps it was just an instinct that told him something was wrong. For whatever reason, even though Una had only been missing for a short time, both Patrick and his son John became very concerned very quickly by the news that Una wasn't home.

Patrick set off in the car for the Lynskey house, leaving Andrew to cycle behind them. John Gaughan ran across the fields to get his own car and then also went straight to the Lynskeys'. He arrived there at around ten to eight, and got the news that Una still wasn't home. He drove down to see Una's sister, Anne Reddin, but Anne hadn't seen her. He then drove to Una's boyfriend's house, the urgency of the search increasing.

Patrick Kelly had been in bed for about ten minutes when John Gaughan arrived. He told him he hadn't seen Una since the previous night. He too was extremely worried to hear she seemed to have disappeared after getting off the bus. On hearing the news, Patrick went straight over to the Lynskeys' house and when he found that Una still wasn't home he went directly to Dunshaughlin Garda Station and formally reported Una missing. The time was 8.20pm. Una had last been seen just ninety minutes previously. Already, people were out on the lane looking for her. Already, the gardaí were on the case. With such a quick reaction to her disappearance, whoever had captured and killed Una was placed under immediate pressure.

The word spread quickly throughout the local community, and people began exchanging stories of having heard screams and having seen a strange car in the area.

Soon a large crowd had gathered near the ESB pylon on the lane, and gardaí were gathering information about Una's last known movements. It was at this time that Dick Donnelly, Marty Kerrigan,

Martin Conmey and his girlfriend arrived on the lane again, having left the pub.

They were surprised to find the road was blocked with cars and people. 'There was a whole heap of them standing where I had seen the Zodiac parked earlier,' Dick said. 'John Gaughan came to Kerrigan's side and said that Una Lynskey was missing, that she didn't come home.'

Dick Donnelly told John about the Zodiac car they had seen parked on the lane earlier. After talking to the gathered crowd for about ten minutes, the men drove on. They collected Irene Ennis from her house on the lane, and continued their evening of socialising. When they returned to the lane later that evening they heard that Una was still missing.

At that point the men joined in the search. For many of the younger local people, the disappearance of Una and the resulting search was all a bit of an adventure. There was an air of excitement around the area, as people talked about what they'd seen and heard, and discussed possible scenarios. At this early stage, despite the large number of people searching for her, most people didn't really believe that anything bad had happened to Una. People didn't go missing in 1971, and they certainly weren't murdered. It wasn't until days passed without a trace of the pretty teenager that it started to sink in that something really serious might have happened to Una Lynskey.

Two days after Una disappeared a memo was sent out to all Garda stations asking them to be on the alert for 'all Ford Zodiac motor cars with the Reg. No. finishing with 00'. The memo directed that the drivers of such cars 'should be interviewed and asked to account for their movements between 6pm and 7pm'.

Both local and national media descended on the quiet country lane. Journalists found that they didn't need to knock on any doors: they could interview all the local people as they hunted in the bushes, fields and outhouses for any trace of Una.

By 14 October, all the neighbours had exchanged stories about hearing screams and seeing a strange car in the area. Both local and media speculation increased about the driver of the Zodiac, and his involvement in Una's disappearance.

At this point, a team of specialist gardaí unofficially known as the 'Murder Squad' was brought in to take over the investigation. They were led by Detective Superintendent Dan Murphy and Detective Sergeant John Courtney.

Everyone who lived in the area was asked to make a statement. Some people were asked for second and third statements in order to get more detailed descriptions of what they had seen. And so, when Dick Donnelly, Marty Kerrigan and Martin Conmey were approached by gardaí after the initial interviews had been done, they thought nothing of it.

'We just figured that it was because they'd seen the strange car on the lane, and that gardaí thought it was important to know more about it,' said Mary Conmey, Martin's sister. 'At this stage, all anyone could talk about was this strange car. It just didn't occur to us that the investigation might be focusing on anyone else.'

But at some indefinable point in the Garda investigation, the focus had most certainly switched. Detectives later admitted that they never found the man in the strange Zodiac, and that they had no idea who he was, what he was doing on the lane, or what happened to the girl that James Donnelly had seen struggling in the back seat. However, they said that every line of enquiry had been investigated thoroughly, and they had followed the evidence to find their prime suspects.

In the course of taking statements from locals, two witnesses had told gardaí that they saw Dick Donnelly's car driving away from Fairyhouse Road towards the Dublin/Navan Road around the time Una disappeared. This directly contradicted the evidence given by the three men. Even though there were a number of other statements backing up the evidence of the men, the anomaly was enough for the detectives' spotlight to move away from the strange Ford Zodiac and shine directly upon Dick Donnelly, Martin Conmey and Marty Kerrigan.

It was almost two weeks after Una went missing when the Murder Squad descended on the three men simultaneously and asked them to come to Trim Garda Station for further questioning. It was a carefully planned and successful operation and within an hour all three men were in separate rooms in the station, being questioned closely about their movements on the night Una Lynskey went missing.

They were brought in at 10pm on Monday evening and not released until Wednesday night. By the time they left the station, both Martin Conmey and Marty Kerrigan had made some sort of confession to killing Una Lynskey. Dick Donnelly had not. What happened in those intervening 48 hours has been the source of much contention ever since.

A few things are agreed by both sides. In the time between Martin Conmey being brought in at 10pm on Monday night to him making his first signed confession at around 7.30pm the following evening, he had been questioned constantly and had had no sleep. Considering he was brought into the station after a full day's work, this meant he had not slept for around thirty-six hours when he signed his statement. Marty Kerrigan was also questioned constantly, he too got very little sleep, and he too signed a confession—at 1.05 on Wednesday morning.

Dick Donnelly, meanwhile, was interrogated from the time he went into the station until 7am the following morning. The interrogation resumed again at 11.30am on Tuesday and continued without interruption until 5am on Wednesday morning. Dick, however, left the station having still refused to admit that he ever saw Una on the lane.

That is about where the agreement ends. During their forty-eight hours at the barracks, all three men said they were physically and mentally abused by the gardaí. Every garda who was present at the time vehemently denies this.

It started with Martin Conmey, who was initially interviewed by Detective Sergeant John Courtney and Garda Brian Gildea. During the court case, Martin said that as soon as he walked into the small interview room the casual friendliness of the gardaí changed, and Garda Gildea immediately started calling him a murderer and saying that 'the game was up'. He described how Gildea banged the table with his fists and gritted his teeth at him.

'I felt like I was going to get hammered to death inside in the barracks,' said Martin later. 'I was frightened and upset by the way they were carrying on.'

However, Garda Gildea denied that he had attempted to intimidate Martin Conmey. He said he didn't call him a murderer, but admitted that he may have 'tapped' on the table a few times to emphasise a point. He said that was the extent of any aggressive behaviour.

Martin stuck to his original statement, saying that he and the other two men had arrived on the lane from the Dublin/Navan Road direction and had not seen Una at all that evening. After four hours of questioning, having made no dent in Martin's statement, Gildea and Courtney left and Inspector Hubert Reynolds came in to talk to Martin. The young man said he immediately felt more at ease because Reynolds seemed to be much friendlier than Garda Gildea.

However, he said that after some time, Reynolds, too, appeared to get 'fed up' and started pressuring him to tell him the truth, saying that if he didn't he would 'let the other two back into you again'. Inspector Reynolds denied saying this.

Martin said that he then became very frightened and upset because he was afraid of Garda Gildea. He finally said that he had seen Una Lynskey that evening. He said that they met Una just at the bridge on Portwerstown Lane. Dick asked her if she wanted a lift, and Marty Kerrigan opened the passenger door to let her in. Una sat in the front seat alongside Marty Kerrigan and Dick Donnelly.

Dick drove the car towards Una's house but passed the turn for the cul-de-sac. As they approached the Dublin/Navan Road end of the lane, Martin said Una began to shout and asked, 'Where are you taking me?' Nobody answered. Una then started trying to get out of the car, and Marty Kerrigan caught her hand and she fell over with her face against the glass. Una then went limp. At that point they had reached the junction at the Dublin/Navan Road, and Dick Donnelly told Martin to get out of the car. He did so, and then walked back the lane to his house.

As soon as he was finished speaking, Inspector Reynolds asked Martin Conmey if he would make a written statement about what he had said. Martin said no, that he didn't want it written down. He then said, 'What would happen to me if I made a statement and told you lies?' Inspector Reynolds asked him if he had been telling lies, and Martin said no, that what he had just said was true.

Inspector Reynolds said then that he just wanted Martin to tell him the truth, at which point Martin started pulling at his hair with his two hands. He said 'I want to tell you the truth, but I can't, I can't.'

When he was asked in court what he meant by this, Martin Conmey said: 'I can't explain the way I felt that time. I knew it was wrong, that it was lies, like.' In court, Martin said repeatedly that everything he had said to Inspector Reynolds was a lie, that he was just trying to say what they wanted him to say so that they'd let him go.

Inspector Reynolds then left the room. When he returned a short time later, Martin Conmey immediately told him that what he had said was not correct: that he had not seen Una at all that evening.

He was left alone after that for a short while, and then Garda Gildea came back into the room along with Detective Sergeant John Courtney. Martin said in court that Garda Gildea 'was even rougher looking and had more of a vicious look on his face' when he returned.

'I was sitting down at the table at this time,' he said. 'Garda Gildea dragged me out of the chair, pushed the table out of the way and pulled me out in the middle of the floor and said "Are you going to tell me?" I said my first statement was right and he got vicious and he hit my right eye. He repeated the same question again. I said my first statement was right. He shook me. I fell to the ground. I couldn't get up and he lifted me up by the hair and pulled me up by my left side lock. The hair gave away in his hand. I didn't know what I was doing I was that frightened. I was never in a barracks before, I never knew what Guards could do—that they could treat people like that.'

When he was questioned in court, Garda Gildea categorically denied any of this abuse. He said at no time did he ill-treat Martin Conmey, punch him or grab him by the hair. The evidence of all the other gardaí backed this up—none of them witnessed any physical or mental abuse or aggressive behaviour of any type.

Shortly after being interviewed by Garda Gildea, at around 7.30pm on Tuesday evening, Martin Conmey agreed to make a written statement confessing to having abducted Una on the night she went missing.

In his statement, Martin repeated what he had told Inspector Reynolds. Later, in court, he said that the statement was written through a combination of the gardaí asking him questions and him agreeing to whatever they said. The gardaí who were present categorically deny this.

In whatever way the statement came to be written, it is clear that some parts of it were patently untrue. Martin said that he and Dick Donnelly had driven from Coyle's farm up behind Porterstown Lane and had come down into Ratoath village. There, they came across Marty Kerrigan who was sitting on his blue scooter outside Maher's pub. On seeing his two friends, Marty Kerrigan got in the car with them. They then drove down Fairyhouse Road and turned right onto the lane, where they met Una Lynskey.

All of the above was later accepted as untrue by the gardaí. A huge number of witnesses—including Garda McKeown—had seen the three men on the other side of Porterstown Lane, which meant there was no way they could have picked up Marty in Ratoath. And yet, inexplicably, aspects of this untrue statement later popped up in the statement of someone who was not even present that night in the garda station—John Gaughan, Una's cousin.

In describing what he saw on the evening Una disappeared, John

Gaughan said he met Marty Kerrigan in Ratoath at around 6.20pm, when he was on his way home from work. 'About a hundred yards on the Ratoath side of the national school we met Martin Kerrigan of "The Bush",' said John Gaughan. 'He was riding a blue scooter. Martin Conmey of Porterstown previously owned this bicycle. He was on his own and driving towards Ratoath village. The bicycle was very noisy. I'm not sure if anything was said about Kerrigan's presence on the road. Kerrigan was wearing a brown jacket. He was not wearing either a coat, helmet or gloves.'

There was never any explanation as to why or how John Gaughan had said this in his statement when it could not have happened. Certainly, it would have been a useful sighting to the gardaí if Martin Conmey's first confession had stood up to scrutiny—a second witness confirming what Martin had said. But Martin's statement, however it came to be written, wasn't true. So why did John Gaughan say what he did?

He wasn't questioned about it by the defence team during the court case. However, when he was being examined by the prosecution there was a very curious exchange between him and the barrister Patrick Smyth, in which they talk about a 'Garda Martin Corrigan' being in Ratoath on a scooter.

'Earlier that evening did you meet Garda Martin Corrigan?' asks Patrick Smyth, prosecutor.

'Yes,' says John Gaughan.

'Can you remember when that was?'

'It would have been between a quarter and twenty past six. I was on my way home from work and I met him about three hundred yards on the Ratoath side of Fairyhouse Road. He was going towards Ratoath.'

'What way was he travelling?'

'He was on a small motor bike, or scooter.'

This entire exchange is extremely strange. First, the local people were not familiar with any Garda Martin Corrigan working in the area at the time. Second, John Gaughan makes no mention of seeing a Garda Martin Corrigan on a scooter in any of his statements. And yet, when he is asked about it by the prosecutor, he doesn't seem surprised and answers fluidly.

The issue of the mysterious Garda Martin Corrigan on his scooter was not noticed by the defence team, and the question of John

Gaughan having seen Martin Kerrigan on his scooter was never brought up by either side. It is, at the very least, perplexing. To this day, the only mention of either sighting lies buried in court documents in the National Archives.

In addition to what he had told Inspector Reynolds earlier, detectives said that Martin Conmey also told them that the day after Una disappeared he was worried that she might not be all right. He approached Dick Donnelly and asked him what had happened to Una after they dropped him off at the end of the lane. 'She is not all right,' Dick replied, 'Myself and Kerrigan took her to Clonee and went out the Lucan Road and hid her at the railway bridge near Lucan.'

The detectives, unsurprisingly, took this admission very seriously. Later that evening, close to midnight, Martin Conmey and Marty Kerrigan were brought into the same room. Detectives told Martin Conmey to tell Marty Kerrigan what he had been saying earlier.

'Do you remember Richard Donnelly telling us that he had hidden Una Lynskey at a bridge near Lucan?' said Martin Conmey.

Marty Kerrigan hesitated and Martin Conmey repeated the question two more times, saying something like: 'Martin, you must remember that.'

Finally, Marty Kerrigan said yes, he did remember. He went on to make a statement at 1.05am on Wednesday. He told gardaí that he and Dick Donnelly had driven out to a bridge between Clonee and Lucan. However, Marty said it was he, not Dick, who had lifted Una's body out of the car and laid her in the bushes under the bridge.

Over the course of his detention in the station, Marty Kerrigan also told gardaí that he and Dick had driven Una to Rathbeggan and left her at a tree near a wood there. Then his story changed again and he said that they had left her in a pond.

It is worth noting that Una's body was not found in any of the areas the men talk about in their statements. And nowhere in any of their confessions do they reveal how Una died.

After making these statements, both Martin Conmey and Marty Kerrigan were mostly left alone for a few hours. Detectives now had to focus on the final corner of the triangle. Because in another room in the building, Dick Donnelly was steadfastly refusing to admit that he had seen Una on the lane that evening.

He was submitted to intense interrogation from the investigating officers. During his time in the station, Dick said he was badly beaten by Garda Brian Gildea. He said he was repeatedly punched in the head and stomach as the garda asked the question: 'Where is Una Lynskey?' This was strongly denied by Garda Gildea, who said he wasn't even in the room with Dick Donnelly at the time of the alleged assault.

When Dick still hadn't made any admissions by Wednesday afternoon, he said that Garda Gildea came into the room on his own. 'He said "Where is she?"' Dick recalled during the trial. 'I said, "I don't know where she is." "Now," he said, "you'll tell me now." And he picked up the poker.'

Dick went on to describe how Garda Gildea then hit him on the back with the poker he had taken from the fireplace.

The court later heard evidence from Dr John Clarke, who treated Dick Donnelly on the day after he left the station. Dr Clarke told the judge that he found four abrasions on the inside of Dick's left arm. There was an area of bruising fourteen inches long and two inches wide beneath his left shoulder blade. Over the ribs there was an area of reddish bruising. Above the right shoulder blade there was an area of bruising. His right jaw joint was swollen and tender. And in both ears there was haematoma of the ear lobes. 'They were bluey-blacky and obvious to anybody looking at them,' said Dr Clarke of Dick's ears.

Asked how the injuries were likely to have been caused, Dr Clarke replied: 'As a result of blows or probably by means of fists and probably the long red marks on his chest were caused by some long, blunt instrument. I would say they had been caused anytime between a couple of hours to maybe twenty-four to thirty-six hours previously.'

However, a stream of garda witnesses denied that these injuries had been caused to Dick Donnelly during his time in garda custody. They pointed to the fact that he had been out socialising the night before he was taken to the station. They said he was refused entrance at the door to the dancehall and that he had tried to burst his way through the door, before getting into a fight involving about twenty people at the dance. The gardaí believed this was how he had sustained his injuries. Dick Donnelly said he hadn't seen, or been involved in, any such row.

It had taken until Tuesday for the young men's families to realise that they were being questioned in Trim Garda Station. They visited them immediately and later said they were shocked at their physical and mental condition. Marty Kerrigan's family said that they found him almost naked, curled in a ball on the floor of his cell and deeply traumatised. Gardaí denied this.

In all the time the three men were at the station, they were not at any time formally cautioned. The gardaí said this was because they were not under arrest and that they were free to leave at any time over the forty-eight hours they were in the station, but they did not ask to do so.

This contention does not seem to tally with the fact that, having seen Marty in the station, the Kerrigan family applied for a Habeas Corpus: an official court order that would determine whether the gardaí had lawful authority to hold him in custody. It seems reasonable to assume that if Marty Kerrigan could have left the station at any time, there would have been no need for his family to apply for this order.

In any case, shortly after the application was lodged, the three men were released. Martin Conmey was the first to leave the station, and his father drove him home. The other two men were let go a little later, but they had no mode of transport to travel the twenty miles back to their homes.

Gardaí later said that they didn't drop them home because they thought they had got a lift. The men walked thirteen miles in the dark before they managed to hitch a ride with a neighbour.

All of the families and friends of the young men later said they were shocked at their physical condition. Mary Conmey, Martin's sister, recalled the scene when Martin and Dick arrived to her house.

'I remember the kitchen with all these people in it and Martin was sitting at the kitchen table and his face was so white. It was all swollen but he was pale underneath it and patches of hair were missing. His whole self seemed to have changed. He just looked stunned or shocked, like he didn't know what was going on.

'I couldn't stop looking at Dick Donnelly's ears. They were completely blue and black. I'd never seen anything like it. They just looked so strange that I couldn't stop staring at them. It was a very frightening scene, even though we were sitting in my own house. I just kept thinking that the gardaí were supposed to be there to protect us and find the person who had taken Una. And then I'd look at Dick's ears and it was just so frightening.'

However, after the court case a full internal Garda investigation into the interrogation of the three men found that no physical abuse had occurred at the station. In his report to the Garda Commissioner, Chief Superintendent R. Cottrell said: 'I am satisfied that all concerned in the investigation into the death of Miss Una Lynskey and the taking of statements in reference to that matter acted in a proper manner towards the persons in custody. I am satisfied that the gardaí did not behave in an untoward manner in their dealings with the suspects questioned and consequently find no substance in the allegations made against them.'

Even though they knew that the men had signed statements, the families were still not overly worried. 'No one realised the importance of it, because we figured that if Una turned up then it would be all over and the truth would come out,' said Mary Conmey.

However, as the news reached the local community that the three men had been held for such a long period of time, rumours began to abound about their involvement in Una's disappearance. The Lynskey family, in particular, appeared to have received sufficient information to convince them that the three men had had something to do with Una's abduction.

Over the following weeks, the Conmeys, Kerrigans and Donnellys all became accustomed to cars driving slowly past their houses at night, gunshots being fired in the air, and the word 'Murderer' being painted on the roads outside their houses. The families made complaints to the Gardaí about the harassment but it continued nonetheless.

Then, two months after she had disappeared, Una Lynskey's body was found in the Dublin Mountains.

Farmer James Williams was cleaning a drain on the road at Glendu on Friday, 10 December 1971 when he noticed some bushes in an area where he knew that they should not be.

'I decided to have a closer look,' Williams told gardaí. 'I believed that there may have been a dead sheep buried there.'

Williams got a shovel and pushed the bushes back, revealing a layer of rotten felt and an old grate. He removed the felt and was startled to find a human skull. He informed gardaí immediately.

The State Pathologist, Professor Maurice Hickey, was called. He found that decomposition was at a very advanced stage. However, he could determine that the skeleton was that of a female who had been five-foot two-inches in height. The body was fully clothed in a coat, cardigan, dress, slip, pants, tights and bra. All the garments appeared to be in their proper position.

Hickey found that none of the bones of the body had been broken, which suggested that the woman had not been hit by a car. The small bones around the neck had not been fractured, as would often happen in the case of strangulation. Because of the stage of decomposition of the body, Hickey said that he was unable to determine the cause of death.

He also found a heart-shaped watch on the wrist, and a gold ring with a red stone on the ring finger of the right hand. The treasured presents of a young girl in love. The jewellery helped to make a positive identification, and gardaí were then sure that they had at last found the body of Una Lynskey. They made the journey to Porterstown Lane to break the news.

The word spread quickly and the underlying tension in the community now became thick in the air. There was no more talk of a missing woman: Una Lynskey had been killed, and her family were very angry about it. Apart from the interrogation of the three men many weeks previously, the investigation didn't seem to be going anywhere. No one had been charged.

Despite the insistence of Dick Donnelly, Martin Conmey and Marty Kerrigan that they had nothing to do with Una's death, the Lynskeys were convinced otherwise. They were growing increasingly frustrated that the three people they believed had murdered Una continued to walk free around the community. Their sense of impotence was fostering a strong desire for action.

The Lynskeys' open hostility towards the three men had also led to a certain amount of anger in return. While the three men understood the source of the Lynskeys' frustration, they were growing tired of being targeted for a crime they maintained they had not committed. They resented the Lynskeys' overt aggression.

The result of all this was that the area around Porterstown Lane was now full of very angry young men, half of whom wanted to revenge a loved one, half of whom were determined to defend their good name. The situation was becoming patently dangerous.

The first clash between the two factions came the day after Una's body was found. Eileen Kerrigan, Marty's older sister, drove Marty into Ratoath on the night of 11 December. She parked outside Ryan's pub and went into the lounge, leaving her brother in the passenger seat.

She had a quick word with the barman, and as she turned to leave she heard some voices behind her saying 'Kerrigan is outside'. Before she had time to react, she was pushed aside by James Lynskey, who was joined by a crowd of about five other men, including John Gaughan, Sean Lynskey and Patrick Kelly.

She followed them outside and saw Patrick Kelly running over to the passenger side of the car and shaking his fist at Marty, saying 'You're dead'.

James Lynskey then made a movement to drag Marty out of the car, and Eileen tried to pull him away. As she struggled with James, another member of the gang jumped on the bonnet. In the confusion of the moment, Marty Kerrigan managed to slide into the driver's seat and start the car. He drove away, leaving the men panting angrily in his wake.

Four days later, on 15 December, Una was buried. The Lynskeys were consumed with grief. The loss of their daughter and sister, in such horrific circumstances, was almost too much to bear. They visited the grave regularly, taking any opportunity to be close to Una. It was during one such visit, on 19 December, that Winifred Lynskey had a run-in with Marty Kerrigan. Winifred later told her furious sons how Marty jeered at her across the graveyard and made a V-sign at her.

Una's sister, Anne Reddin, later recalled how that had been the first day in a long time that her brothers and her cousin, John Gaughan, appeared to be happy. They were joking and relaxed and didn't have the haunted expressions to which she had become accustomed. But their attitude changed dramatically when Winifred Lynskey told them what had happened in the graveyard that day. 'I thought there was a look of despair in their eyes,' said Anne.

However, rather than attempt any physical retaliation, Una's cousin John Gaughan said that he would make a complaint to the Gardaí about the incident. After doing so, John went to the Country Club in Dunshaughlin, where he had a few drinks with Patrick Kelly, and Sean and James Lynskey. John later said it was the first time he had relaxed properly since Una's body had been found.

But it was a shaky calm, and the anger of the Lynskeys continued to simmer just under the surface. That night the delicate impasse was shattered—with fatal consequences.

Marty Kerrigan and Dick Donnelly were also out for a few drinks that day. They had been the first people in the door of Maher's pub in Ratoath at 4pm, and had been drinking steadily until closing time. When the bar shut, Marty Kerrigan hung around on the street for a while before he spotted Patrick Kelly's car parked nearby. He began shouting at Patrick, venting his anger at everything that had happened to him. His friends had to hold him back and eventually managed to pull him away.

Marty then went over to speak with Garda Harty, who was also parked in the village. After a short conversation, Garda Harty offered to drive Marty and his friends to a local dance in Kilmoon, near Ashbourne. The men gratefully accepted the lift, and sped off in the car.

When Patrick Kelly returned from the village at around 11pm he went straight to the Gaughans' house, where he found John Gaughan sitting with James and Sean Lynskey and some of their friends. Patrick told them that Marty Kerrigan had insulted him in Ratoath and had kicked his car. In the men's minds, this was the final straw.

Sean Lynskey jumped up, shouting, 'We'll go down and see what it's all about.' The men all rushed out of the house, shouting and roaring their intention to get Kerrigan to confess to what he had done. Their blood was running high. When he was leaving, Sean Lynskey took a bread knife that he had been using to cut an apple tart and put it in his pocket. The men piled into two cars and sped off in the direction of Ratoath.

In the meantime, Marty Kerrigan and his friends had travelled in Garda Harty's car as far as the Old Barracks crossroad. There, they had come across the scene of an accident. Garda Harty got out of the car and took both of the drivers into a nearby house to speak with them. While they were waiting for him to return, Marty Kerrigan and his friends also got out of the car.

As they stood there in the dark empty countryside, two cars came speeding up the road, one driven by Patrick Kelly, the other by John Gaughan. Young men spilled out of both vehicles and a fierce battle between the two groups ensued. Only John Gaughan remained in his little green Mini, and watched as James Lynskey ran straight for Marty Kerrigan, dealing him a heavy blow.

Marty fell to the ground, cracking his head off the tarmac. He waved his arms in the air, trying to defend himself. Paraic Gaughan, Una's cousin, who used to be James Lynskey's best friend, now found himself struggling with his cousin, trying to pull him away from Marty Kerrigan. In the middle of the scuffle Paraic turned around and saw another serious fight. He ran over to try to break it up.

Sean Lynskey then grabbed Marty Kerrigan by the hair and dragged him three or four feet across the ground towards where John Gaughan was waiting in his car. Sean bundled Marty into the car headfirst, so that his feet were still sticking out. John started the engine and drove slowly up the road as Sean ran alongside the car, pushing Marty the rest of the way in before jumping in himself. James Lynskey followed him into the back seat, and John Gaughan revved the car and sped away from the brawl.

Paraic Gaughan was one of the first to realise that Marty had been taken. In the midst of the roaring angry battle he saw a pair of black shoes on the road about three yards from where John Gaughan's car had been parked. He picked them up and gave them to Marty Kerrigan's father twenty minutes later. They were to become Martin Kerrigan Sr's last link to his son.

The little green Mini was speeding in the direction of the mountains. Marty Kerrigan was lying on his back on the floor of the car, his head resting on the tubular bar under the front passenger seat. The Lynskey brothers both had a firm grip of Marty's hair and each held one of his wrists.

The men started questioning Marty about who had killed Una, and why they had done it. Every now and then they would shake Marty's head up and down, hitting his skull off the bar. Sean Lynskey told him that John Gaughan had a shotgun in the car with him and at one stage Gaughan said, 'Don't kill him in the car. We will push him over a cliff.'

Despite his fright, for the first stage of the journey Marty repeatedly denied that he had anything to do with Una's death. As his fear and pain increased, he then said that Dick Donnelly and Martin Conmey had done it. 'He kept saying that and settled with that story,' Sean Lynskey said later. 'He did not go into any detail as to how the incident took place.'

Once again, despite being put under the most extreme, frightening pressure, Marty Kerrigan appeared unwilling—or unable—to say what had really happened to Una.

Halfway to the mountains, John Gaughan pulled in at a petrol station. When the engine stopped, Marty started to struggle and shout for help. Sean Lynskey clamped his hand over Marty's mouth and stuck his fingers up under his lip, tearing the delicate tissue. Marty stopped shouting. As they drove away from the station and began to travel up the mountains, the men all noticed that Marty had suddenly become very quiet.

'Kerrigan remained silent. I do not know whether he was breathing or not,' said Sean Lynskey. 'There was no movement from him. I formed the impression he was play-acting. When we reached the place where my sister's body was found, John Gaughan stopped the car and opened the passenger door. James and I pushed him out of the car onto the grass margin. He appeared to be unconscious and did not offer any resistance to the fall out onto the grass. James got out of the car and put his hand on his chest and said his heart was beating. He then shoved him into the dyke, which was only about one foot in depth.'

The three lads later told gardaí that they were convinced that Marty Kerrigan was alive when they left, and that he was only 'up to his old tricks' by pretending to be unconscious. Leaving the 19-year-old lying on the same spot that Una Lynskey's body had been discovered just one week previously, the men set off for home.

A huge crowd of people, many of them hostile, had gathered outside John Gaughan's house. The abduction of Marty Kerrigan was seen as unacceptable by the community. When the little green Mini pulled up to the house the crowd jeered and shouted angrily. The three men ran inside, and found the gardaí already waiting for them.

At first, when Superintendent Moore questioned them as to Marty's whereabouts, John Gaughan replied that they had left him on Fairyhouse Road and he had been picked up by another car. But after the superintendent left the room, John told Garda Harty that they wanted to tell him the truth.

Garda Harty asked if Marty was dead, and John said he did not think so, saying that Marty hadn't really had 'a good going over'. John described how Marty was very quiet when they left him in the mountains, but said that he thought he was 'only play-acting'.

With the fervour of the crowd outside increasing, the gardaí decided it was best to get the three men to the safety of the garda station. In the meantime, a team of gardaí was sent up the mountains to get Marty Kerrigan.

At 3am, two officers from Dundrum found Marty's body lying on the small, significant patch of grass. He was dead. His trousers were ripped at the seams and his shirt torn open so that his thighs and abdomen were exposed. The skin had been torn from his nose, and his lips, scalp, shoulders, arms and chest were all bruised.

The most sinister injury, however, was not discovered until later. There was a jagged cut, three inches long, along the left side of his scrotum. The wound was inflicted after death and was effectively an attempted castration.

The gardaí phoned in the news to Dunshaughlin Garda Station, and detectives went to tell the three men.

When James Lynskey heard he buried his head in his clasped hands and remained this way for about a minute. He then gave a deep sigh and said: 'Ah Lord,' adding after a minute or so, 'I don't know how he could have died. It must be very easy to kill a person.'

John Gaughan, too, looked extremely shocked at the news. 'The last thing we intended to do was to kill him,' he said. 'We only intended to frighten him. I never thought he was dead. I was sure he was putting it on. Jesus Christ, is it that easy to kill a man?'

Of the three men, Sean Lynskey was the only one who did not immediately show remorse. 'I do not care if I am strung up in the morning,' he said.

Now that Marty's death was official, the gardaí had to break the news to his family. That night the Kerrigan sisters had also been on the way to the dance in Kilmoon when they heard that their brother had been abducted by the Lynkseys.

'We went back home immediately when we heard it,' said Kathleen Kerrigan. 'We were very worried, but we didn't ever think they'd kill him. We knew he might be badly beaten but not killed.'

After waiting anxiously for a while in their house the Kerrigans decided to go to John Gaughan's house to see if there was any news. They were there when the three men came back in their car, minus Marty, and ran straight into the house.

'The gardaí told us to go home at that stage, and we did,' said Kathleen. 'A few hours later they came with the news. We were in the kitchen, me, my father and my two sisters. And they told us Marty was dead.'

There was a brief silence after she recounted the memory. When she talked again, it was almost in a whisper. 'You just don't believe it at the time,' she said. 'It's pure shock, you know. It didn't sink in at all. My sister Eileen had to go to identify the body, because my father wasn't able. He wasn't able for anything much after that. It just destroyed him. On the day he died, many years later, he mentioned

Marty again. It never left him. It destroyed all our lives really. Because we had this person who we loved so much and he had been killed for something we knew he didn't do. And there was nothing we could do to fix it. It was all such a terrible mistake.'

The murder trial of John Gaughan and James and Sean Lynskey took place in March 1972. The men pleaded not guilty.

The court heard evidence from the State Pathologist, Professor Maurice Hickey, that Marty Kerrigan had died when something interfered with his breathing, causing asphyxia. Hickey said that the pressure of a person's hand applied over the mouth and nose could have caused death. He said that Marty Kerrigan probably died between midnight and 2am.

The issue of the jagged cut around Marty's groin was less straightforward. Hickey found that this wound was inflicted after death and unlike the other wounds it was caused by an implement with a sharp cutting edge. He said that the wound was made at least ten to fifteen minutes after death, and that it could have been much later than that.

Hickey had also examined the bread knife taken from the house by Sean Lynskey on the night of Marty's death. He said that it was unlikely that the bread knife had been used to make the wound unless that knife had been cleaned very carefully afterwards—there had been no trace of blood on it.

The men all denied having had anything to do with the wound. They said that they did not tear open Marty's trousers, but that they must have ripped at the seams when they bundled him into the car.

To this day, it has never been discovered who made the jagged cut in Marty Kerrigan's groin. Because it could not be proven that the men had made the wound, there was nothing to prove that Marty Kerrigan was actually dead when they left him in the mountains.

The prosecution's case was that Marty Kerrigan could have died after the men left. They painted a picture of him, semi-conscious and drunken, standing up and falling back down again, effectively asphyxiating himself.

The jury took ten hours to come to their decision. They found the men not guilty of murder, but guilty of manslaughter. In handing down his sentence the judge said he was taking into account the previous good character of the three men, and he commented on the enormous tragedy of both deaths.

Sean Lynskey and John Gaughan were sentenced to three years in prison. James Lynksey, who was only 18, was sentenced to two years' detention in St Patrick's Institution.

Marty Kerrigan was buried alongside his mother in the local grave-yard. His father, Martin Sr, now lies there too.

A week before Marty Kerrigan's murder trial began, Dick Donnelly and Martin Conmey were formally charged with the murder of Una Lynskey. The men and their families were completely taken aback. After Una's body was found they had believed that the gardaí would find new evidence and the focus of the investigation would naturally progress.

The men now knew that Sean Reilly and Martin Madden were the two witnesses who had told gardaí that they had driven in the opposite direction down Porterstown Lane that night. They didn't know that the teacher, Mary Collins, had also made a new statement saying she had also seen them on the road.

However, even as the trial approached, the men and their families remained confident that there was no evidence to convict them.

'In a way, my parents were almost relieved that there was going to be a trial because they thought that finally the truth would come out,' said Mary Conmey. 'The way they saw it, if you were under oath then you had to tell the truth. That's what they thought.'

The trial began.

The people who had seen cars on the lane that evening were now the most important witnesses in the case. In order for the statements that were taken from the men in Trim Garda Station to hold any weight, it was essential that it could be proven that Dick Donnelly's car was seen travelling on Porterstown Lane from Fairyhouse Road direction towards the Dublin/Navan Road.

Among the important line-up of witnesses who saw a car on the lane were Paraic and Kathleen Gaughan, the Lynskeys' first cousins, next-door neighbours and close friends. There were also Sean Reilly, Martin Madden and Mary Collins.

In court, both Paraic and Kathleen Gaughan remained firm in their contention that they had not seen any other cars apart from the strange Ford Zodiac on the lane that evening. They were both adamant that they had certainly not seen Dick Donnelly's car on the lane. Their refusal to say otherwise caused a huge rift between their family and the Lynskeys, and both were deeply hurt at the split. That painful divide was never healed, and the relationship between the both families was irrevocably destroyed.

Then it was the turn of Sean Reilly to take the stand. Sean said that he had arrived to his home on Porterstown Lane on his bicycle at around 6.55pm that evening. He heard a car at the gate and guessed it was that of his friend, Martin Madden. He went outside and found that Martin had parked the car in the entrance to his house, the front facing in towards the gate, the back facing onto the road.

Sean sat into the car alongside Martin, and the two young men remained there chatting for a while. Then they noticed a car passing behind them, coming from Fairyhouse Road, going towards the Dublin/Navan Road.

Even though Sean Reilly was one of the witnesses who had told gardaí that this car belonged to Dick Donnelly, he sounded less than convinced about this while he was giving evidence, as the following exchange reveals:

'Do you know whose car it was?' asked the prosecutor.

'I thought it might have been Dick Donnelly's, but I'm not going to swear . . .' said Sean.

'Can you say who was driving the car?'

'Well, if it was Dick Donnelly's car, I should think he would be driving it himself.'

'Apart from the driver, was there anybody else in the car?'

'I thought there was someone in the passenger seat.'

'Can you say whether it was a man or a woman?'

'No.'

'Can you say what colour it was?'

'I couldn't see what colour it was because it was dark.' [Repeats sentence]

'Had you seen that car before?'

'I couldn't see at the time. I couldn't see at the time. If it was bright I probably would have known.'

'Could you see the driver of the car?'

'I could barely see the top of his head.'

'Could you see whether the driver was a man or a woman?'

'No.'

As the evidence continued in this way, the prosecution team made an application to the judge to be able to treat Sean Reilly—a prosecution witness—as hostile, on the grounds that his evidence was not the same as what he had said in the district court.

The judge then asked Sean Reilly if he remembered saying in the district court that Dick Donnelly was the man driving that car.

'I could have,' said Sean.

'Is it correct?' asked the judge.

'It's correct, but I'm not going to take an oath on it,' said Sean.

'You did take an oath on it,' said the Judge. 'This is something you swore in the district court.'

'I don't remember,' said Sean.

'You don't want to swear that again?' asked the judge.

'I'm not going to swear that he was driving when I wouldn't be sure,' replied Sean.

This interaction between the judge and Sean Reilly was heard in the absence of the jury. The judge ruled that Sean could not be treated as a hostile witness, and the case resumed.

A short while later, Martin Madden was called to the stand. It had been a combination of his statement and Sean Reilly's statement that had first led the gardaí to regard the three men as suspects. And yet Martin Madden's evidence on the stand, like Sean Reilly's, is halting and hesitant. He described sitting in his car with Sean Reilly outside Reilly's house when a car passed behind them coming from the Fairyhouse Road direction.

'Can you describe the car?' asked the prosecutor.

'I can't, no,' said Martin.

'Was it a large or small car?'

'I couldn't, I wouldn't be exactly sure.'

'Could you say what colour it was?'

'No. I think it was yellow.'

'Did you know whose car it was?'

'I didn't, no.'

'Did you see who was driving it?'

'I didn't see who was driving it.'

'Did you see into the car?'

'Oh, I didn't see into the car, no. I was looking over a wall, and the wall is about four feet high.'

As the conversation continued, the prosecution team again asked for the jury to leave and they asked the judge to be allowed to treat Martin Madden, their own witness, as hostile on the grounds that he was contradicting what he had said in the district court. In this case, the judge allowed the application.

The prosecutor then put it to Martin Madden that in the district court he had said: 'It was a big car. I couldn't exactly say the make. I thought it was an orange colour. I thought it was Dick Donnelly's car by the sound of it. I thought Dick Donnelly was driving this car. I thought there were two more in the car along with the driver. The third person in the car could have been in the back or front. I thought it was Martin Kerrigan.'

Martin Madden agreed that he had said all of this. However, when he was questioned further, he again lapsed into saying that he couldn't be sure about any of it. It was emerging from the questioning that he had identified Dick Donnelly's car by sound, rather than sight.

'If you thought it was the sound of Donnelly's car, didn't you know it?' said the prosecutor.

'No, I wouldn't be sure of it,' said Martin.

'Why think it was the sound of Donnelly's car?'

'Because it was a heavy sound. It made the noise of any other big car, like.'

The defence team saw an opportunity, and didn't let it pass up. On cross-examination they focused on how exactly Martin Madden had identified Dick's car.

'Your reason for saying you thought it was Dick Donnelly's car was because of the sound of it?' asks the defence barrister.

'Yes,' says Martin Madden.

'Nothing else?'

'Yes.'

'Most of the cars around there are smaller models than his?'

'Yes, that's right.'

'And simply because it appeared by the sound to be a heavier car than your neighbour's, you thought it might be Dick Donnelly's?'

'Yes.'

Interestingly, Martin Madden also gave evidence as to having seen Dick Donnelly's car parked outside Donnelly's house later that evening, around 7.25pm, which directly backs up Dick Donnelly's own version of events. He said he saw Marty Kerrigan sitting in the front seat on his own. There is a striking difference in the way Martin Madden delivers this evidence. There is no hesitation or confusion. He is clearly sure about what he saw.

The prosecution had one more reliable witness in their ranks: Mary Collins, a respected school teacher in the area. Mary had given a number of statements to gardaí after the night Una disappeared, and as was practice, the most pertinent aspects of each statement were put into one long statement and delivered to the prosecution team.

In the case of Mary Collins, this had a very peculiar result. At the beginning of her statement she appears to be adamant that she did not see any car other than the strange Ford Zodiac on the night in question.

'I met no car other than the chocolate car I saw when speaking to Kathleen Gaughan,' she said. 'If I met any other car I am quite sure I would remember. I cannot recall a car passing near Maddens' or Reillys' on that evening going in the direction of the Navan Road.'

However, later in the statement she directly contradicts herself, saying: 'I had just reached the entrance gate to Madden's house when a large car, very broad and well down on its springs, passed me. I looked to my left and saw what I thought to be three hairy-looking youths in the front seat of this car. The car appears to be the same car that I have seen since in Porterstown Lane and being driven by a Donnelly chap from Fairyhouse Road. It is a gold-coloured Zephyr.'

Quite clearly, these recollections are directly in conflict with each other. There is no explanation for this. To add to the mystery, when Mary Collins took to the stand, she did not talk about her very vivid description of the 'three hairy-looking youths' she had seen on the road, and the prosecution did not push her on it, even though this surely should have been an integral part of their case.

Instead, when she was asked if she saw another car on the lane, Mary replied: 'I am not sure, was it that evening or the evening before a car passed me.' She made no mention of the colour, the make, or the occupants. And that was the extent of her evidence about having seen Dick Donnelly's car.

There were a number of garda witnesses attesting to their role in the investigation. Among them was Detective Inspector William Byrne, who gave evidence that he could find no fingerprints belonging to Una Lynskey in Dick Donnelly's car.

Martin Conmey and Dick Donnelly then took the stand and recounted their experience in Trim Garda Station, with Martin explaining that the physical intimidation and abuse he encountered was the reason he signed his statement.

The gardaí who were present in the station that night all denied these allegations. It was during this phase of the court case that Detective Sergeant John Courtney was questioned about the strange Ford Zodiac that was driven by the middle-aged man, and why it had suddenly been ruled out of the investigation.

'Inspector, at this time when you had these men in the station were you aware that a number of witnesses had identified a man in a Zephyr car, between the age of 45 and 50 with grey hair, a beard, reddish face and stout?' asked the defence barrister.

'There was mention of some gentleman and about a car coming out at Fairyhouse Road and that it was a middle-aged man driving,' replied Detective Courtney.

'Two witnesses so far have given evidence of seeing such a man around Porterstown during the hearing of this case?'

No answer.

'You have heard the question?'

'Yes.'

'Was that investigating every aspect?'

'Everything that came up was thoroughly investigated.'

'Was that man discovered?'

'No, he was not.'

'Have you any clue as to who he was?'

'No, I do not.'

This set of questioning was effectively the last time the middle-aged man in the Ford Zodiac was mentioned during the case. All focus now was on the three young men.

As the trial began to draw to a close, the prosecution produced one more witness, who proved to be extremely important in the case. His name was Thomas Mangan, and he maintained that Martin Conmey had confessed to him about killing Una Lynskey.

Mangan came from Belmullet in Co. Mayo but was working as a labourer in Dublin and living in digs in Clondalkin. One month after Una Lynskey disappeared, Martin Conmey asked Thomas if he could move into the digs with him. Thomas agreed, and the two men began sharing a room.

According to Thomas, before Una Lynskey's body had been found, Martin Conmey came into the bedroom and announced that he and Dick Donnelly had killed Una by accidentally hitting her with their car. Thomas recalled how Martin told him that they were driving down

Porterstown Lane at forty-five miles an hour, when they came to the sharp bend. They struck Una with the front of the car and she collapsed on the ground. They then lifted her into the back of the car. Only Martin Conmey and Dick Donnelly were in the car. Martin went on to say that they kept driving and 'left her inside a fence in a ditch near a mountain'.

Thomas said Martin never said how they got to this ditch near the mountain, or what mountain exactly he was talking about.

Even though Thomas said that Martin Conmey revealed this to him before Una's body was found, he said nothing about it to the gardaí until he was brought into the station for questioning in January. He was in the barracks from 3.30pm until 11.30pm, during which time he made the statement. He flatly denied a suggestion by the defence barrister that he was frightened of the gardaí, that he used to hide behind a mixer at work when they came around, or that when he returned from making his statement in the station he was unable to eat his dinner because he was so upset.

Thomas was not questioned about the fact that State Pathologist Professor Hickey had ruled that Una could not have died from being hit by a car.

Shortly later, both sides rested their case and the jury was told to retire. They now had a daunting amount of information to deal with, having been presented with a number of entirely different scenarios, none of which really explained what had happened to Una.

At one point it had been said that the men had left Una's body in a pond. Then it was said that Marty Kerrigan and Dick Donnelly had hidden her under a railway bridge near Lucan. Then, in the alleged confession to Thomas Mangan, Marty Kerrigan was left out of the scenario altogether and it was Martin Conmey and Dick Donnelly who had knocked Una down on the lane and then dumped her 'in a ditch beside a fence near a mountain'. For a case that focused so specifically on every minute, there was no real clarity about when any of these scenarios was supposed to have been carried out.

In his summing up, the judge pointed out that one of the first things the jury had to decide was whether it had been proven that Dick Donnelly's car was seen driving down the lane from Fairyhouse Road direction that evening. To decide on this, the jury had to rely on the decidedly shaky evidence of Martin Madden, Sean Reilly and, to a much lesser extent, Mary Collins.

The jury also had before them the scenario presented by the three young men, in which they drove onto the lane at around 7.20pm from the Dublin/Navan Road and never saw Una at all. There were a number of witnesses to back this up.

One thing that the jury was never truly asked to consider was the role of the strange Zodiac in the murder of Una Lynskey.

For twelve hours they deliberated. At one point they returned to ask for a definition of manslaughter, at which the families of the two men looked at each other in alarm. For the first time in the entire case, it occurred to them that Martin Conmey and Dick Donnelly could actually be convicted of this crime.

And they were. In the early hours of the morning the jury returned to the court and found the men not guilty of murder, but guilty of manslaughter. The judge sentenced both men to three years in prison. At the back of the courtroom, David Conmey's legs gave way under him as he collapsed. The Lynskey family cried with relief. The incredible tragic saga had reached an end.

Both Dick Donnelly and Martin Conmey appealed their convictions. Dick's appeal was successful and his conviction was overturned. Martin's was not, largely on the grounds of Thomas Mangan's statement and the fact that he had signed a confession in Trim Garda Station. Martin served most of his three years in prison, before trying to return to his normal life.

But for everyone who was involved in the case, the wounds were deep and wouldn't easily heal.

The Lynskey family moved away from Porterstown Lane, the memories of everything that had happened making it too difficult to stay.

For years and years, the Donnellys, Kerrigans and Conmeys were unable to speak, even to each other, about the two murders. Only relatively recently have they found the strength to talk, a little, about that fateful night in October 1971, and everything that followed.

While Dick Donnelly was somewhat appeased to have won his appeal, Martin Conmey and his family remained tortured by Martin's criminal record. In 1997, Martin Conmey made another application to the courts to have his conviction overturned. Ten years later, it is still working its way through the legal system.

The Kerrigan family also hired a private detective to look into the case. His name was Billy Flynn, the man who helped uncover the Garda corruption scandal involving the McBrearty family in Donegal.

Having trawled through the evidence, Billy Flynn is on record as saying he believes the three men were innocent.

In a quirk of fate, Una's cousin, Paraic Gaughan, married Martin Conmey's sister Mary. Paraic talks quietly of the enormous pain and division that the two murders caused. Almost forty years later, he says there are still so many people who are deeply affected by the events of that winter.

And, Paraic says, even now he still cannot forget the face of the man he saw in the Ford Zodiac that night. 'I was a good sleeper until it all happened and for years afterwards my sleep was disturbed,' he said. 'When I closed my eyes, I just used to see his face in my mind. I still see him. Maybe that's a good thing. Maybe one day I'll get to identify him.'

Many of the people who were involved in the case are now dead. Many other people don't want to remember. But, still, so many questions remain.

Among the stacks of conflicting statements and vague, hesitant evidence, it becomes almost impossible to distinguish truth from fiction. But one fact is startlingly clear. At approximately the time Una Lynskey was abducted and murdered, an independent witness saw a girl struggling with a man in a car that was being driven out of Porterstown Lane. And this man was never found.

Who was he? Who was the girl? More questions. No answers. Just the awful possibility that maybe, just maybe, the real truth of what happened to Una Lynskey has never been told.

Chapter 3

The Murder of Phyllis Murphy

Phyllis Murphy was looking for the perfect man. Someone who didn't smoke. Didn't drink. Didn't curse. A gentleman. A kind, tender person who would love her and care for her and treat her with respect. One week before she was savagely beaten, raped and killed, Phyllis sat with her sister over a cup of tea and said that she was willing to wait. She was saving herself for him. She knew he was out there. The perfect man.

'I told her there was no such thing,' says Barbara Turner, Phyllis Murphy's eldest sister. It is twenty-eight years and one day since Phyllis was murdered, and we're sitting in front of a roaring fire in the Turner household, the crackling flames challenging any wisp of cold that might find its way in from the bitter winter afternoon. Barbara smiles ruefully, and makes a sad, exasperated clucking sound with her tongue. 'I told her that just because a man would have a drink or smoke or use bad language didn't mean he was a bad person. I told her that you won't get a lad who is that perfect and usually if they're that good then they're probably hiding something. No one is perfect. But Phyllis was very particular.'

That sisterly conversation is still vivid in Barbara's mind. It was the first proper chat she'd had with Phyllis in quite a while. It was also the last. One week later, her sister was targeted by a man whose most minor crimes were drinking, cursing and betting on horses. A family man, quiet and unassuming. A person who could wrap his hands around a woman's throat and squeeze the life from her, before callously dumping her bloodied and bruised body in a ditch in the mountains in the black cold night of winter. A killer whose own DNA would ultimately definitively link him with his victim, but who would never, once, say sorry for his brutal crime. Phyllis Murphy was looking for a perfect man. Instead, she found John Crerar.

It was 22 December 1979—almost Christmas Day, with only a few precious shopping hours left. Phyllis Murphy was taking advantage of every minute. Standing just over five feet tall, and wearing a grey coat over denim jeans and soft cosy mittens, she cut a petite and vulnerable figure as she wandered down the streets of Newbridge in Co. Kildare looking for last-minute presents.

Her first stop was Blake's hairdressers on Main Street where she had an appointment at 12.30pm. She was taking her straight chestnut hair to task by getting a perm. Perms were in fashion, and Phyllis had an exciting new love interest on the scene. The hair appointment, therefore, was very important.

The third youngest of ten children, 23-year-old Phyllis was not yet married. She had recently broken off a long engagement and was starting to see another young man. She had discussed this excitedly with her sister, Barbara Turner, just the previous week.

'She came in to see me and for the first time in ages neither of us were rushing anywhere and we had a long chat,' says Barbara. 'She was talking about her future and how she was going to meet this new lad, and I remember saying good luck with him, because it had been hard when the previous relationship finished. She was a virgin and she was very, very adamant that she was going to be a virgin when she got married. She was still a virgin when he got to her. It was terrible. Such a shame, you know, that someone else took that from her.'

Innocent of the fate awaiting her, Phyllis came out of the hairdressers on Saturday afternoon, delighted with her new style. She strolled into a few shops, picking up a new pair of tan boots for herself on the way. By about four o'clock, satisfied she had everything she needed, she went to the house where she lodged with friends of the family, the Martins.

Phyllis only spent some of her time staying in Newbridge. After completing her Group Cert in the Presentation Convent in Kildare town she had found a job as a cutter in the Curragh Knitwear Factory in Newbridge. She also sometimes stayed in Rathangan, as a companion to her friend's mother, and spent the rest of the time in the family home in Rowanville in Kildare.

On this last Saturday of her life she planned to stay at home with her family. She returned briefly to her lodgings in Newbridge to freshen up and collect an overnight bag and the rest of the Christmas presents she had bought for the family. Then she set off down the road towards the bus stop, where she planned to catch the 7.10pm bus home to Kildare.

En route, she called in to see her brother Gerard, who lived just a few doors away. He remembers that she was in great form, and full of excitement about the Christmas presents she had bought for her nieces and nephews. She refused to sit down, saying that she wanted to call into the Lukers' house down the road and she was anxious not to miss the bus. She wished her brother a happy Christmas before setting off again. It was the last time Gerard Murphy saw his sister alive.

Barbara Luker, a good friend of Phyllis's, lived just opposite the Keadeen Hotel a short distance from the bus stop. That Saturday evening when Phyllis knocked on the door, Barbara wasn't home. Her mother, Margaret, invited Phyllis inside. The two women had a short chat about the Christmas and their plans for the holidays, before Phyllis decided to take her leave. She asked Margaret to pass on a message to Barbara that she would meet her that evening in Kildare town to go to a dance.

It was just after 6.30pm when Phyllis left the Lukers' and walked down the road to the bus stop. In one mittened hand she held the 60p bus fare. Her arms were full of bags and presents. It was already dark, and freezing cold. In the shadow of the Keadeen Hotel, a car pulled up beside her.

Until that point, John Crerar had been having a largely unremarkable day. Conscious of the fast-approaching Christmas, he and his wife Carmel had spent a few hours shopping in Newbridge, before returning to their house at Woodside Park in Kildare town—just a short walk from where Phyllis Murphy's sister Barbara was building her new house.

That evening, Crerar headed down to McWey's pub in Kildare to have a few drinks before he started work at 8pm. There he met his colleague Patrick Bolger, who had also been shopping that day and had stopped off in the pub with his family on the way home. Bolger, too, was starting work at 8pm. The simple twist of fate that led his name to be pencilled in on the roster alongside Crerar was destined to change Patrick Bolger's life forever, and eventually lead to Crerar being arrested.

However, for both Bolger and Crerar that Saturday had been a very average day. Indeed, to any casual observer every day was average for 31-year-old John Crerar.

Standing at just five-foot seven-inches tall, with fair, wispy hair and a ruddy complexion, he easily went unnoticed in a crowd. An unthreatening, unassuming, unremarkable individual. Originally from Cloughjordan in Co. Tipperary, Crerar left school at the age of 14 and joined the defence forces in 1966. He had been married for eight years when he retired from the army with the rank of sergeant in 1979, and started working as a security guard with Provincial Security at the Black and Decker plant in Kildare.

He had never officially come to the attention of authorities, although locally there were whispers about his 'womanising' ways. However, unbeknownst to most people, one young girl in the area was already actively and fearfully avoiding John Crerar. Although she had never filed an official criminal complaint against him, she was later to tell the gardaí that Crerar had sexually assaulted her in the early 1970s. This allegation has never been proven, but if true it would lend serious weight to the contention of some detectives that John Crerar has killed more than once.

No one in the festive crowd gathered in McWey's pub on that wintery Saturday evening suspected that among them sat a man who was about to beat, rape and murder an innocent woman. Perhaps even Crerar himself was not planning, or conscious of, what he was about to do. He seemed in excellent spirits when he rang his two colleagues in the Black and Decker plant and joked that he had decided to continue drinking instead of going to work. Or perhaps he was already creating an alibi for himself, deliberately allaying any suspicions that might form in their minds if he was late for work. Perhaps John Crerar was already carefully planning what he wanted to do.

As he was leaving McWey's, Crerar agreed to give his friend Peter Rooney a lift back to his home in Maryville. He waved goodbye to Rooney and was just a short distance from his own house, where his wife was preparing his tea. But he didn't go home. He went north. Four miles out of his way. To Newbridge. To where Phyllis Murphy was walking towards the bus stop with her 60p clutched in her mitten.

As he drove, no one knows what was going through his mind. He may have been feverishly scanning the road, looking for vulnerable prey. Or maybe he was looking for someone in particular, and just happened to spot Phyllis Murphy standing alone at the bus stop. Was he suddenly overcome with a violent sexual impulse to attack her? Or did he wake up that morning—or the previous week, or the previous month—and begin planning an attack? Had he done it before? While detectives have their suspicions, no one knows for sure. What is certain is that sometime between 6.30pm and 6.45pm on 22 December 1979, John Crerar pulled up beside Phyllis Murphy outside the Keadeen Hotel.

The Murphys knew the Crerars the way neighbours know neighbours; they weren't necessarily great friends, but they were very familiar with each other.

'We all knew him,' says Barbara Turner. 'His house is just up the road.' She points out the window to where the cold wind is buffeting the trees and twirling dead leaves in the air. 'Phyllis and another sister of mine, Breda, babysat for him, and he and his wife would have gone out a few times with Claire, my sister, who lives next door. We all knew him, although not as well as we knew his wife. He was a secretive type of man, he didn't talk much.'

However, while Crerar later admitted that he knew the Murphy family and that he would have recognised Phyllis as one of the 'Murphy girls', he vehemently denied ever having even spoken to her, or that she ever babysat for him. By his account, they were virtual strangers. But anyone who knew Phyllis knew she would never have got into a car with a stranger.

'She was very fussy about that,' says Barbara. 'Very careful of strange men. But she did know him, and I suppose it was a very cold night and maybe she thought she'd get home a bit quicker. When someone you know well, who you babysat for, stops and offers you a lift, you don't think he's going to kill you. Do you?'

She looks at me, wondering. 'Maybe you would, nowadays, with everything that happens. But then, maybe you wouldn't either. Maybe you would just think that this was someone you knew, and no one expects to know a killer.'

There is no evidence to tell gardaí what happened immediately after Crerar's car rolled up beside the bus stop in the black, bitter night. He may have leapt out and immobilised Phyllis with an unexpected blow before bundling her into the car. But it is more likely that he played the role of a friendly unthreatening neighbour just offering her a lift.

The fact that there was no sign of any struggle at the bus stop—no torn bits of wrapping paper, no drops of blood—certainly suggests that Phyllis got into the car willingly. In fact, long before Crerar was pinpointed as the killer, gardaí were working on the theory that Phyllis might well have been abducted by someone she knew.

Gardaí also have no way of knowing for sure when Crerar began his assault on his victim, when or where he raped her, and at what point he finally killed her. However, a trail of evidence left enough details for detectives to form a rough idea of what happened when Phyllis decided to get out of the cold and into Crerar's car.

He drove four miles to the outskirts of Kildare town. At some point, he started to hit her. Any trace of gentlemanly behaviour was gone. He hit her hard. She was later found with 25 injuries to her body, including bruising and abrasions to her head, face, neck, chest, arms and legs.

At Colgan's Cut, an area of open ground close to the Curragh, it appears that Crerar stopped the car. And it is thought that at this point Phyllis made a desperate bid to escape. Following the trail of evidence, detectives believe she may have run, panting with fear through the furze bushes, dropping her bags and Christmas presents as she went. If she screamed, no one heard her. The wide, flat, black expanse of the Kildare countryside must never have felt so isolated, so terrifying.

It is at Colgan's Cut that gardaí believe the murder most likely took place. If Phyllis had managed to escape, Crerar caught her. He flung her to the ground. He punched her repeatedly in the face and chest, causing severe bruising around both her eyes, damaging her jaw and chin and cutting her lip. She fought him fiercely, and held up her arms to try to ward off the blows. She was later found to have a number of defensive injuries on her arms and wrists.

Her legs were also badly bruised. The pathologist reported bruising on the inside of her thighs and knees 'consistent with forcible parting of the legs' and bruising in the pelvic region, consistent with her having been raped. Other bruising on her arms indicated they had been held tightly during the attack.

Finally, after subjecting Phyllis Murphy to the most intimate, degrading violence, Crerar wrapped his hands around her neck and squeezed as hard as he could. In doing so, he compressed the vagal nerve, causing her heart to stop suddenly. The end, at least, was quick.

He got up. He doesn't appear to have been shocked at what he had done. Certainly, he was calm enough to immediately form a plan.

Detectives believe he collected what he could of her bags and presents, squinting in the dark, hoping not to miss anything. He then picked up Phyllis's limp, beaten body and put her in the boot.

It is possible that Crerar may not have hidden Phyllis's body immediately. He was later to take an unscheduled two-hour break from work, and he could have driven to the mountains then or at some other time over the following days. However, it is thought that it is most likely that immediately after killing her, Crerar turned the car around and drove twenty-four miles east, towards Wicklow and the mountains.

Twenty years later, gardaí made the same journey. Careful not to go over the speed limit, they discovered they could drive to where Phyllis's body was found and return to Kildare well within an hour and a half—a time frame that would have allowed Crerar to drive home for some tea before arriving at work, over 40 minutes late.

When he reached Ballinagee, a densely forested area close to the Wicklow Gap, Crerar stopped the car. He lifted Phyllis out of the boot and removed any clothes left on her body, storing them in his car. He left her lying on her back at the foot of an embankment below a spruce tree, her newly permed hair sinking into the mud and the leaves. Her left arm was thrown over her head, her right hand lay on her chest, almost as if she was in a restless sleep. Crerar threw a few branches over her body, in a haphazard attempt to cover her. Temperatures in the dark night had dropped below freezing, but—if Crerar even noticed—he could never have guessed that the elements themselves were conspiring against him. Over the next few hours and days, the sub-zero conditions preserved Phyllis's body along with vital trace evidence left by her killer.

Crerar drove two and a half miles back towards Wicklow, stopping at Lockstown Upper on the Glendalough road to set fire to Phyllis's clothes. Perhaps conscious of the time, and panicking now, he didn't wait to make sure that everything was burnt properly. Gardaí were later able to identify the charred remains of Phyllis's coat and jeans from among the ashes.

He drove on, getting closer to home. At Brannockstown, he threw Phyllis's Christmas presents over a high wall, sloppy and impatient now in his efforts to be done with his crime. Finally, he returned to the domestic warmth of his house, and casually said hello to his wife. He calmly had some tea, drove to work, and began living a lie.

After leaving McWey's pub at around 6.30pm earlier that evening, Patrick Bolger had gone home for his tea, changed into his uniform and driven to work, arriving at the Black and Decker plant around eight o'clock. He said goodbye to a co-worker, Sean Phelan, who was just finishing his shift. Phelan would later admit that he shouldn't have left Bolger alone. There were strict company rules that two security guards had to be on duty at all times—and when Phelan was leaving just after 8pm there was no sign of John Crerar.

At around twenty minutes to nine, Crerar finally arrived. 'He pulled up outside the security hut in his car and said there was something wrong with it,' Bolger later told a hushed courtroom, going on to describe how Crerar told him that he had hit a bump in the road and the battery fell out. Crerar got out of the car, lifted the bonnet and 'did something with the battery', before shutting the bonnet again. It was then that Bolger noticed Crerar wasn't wearing his uniform.

'He said, "I'll be back after a while, I'm going down to O'Leary's to play darts", and then he went off,' said Bolger. 'He came back around twenty-five or twenty to eleven that night.'

When he returned, Crerar sat down in a chair in the security hut and fell asleep for a while. His actions that night weren't sufficiently troubling to keep him awake.

Bolger continued to keep watch on his own, as he had been doing for most of the night. As his friend slept, it occurred to him that Crerar's story about the broken car battery wasn't all that convincing. Maybe, thought Bolger, Crerar had stayed on in the pub for a few Christmas drinks.

It was this thought—that there was an innocent reason for Crerar's delayed arrival to work—that led Bolger to lie to the police in the following weeks, unwittingly giving a savage rapist and murderer a watertight alibi for twenty years.

The next day, word came that Phyllis had never shown up for the dance in Kildare. Straight away, alarm bells rang.

'When we got that word, immediately we panicked,' says Barbara, shaking her head. 'Because she wouldn't be the type. If she said she was going to be in a place, she'd be there, or she'd let somebody know if she couldn't go. That was just the way she was.'

Phyllis's brother Gerard and a family friend, Michael Martin, straight away reported her disappearance to the gardaí in Newbridge.

But Phyllis was 23 years old, and she had only been missing for about twenty-four hours. The gardaí, perhaps unsurprisingly, were initially not inclined to take the matter too seriously.

On Christmas Eve, as the Murphy family were frantically contacting friends and relatives and convincing the local media to alert the public to Phyllis's disappearance, a young boy walking at Colgan's Cut came across a brand new pair of tan ladies' boots and a child's cardigan strewn on the ground. Thinking that there was little chance of finding the owner, the boy picked up the items and brought them home.

On Christmas Day, all the men in the Murphy family went out searching for Phyllis. When they reached Colgan's Cut, they scoured the area for any clue as to where she may have gone. But they found nothing, no trace of the horror that had occurred there just two days previously.

In desperation, they went to a diviner, who told them to focus their search around Old Kilcullen. 'We headed off there, searching like mad things, out of our minds with worry,' says Barbara. 'We had some of the Civil Defence men with us as well, and we searched all the outhouses and went to people's doors with photographs. All the time, our search was moving towards Wicklow and the mountains. We told the gardaí what we were doing and they let us off. I think they thought we were mad. It was twenty-seven years ago, and it didn't seem possible to most people that anything bad would have happened to Phyllis. But we knew. I knew. From the very beginning, really, I was looking for a body.'

Finally, on the morning of St Stephen's Day, a man out shooting game in the grounds of an estate near Brannockstown spotted Phyllis's overnight bag and Christmas presents in the undergrowth.

'It was a miracle that he saw it,' says Barbara. 'It was dumped over a big high wall and hidden deep under all this growth. He handed it in to a garda's house around there and it was identified as being Phyllis's straight away. So then everyone knew something awful had happened. Then it really started.'

Hours after the news emerged that Phyllis Murphy's belongings had been found, the boy who had found the boots realised the significance of his discovery and handed them in to the gardaí.

A full-scale Garda investigation was launched, and under the direction of the then Detective Inspector Sean Camon, gardaí joined the Murphys in their search. The hunt was moving slowly, inexorably towards Wicklow, and the mountains.

'Everybody, the whole town, went searching,' says Barbara. 'We had a bus that would collect people every morning. The search was heading all the time towards Wicklow, until one day, for some reason, the bus turned back. And nobody to this day knows who told it to go back. But we think now that we were getting too close to the body, so an effort was made to divert us away.'

That effort, the Murphys believe, was made through the planting of evidence. During a second search of Colgan's Cut, a number of Phyllis's belongings were found. The belt of her coat was discovered hanging openly on the side of a bush. Her mittens were spotted lying very visibly on the ground, with the 60p bus fare still hidden in one. Those who had searched the area before could not understand how they had missed such vital, visible evidence.

'My husband would have seen them. You couldn't miss them, the way they were found. So we think they were put there after the first search, to bring the attention away from Wicklow,' says Barbara.

If the Murphy family's suspicions are correct, it could mean that for some reason Crerar had kept some of Phyllis's belongings after he murdered her. Many top criminal psychologists have documented the compulsion of some killers to take a souvenir or trophy from their victims after their death. The items remind the killer of the personal aspect of his crime, allow him to relive the murder itself and give him a physical link to his victim. While there is no evidence to prove that Crerar did intentionally keep Phyllis Murphy's gloves and coat belt as souvenirs, it could be one explanation for their sudden reappearance in an area that had already been painstakingly searched.

Another possibility is that—like the boy who had found the boots—an innocent passer-by had picked up the items without realising their significance. Later, perhaps embarrassed by his or her actions, or unwilling to risk becoming involved in the investigation, that person could have decided to return the items anonymously.

Alternatively—although the Murphys vehemently deny this could be the case—maybe the items really were there all along, and were simply missed by the first team of searchers.

Regardless of why they suddenly appeared, the discovery of Phyllis's belongings gave a fresh impetus to the gardaí and the many hundreds of locals who had joined in the search.

By 7 January, over 3,000 people had answered a questionnaire about their movements on the night of the twenty-second. Farmers living within a twenty-mile radius of Newbridge were responding to a plea to search their land and their outbuildings for any trace of Phyllis. The disappearance of the young woman from Kildare had captured the attention of the nation.

However, hopes that Phyllis would be found alive were fading fast, and by the end of the first week of the new year, gardaí were privately admitting that the chances of finding her were very slim. 'We can't think of calling off the search yet, but it's very hard to hold out much optimism,' said one senior officer at the time. 'The outlook is very bleak.'

In the days after he killed Phyllis Murphy, John Crerar made sure to attract as little attention as possible. However, he mildly piqued the curiosity of his colleagues when, shortly after news emerged that Phyllis had disappeared, the ex-soldier set about vigorously washing the interior of his car.

'He explained to me that seemingly his wife had spilled cream or milk in it and it was stinking because of that,' said his co-worker Sean Phelan, describing the scene to the jury over twenty years later.

Phelan told how Crerar drove his car about a hundred yards away from the security hut into the car park of the Black and Decker plant before starting to clean it. There was no hot water in the security hut, but there was a kettle, a mop and a bucket. Phelan described how Crerar repeatedly boiled the kettle, put the water in the bucket, and carried it the hundred yards to his car, the hot water splashing over the sides and quickly turning icy in the freezing winter air.

'He must have done that several times,' said Phelan. 'It struck me as very odd. Given the quietness of the day, he could have parked his car close to the hot water and the cleaning materials. I can't remember how long [it took] but to me it was an inordinate length of time to spend cleaning a car.'

This behaviour alone may have been enough to raise the suspicions of the gardaí. However, Crerar officially became a suspect on the twelfth day of the investigation, when he replied to a Garda question-naire stating that he did not know Phyllis Murphy. The gardaí already knew from talking to the Murphy family that Phyllis and her sisters had sometimes babysat for Crerar. This simple lie—when the truth should not have been any threat—brought John Crerar strongly into the gardaí radar.

Then, during the course of door-to-door enquiries, a young woman told a garda sergeant that Crerar had assaulted her some years previously. She had never reported the crime—and to this day it has never been officially investigated or proven—but the garda sergeant was sufficiently convinced to write a note on John Crerar's file, urging other officers to treat him as a suspect.

On 16 January 1980, two days before Phyllis's body was found, Detective Sergeant Joseph Higgins and Detective Garda John Canny sat down with John Crerar in Kildare Garda Station to take a statement. In the course of the interview, Crerar told the gardaí he had been in work from 8pm on the night of 22 December until the following morning, and had been at home before that. He admitted to knowing the Murphy family, specifically Phyllis's sister Patricia, whom he knew from when she was working in the Jet station in Kildare. 'I do not know Phyllis Murphy to speak to,' he told the detectives. 'I know her father and sisters. I cannot even remember speaking to Phyllis Murphy in my life.'

Conscious of the warning written on top of Crerar's file, detectives asked his wife to corroborate his story. She confirmed that her husband had indeed been at home before going to work.

However, it was Patrick Bolger's statement that really forced detectives to cross Crerar off their list of suspects. Bolger did not want to jeopardise his friend's job by admitting he had been forty minutes late for work. When detectives asked him if John Crerar had started his shift with him at 8pm, Bolger lied. He said yes.

'The alibi came very early,' says Barbara Turner. 'We knew from the beginning that they had John Crerar down as a suspect, because they asked me if I knew him. I think he was one of the first to be brought in because he was known in the area, if you know what I mean. A known womaniser, if you'd like to call it that. There'd been complaints about him from women. But then they said that he had an alibi and he was clear, and we didn't have very much to do with him after that. He kept a very low profile then. He would never be around much, even though we would regularly meet his wife and children on the road. The gardaí had loads of suspects at the time, but how do you know? You never think anyone you know is a killer.'

It was just before noon on 18 January when Phyllis Murphy was finally found by one of the search teams. She had been lying in her frozen makeshift grave for twenty-eight days.

The area was immediately sealed off. The head of the 'Murder Squad', Chief Superintendent Dan Murphy, arrived to take charge of what was now officially a full murder investigation.

'The gardaí were pulling up to the door when it came on the radio,' says Barbara Turner. 'They tried to get to us in time, but the news just spread so quickly. We were so lucky to find her. That month she went missing, it was pure hell. Oh gosh, could you imagine if we hadn't found her?'

Barbara looks into the fire, a small smile on her face as she remembers the relief the family felt at being able to bring their sister home. Then the smile fades.

'Of course, by finding her we then knew what had happened to her, you know. Even though my brother tried to protect us from it. He told us she was fully clothed, because of course he didn't know it would be on the television, what really happened.'

Barbara sighs, a breath full of sadness and pain. 'And then my two brothers had to identify her. And that had a bad effect on them. Even to this day, you know. They can never forget seeing her that way.'

A silence falls in the room, broken only by the spitting of the burning wood. The effect of John Crerar's murderous actions continues to cause sad silences in the lives of the Murphy family. An act of brutality, completed in minutes. Grief that has spanned almost thirty years.

The Murphy brothers went to Naas General Hospital to identify Phyllis before the State Pathologist, Dr John Harbison, began a post-mortem examination on her body, just ten hours after she had been found.

Silence fell in the room as Harbison used twelve cotton buds to take swabs from Phyllis's body. They would later test positive for semen, confirming detectives' suspicions that she had been raped. The swabs were put into protective vials and placed in a locker in a garda station, where they remained for eight years.

Two days later, an estimated 2,000 people attended Phyllis Murphy's funeral.

In the weeks following the discovery of Phyllis's body, gardaí set about getting voluntary blood samples from fifty men who were considered to be suspects in the investigation.

On 6 March, despite the fact that he had an alibi, gardaí asked John Crerar for a blood sample. Perhaps feeling confident that he had successfully covered his tracks, Crerar agreed.

None of the fifty blood samples turned up any evidence for gardaí at the time. However, they carefully placed the stain cards in an envelope and stored them alongside the cotton buds in the Garda locker.

Over the next few months, detectives reviewed 22,000 question-naires, interviewed hundreds of people, and chased down every lead. In December 1980, the investigation stepped up when twenty new detectives were assigned to the case, led by Detective Superintendent John Courtney and Detective Inspector Gerard McCarrick.

The following month, in early January, it seemed that there might have been a breakthrough in the murder hunt when a farmer from Kildare walked into Clondalkin Garda Station and said he had new information. The man told gardaí about a Datsun car that he had seen parked near the Wicklow Gap soon after Phyllis Murphy had disappeared. John Crerar was driving a Datsun car at the time Phyllis disappeared. But John Crerar had an alibi. The lead had gone cold.

In 1988, the blood and semen samples were moved from the locker at Naas Garda Station to another locker at Kildare Station. They were not touched again until 1997, when Detective Inspector Brendan McArdle came looking for the evidence he believed would solve the murder.

Brendan McArdle was a uniformed garda when Phyllis Murphy went missing. He was one of hundreds of officers who searched for her body. Although later promoted to the ballistics section of the Garda Technical Bureau in Dublin, he did not forget the case.

In 1997, McArdle learned about groundbreaking new DNA technol-ogy that would allow a DNA profile to be determined from a tiny sample of blood or semen. It occurred to him that there was a possibility this new process could be used on the old samples taken from Phyllis Murphy's case. To his delight, when he contacted gardaí in Kildare, he found that both blood and semen samples had been meticulously preserved.

In July 1997, McArdle handed over the samples to Dr Maureen Smyth in the State Forensic Science Laboratory, who conducted fresh analysis on the cotton bud semen samples. By January 1998 she had determined that nine of the twelve swabs could yield DNA results using the polymerase chain reaction (PCR) method.

Swallowing a growing excitement, McArdle travelled to the Forensic Alliance Laboratory at Abingdon in Oxfordshire, where he handed the swabs to scientist Matthew Greenhalgh. The following month, Greenhalgh phoned McArdle to tell him the PCR test had worked. They had succeeded in extracting a full DNA profile from the semen.

It was a huge step forward in the investigation, but the DNA profile was useless unless it could be matched to the killer. At that time there was no DNA database in this country. (It is thought that one might be introduced in 2008.)

For detectives on the trail of Phyllis Murphy's killer, the absence of a database meant they did not have the option of quickly comparing their newly discovered DNA profile from the cotton swabs with the DNA records of hundreds of convicted rapists and murderers in the country.

However, they did have one other option—the stain cards containing blood samples from fifty men who were considered to be suspects at the time of the murder. In September 1998, McArdle delivered twenty-three stain cards to Matthew Greenhalgh, who successfully extracted DNA profiles from all of them and compared them with the results from the semen swabs. There was no match.

Refusing to give up, in February 1999 McArdle handed over the rest of the stain cards—one of which contained John Crerar's blood—along with twelve new samples from people who had more recently become suspects in the investigation. The net was tightening.

Four months later, the call came. Greenhalgh had found a match. The semen sample matched a blood sample taken from a man named John Crerar.

Dr Maureen Smyth would later conduct comparative analysis on the DNA profile. She would find that there was a one in seventy-six million chance that the DNA belonged to someone other than John Crerar. The following year she carried out further tests, using a more discriminating method of DNA, and concluded that the chance of another person having the same DNA profile was one in a thousand million.

In June 1999, detectives didn't have this definitive data. They knew, simply, that they had a match. And that gave them a prime suspect for the murder of Phyllis Murphy. They began meticulously planning the arrest.

Early on the morning of Tuesday, 13 July 1999, 51-year-old John Crerar awoke in his house in Kildare. He put on a mustard open-neck shirt, cream trousers, black runners and a blue and black waterproof jacket. He could not have known he would still be wearing those clothes the following day, during one of the most high-profile court appearances in the history of the State.

Crerar shut the door on his house in Kildare, and drove to the Seisiún Stud, where he worked as a security guard. His last journey as a free man.

Just before 7.30am, three detectives quietly pulled up to the Seisiún Stud in an unmarked patrol car. Detective Garda Mark Carroll approached Crerar, and calmly informed him that he was being arrested in connection with the murder of Phyllis Murphy. Crerar gasped with shock. After twenty years he must surely have believed he could never be linked to the crime. But he did not demur. He said nothing at all as he allowed himself to be shepherded into the patrol car and brought to Naas Garda Station.

Fifteen minutes later, in an interview room in the station, Crerar was told that a sample of his blood had been examined, and that the results suggested that he was the man who had left traces of semen on Phyllis Murphy's body.

Down the hallway, in another interview room, Patrick Bolger was being presented with the same evidence. The realisation that he had provided an alibi for a murderer dawned with quick horror on Bolger, and he immediately admitted to detectives that he had lied in his previous statement.

Unaware that his indubitable alibi was crumbling to pieces a few doors away, Crerar sat in the interview room struggling to register what was happening. He looked up as the door opened again and Detective Mark Carroll came into the room. Carroll asked him if he would provide fresh samples of his blood, saliva and pubic hair, making it perfectly clear that he had a right to refuse the request. Crerar—somewhat bafflingly—signed the consent form.

Maybe his success in eluding capture for twenty years had led him to arrogantly believe that he could never be linked to the crime. Maybe he thought that to refuse would make him appear guilty. Evidently, he was not aware of the latest advances in DNA technology. As he picked up the pen and turned to the consent form, Crerar was effectively signing his own life sentence.

The doctor had not yet arrived to take new blood samples by the time another Garda car was pulling up outside Barbara Turner's house in Kildare town. It was 8.30am when Garda Finbarr McPaul walked up to the door to deliver the news.

'He said they'd arrested someone,' says Barbara Turner, shaking her head as if still in disbelief. 'He asked if I wanted the gardaí to tell the rest of the family but I thought it would be better if we got them all here. So I rang them and told them I had news, and they came over to the house. We were all just in shock. A few minutes later it came on the radio, and it was then that everyone burst out crying. It made it so real, to hear it on the radio. It was just unbelievable.'

Within hours, the country's media had got hold of the story, and recognised it as probably the biggest Garda coup of the century.

'It just all went mad, with cameras and reporters and everything,' says Barbara. 'They all descended here, and it was actually a bit scary. But I decided to talk to them because I had always talked to reporters, all through the years. I talked to them to keep Phyllis's name alive and because I thought that if her name came up in the newspapers or on the television then whoever had killed her—if they saw it—maybe it would torment them a little. You know, that's the way I felt. We had to live with it every day, and I felt they should not be allowed to forget what they had done. Why should they get away scot-free?'

That evening, after the new blood samples were tested and found to be a perfect match with the original, John Crerar was officially arrested and charged with the murder of Phyllis Murphy. He answered, simply, dully, 'not guilty' when informed of the charge.

In Kildare town, the Murphy family were finally given the name of the man who had murdered their sister. Barbara Turner looks pensive as she remembers. 'We were hoping all the time it wasn't someone we knew, you know?' she says. 'Even when we heard that someone had been arrested, we never even thought for a second it would be him.' She sighs. 'It was awful. To think he had been living just up the road from us all this time. And that some of us had babysat for him. We still meet his family on the road all the time, and it's very awkward. We never wanted his family to suffer.'

The next day, plain-clothes gardaí accompanied Crerar in a maroon unmarked car on the short drive to Naas District Court from Naas Garda Station, where he had stayed overnight. Already a large, indignant crowd had gathered outside the courthouse, and they jeered and jostled as Crerar was led in handcuffs into the packed courtroom.

The ex-soldier appeared agitated and didn't look at the public gallery. He sat hunched over in his chair, covering his head with his hands throughout the four-minute hearing, and remained seated with his head bowed even when the rest of the court rose for Judge Thomas Ballagh's entrance. As he was led again from the courthouse, an even larger crowd had formed, waving their fists and shouting abuse at this man, a married father of five who had raped and killed a young girl all those years ago. Crerar tried ineffectually to cover his face with his hand, shielding himself from the flashing cameras and hostile public as he was ushered past two lines of gardaí and escorted to a waiting Garda car.

The following day gardaí were prepared for the public reaction to Crerar, and they sealed off the area around the entrance to the Newbridge courthouse to prevent over 200 onlookers from gathering close to the building. At 10.45am Crerar arrived in an unmarked Garda car and again cries of outrage and disgust were hurled from the crowd. Inside, Crerar's solicitor felt prompted to complain to the judge about the behaviour of the onlookers, but the heckling continued when Crerar left the building that afternoon. His comfortable, anonymous life as an unremarkable man was over for ever.

It took three years for the case to come to court. And it took four weeks for all the evidence to be heard. The Murphy family attended every day, every minute of the case—except when State Pathologist John Harbison took to the stand to give evidence. They could not listen to that.

'John Crerar was cool as anything throughout the whole thing,' says Barbara. 'He was just sitting there and you'd know by him that he expected to get off. It didn't seem to bother him at all.'

Finally, after four weeks the jury retired to consider their decision. The next afternoon they returned a unanimous guilty verdict. It was 31 October 2002.

From the back of the court someone cried out, 'Oh, Jesus'. It was one of John Crerar's daughters. The convicted murderer covered his face with his hand, and shook his head as the judge passed the mandatory life sentence and refused leave to appeal. Crerar did not rise when the judge left the courtroom. For many minutes he sat with his head down, his eyes closed.

Standing close by, the Murphy family were completely overcome. 'We didn't know the verdict was in, we were just called and we didn't know why,' says Barbara Turner. 'When he was found guilty it was such a shock. And it was so emotional. It was unbelievable, how emotional it was. I didn't take much notice of him because we were all hugging each other and crying. And then, suddenly, finally, it was all over.'

The Murphys walked as a strong, solid unit from the courtroom, justice finally having been done for their dead sister. Behind them, Crerar's wife, Carmel 'Betty' Crerar, was helped from the Four Courts, leaning heavily on her two sons, and flanked by her three daughters.

Last to leave was John Crerar, handcuffed and in the custody of two prison officers. His head was covered with a cloth hat and a woollen scarf. But he could no longer hide. The country had been given an horrific insight into his life, the acts he had committed, the callousness with which he had covered his tracks, and the deep wrenching pain he had caused both the Murphy family and his own. The country knew now the man he was. Not perfect. Not even close.

Chapter 4
The Murder of Patricia Furlong

The people of Ireland should have been scared. But they weren't to know what was coming.

As the 1980s dawned, a new generation of murderers and rapists was preparing to wreak havoc on Irish society. The relatively recent murder of Phyllis Murphy, which had so stunned the nation, was soon to fade in people's memories as some of the most infamous killers in Irish history made their mark on innocent families.

The eighties also marked the beginning of two decades of murders, disappearances and vicious assaults on women in the country, many of which remain unsolved, and many of which centred around the Dublin/Wicklow Mountains. Commentators began to discuss the 'Vanishing Triangle' that was the Leinster region.

Each new case was greeted with a little less shock, a little more apathy. The realisation was dawning that bad things could happen here too. For the first time, people started locking their doors.

But it took a while for the disturbing new trend of random violence to emerge. It took a while for the fear to set in, and a natural mistrust of others to permeate the island. And so, when 20-year-old Patricia Furlong didn't come home after a night out in Dublin in 1982, her family should have been scared. But they weren't.

'We were more angry than anything else, because she'd got us all worried,' says Angela Furlong, a sad smile on her face. She's sitting at the kitchen table in her house in Dundrum. Her sister Pauline doesn't smile. She just looks sad. They have come together on this autumn afternoon to tell me about their murdered sister, Patricia.

'Even when the Garda car pulled up outside the house the next day, the very worst thing we thought was that she'd been raped,' says Angela. 'It never even occurred to us she'd been killed. You see, there were no murders then.'

But Patricia had been killed. She had been found dead in a field in the mountains by two teenage girls at eight o'clock on the morning of 24 July 1982. She was naked from the waist up, her clothes having been wrenched up around her neck and used as a ligature to cut off her air supply.

Witnesses remembered seeing Patricia in the company of an unidentified man the previous night, a man dressed all in white. For eight years this person evaded capture. For eight years, the Furlong family grieved and wondered.

Finally, in 1990, gardaí arrested a person who had always been a suspect in the crime. A man whose ability to switch personalities, from charming to sadistically violent, meant that every garda who dealt with him never forgot his name. A man who protested his innocence to his death. Officially, he was Vincent Connell. But detectives called him 'The man of a thousand faces'.

Patricia Furlong wasn't supposed to be anywhere near the mountains that night. It was a Friday evening in the middle of the summer, and she had just finished another week's work as a shop assistant in Hafner's Butchers in Dundrum. On the way home, she stopped by her local pub, the Nine Arches, where she had one or two drinks before heading back to her house for something to eat.

There was always something happening in the Furlong family home at 30 Mulvey Park in Dundrum. Patricia was the fifth child in a family of six, and there were only two bedrooms in the house, so there was a constant, comforting barrage of people coming and going, shouting and laughing and talking to each other.

'We were living on top of each other, but it was good because it meant we had to get along,' says Angela, smiling ruefully. 'I think at one stage there were twelve of us living together in the house, because one or two of us got married and hadn't found a place of our own. We were sleeping three or four in a bed at that point. It was always mad, but it was happy.'

Although she was twenty years old, Patricia had no immediate plans to move out of the bustling comfort of 30 Mulvey Park. Despite her age, her sisters remember that there was still a childishness about her, a sort of endearing innocence.

'We had all found jobs as soon as possible after school, that's just what people did then,' says Angela. 'But for Patricia, it didn't mean that she grew up quickly. She was still very young in a lot of ways. You know, she'd go into the pub, and she'd be talking to everyone, she had great time for all the old people. She'd go over to some of the locals and she'd sit on their knee and have a chat with them. She was very childlike in that way. She just got on with everyone.'

When she got home that evening, Patricia had something to eat before running a bath in preparation for her night out. She wasn't intending on doing anything particularly exciting, having decided to return to the Nine Arches for a few drinks with her friends. However, when she came down the stairs, her family whistled in admiration.

'It was the strangest thing, because she was wearing a skirt,' says Pauline, her eyes widening in surprise at the memory. 'It was the first time in a very long time that we'd seen her in a skirt. She used to always wear those trousers that were in fashion at the time, the ones that were so tight you'd be poured into them. But not that night. And she seemed delighted with herself in it.'

Calling goodbye to her family—for the last time—Patricia set off again down the road in the direction of the Nine Arches, her shoulder-length hair swinging gently as she walked.

'She would have been smiling when she left, because she was always smiling. This is what you'd see if you met Patricia on the road,' says Angela, producing a photograph of her sister. The picture is of a grinning young girl with a lightly freckled face, her light brown hair falling straight to her shoulder, her bright eyes looking out from under a wispy fringe. 'See the little gap there?' says Angela, laughing and pointing at the offending space between Patricia's two front teeth. 'She hated that gap, she just hated it. But this is what you would always meet. This smiling face, always in good form.'

A few doors from her house, Patricia came across two neighbouring children out on the street skipping. She offered to turn the rope for them a couple of times, before taking her chance to skip. After a while, flushed and a little breathless, the young woman continued her journey to the pub.

At around 8.30pm, Patricia arrived at the Nine Arches, where she spent a couple of hours chatting with her friends and having a few drinks. It was then that some of the group started talking about going up to Glencullen in the Dublin Mountains, where the Fraughan Festival was taking place that night. One of Patricia's friends, Denis Glenn, offered to drop the rest of them up to the festival and collect them later that night. It seemed like the perfect plan.

At around 12.30am, Patricia and her friends arrived at the festival. Three tents had been erected behind Johnny Fox's pub, and the place was packed with hundreds of people. Patricia launched herself into the crowd, ready for a night of fun.

Standing deep in the throng was Vincent Connell. He was ostentatiously dressed to stand out from the crowd, wearing a white top, white trousers, white belt and white shoes. This contrasted sharply with his mop of slick black hair and clean-shaven face, ensuring that Connell cut a striking figure among the masses.

Beside him stood his fiancée, Mary Creedon, her eyes resting on Connell with a mixture of love and fear. They had travelled to the festival that evening on Connell's insistence. A DJ by trade, and highly ambitious, Connell was hoping to meet a man called Bobby Gahan, from RTÉ, to whom he planned to propose various collaborations for the future.

The couple had had a few drinks in Lamb Doyle's pub beforehand, and as Patricia Furlong waved goodbye to Denis Glenn, they were settling inside one of the beer tents, Connell's eyes scanning the crowd for Gahan.

Then Mary Creedon saw a young girl with brown hair and a fringe appear at the entrance to the tent, accompanied by a group of other girls and guys. Connell followed the direction of Mary's gaze and also spotted the girl. He told his fiancée that he knew the young woman because he had been on a couple of dates with her in the past. He said he was going to talk to her for a while, and that he'd be back shortly.

It didn't even occur to Mary to argue with Connell. She knew better. Although the couple had only met each other in January of that year, Mary had already borne the brunt of Connell's vicious, unpredictable temper.

That month they had gone to a party together where both of them had joined in a sing-song. Halfway through the tune, Connell had started shouting at Mary to shut up. Shocked and upset, Mary had disappeared into the hall, humiliated at how her fiancée had treated her in front of her friends.

Another man at the party had followed her into the hall, and the two had started a conversation. Later, Connell accused Mary of having cheated on him with this other man. Raging and drunk, Connell had punched Mary in the face before wrapping his hands around her throat and pressing her up against the wall. She was gasping for air, and later told the court that she thought he was trying to kill her.

The next day, Mary had a black eye from the assault. Connell phoned her repeatedly, apologising and promising that it would never happen again. Mary told him that it was over, but Connell persisted. As detectives were later to note, Vincent Connell could be extremely convincing and charming when he wanted. Mary eventually capitulated, and the relationship resumed.

And so, when Connell told his fiancée that he was leaving her alone to go and talk with an ex-girlfriend, it didn't occur to her to argue. She watched him weave his way through the crowd towards the entrance of the tent, where the girl with the fringe was now standing on her own, having somehow lost her friends in the hordes of people.

At around 1.30am, a 14-year-old boy who was also at the Fraughan Festival spotted Patricia Furlong standing at the entrance to one of the beer tents. The boy lived close to Patricia in Mulvey Park, and knew her and her family well.

He approached her for a chat, and saw that she was with a tall young man, who was dressed all in white and was wearing his black hair in what the boy described as a 'Shakin' Stevens-style' cut. Patricia seemed to know the man, and the two were quite intimate, cuddling each other and kissing.

The man turned to Patricia and said that they should get going. The boy watched as the two walked towards the entrance of the field and onto the road. They were chatting and laughing, and had their arms linked together. They seemed simply to be a happy couple looking for a little bit of privacy. The boy turned back towards the tent, unaware that he was the last person to see Patricia Furlong alive.

About forty-five minutes after leaving the tent, Vincent Connell returned to where Mary Creedon was standing waiting. She noticed immediately that he seemed to be 'agitated and unsettled', and his behaviour put her on edge. She was learning from experience that Connell was liable to lash out when he was in this sort of mood. He didn't mention where he had been for almost an hour, and she didn't ask.

They left the festival shortly afterwards, Connell's bad form persisting as he drove towards Cornelscourt. Suddenly he turned to Mary and asked her to leave the country with him the following day. He said he had an offer of a job with Radio Clyde in Scotland, and suggested that the two of them could just leave, and make a new life for themselves there.

Mary flatly refused, not backing down even when Connell became angry. The couple travelled the rest of the journey home in silence.

At 8am the following day, two teenage girls were out for an early morning stroll through the mountains. As they approached Corbett's Field off the main Glencullen Road, they noticed what appeared to be a woman sleeping on the grass. However, as they got closer they could see something peculiarly awkward about the way the woman was lying. Then they saw her clothes knotted around her neck, her pale lifeless face, her chest completely still in the absence of breath. Screaming in terror, they ran from the field and alerted the authorities.

Soon a team of gardaí from Stepaside arrived at the scene, and the area was cordoned off and preserved for technical examination. Sergeant John Manley looked carefully at the dead woman. He took in her blue skirt, fanned out on the ground beneath her, and her white shoes, slightly muddied from walking through the field. She was naked from the waist up, and he saw that her blue shirt and white jacket were wrapped tightly around her neck. Her bra was twisted around her left hand. Manley sighed deeply. He knew this could only result in a major murder investigation.

There was nothing on the body or in the vicinity to help gardaí immediately identify the woman, so they drew up a statement with a description of the woman and issued it to the press.

The pathologist, Dr Declan Gilsenan, arrived and did a preliminary examination of the body before the remains of Patricia Furlong were taken to Loughlinstown Hospital for a post-mortem examination.

In the small house at 30 Mulvey Park, the Furlongs were going crazy with worry and frustration.

'It was a Saturday, so we were all there in the house and my parents were going up the wall because Patricia hadn't come home all night,' says Angela. 'We were all so annoyed with her, that she hadn't called to say that she was going to stay in a friend's house or tell us where she was. We spent the day giving out about her, and going in and out of the house to look down the road in case we'd see her coming. My mother was pale with the worry of it, I remember that. But even then, none of us thought for one second that she could be dead. Injured maybe or something like that. But not dead. Because there were no murders then.'

It wasn't until the afternoon that the Furlongs noticed that a few of their neighbours were gathering in groups on the street, and looking over at their house. They didn't know that a young woman's body had been found in the mountains, because they didn't have a radio and they didn't hear the news bulletins.

'Then one of our neighbours came over to us, and said that a girl's body was after being found in Glencullen,' says Angela. 'And just as she was telling us, a police car pulled up outside the door, and they had a doctor in the back seat because my mother had angina at the time, and they didn't know how she'd react to the news.'

The gardaí didn't say immediately that Patricia was dead. They had eventually found identification in the field, but they did not know for certain that it belonged to the dead woman. Instead, they told the Furlongs that there'd been an accident, and they wanted someone to come up and identify the person who had been injured.

'We couldn't believe it, how it all happened,' says Angela. 'Myself, my husband and my dad had to go with the gardaí up to Stepaside, and then my dad and I were put into a room and my husband continued on to Loughlinstown hospital. They didn't tell us she was dead, but going up in the car we knew something really bad had happened. I just kept saying, "Please God, let it be rape", because at least we could cope with that and we could help her through it. But you know, at the same time, that was the worst that I was thinking could have happened. I still wasn't thinking that she'd be dead, because no one just died like that.'

But in Loughlinstown Hospital, Angela's husband was learning differently. He identified the body of Patricia Furlong, and returned to Stepaside Garda Station, where he broke the news to his wife and her father. The three people made the sickening journey back down the mountain to tell the rest of Patricia's family. Their daughter and sister was dead.

'We had no phone in the house, so we had to go to one of the neighbours to ring my brother in Tallaght and tell him,' says Angela. 'Everyone was walking around with the paper, and one of us ran down to the shop to get our own copy. It gave a description of the girl who had been found, and it said that she was wearing a ring with a little green stone in it. And it was strange, it was only when we read that that it really seemed true. We all knew that ring of Patricia's. So it meant it must really be her. She was really dead.'

Both Patricia's sisters say that the next few weeks passed in a blur of shock and grief, as they struggled to cope with the reality that their sister had been murdered. 'It was just a question of survival really, it's all a bit of a blur,' says Angela. 'We were just devastated. A lot of it is a blank in my mind. I think the worst thing, though, was how it affected our parents. I mean, we were bad enough, but I don't think you could realise what it's like to lose a child until you have children of your own. My parents were destroyed. My dad doesn't show emotion very much, and his way of dealing with it was to blame everyone. He'd be down at the pub, and he'd be accusing everyone of having killed her, and we had to keep telling him to stop. It was awful to see him like that.'

Angela pauses then, and swallows. 'But my mother, she was just heartbroken,' she says. And for the first time since the conversation began, her eyes fill with tears. Beside her, Pauline smiles sadly, her own face flushing with emotion. 'She never got over it,' says Angela. 'It broke her heart really. She'd just recovered from cancer, and then, for this to happen,' Angela stops talking again, and bites her lip, forcing the tears back. 'It just killed her really.'

In the weeks following the murder, the Furlong family gleaned some small comfort from the fact that Patricia had not been sexually assaulted before she died, and that she didn't appear to have been beaten either.

'We were very grateful for that, that she didn't seem to have suffered,' says Angela. 'It seems that it took only a few seconds to kill her, and that was it. She wasn't battered beforehand, she wasn't raped beforehand. And you know, we were always thankful as well that she was found. Afterwards we started hearing all these cases of women going missing, and I knew that I would just be a basket case if my sister had just disappeared. I would be out searching for her still. So to this day, we are really thankful she was found. For those families of missing people, the pain must be unbelievable.'

However, the Furlongs could never really rest until Patricia's murderer was found. As the shock began to fade, and they started dealing with the dull, constant loss, they turned their attention to the Garda investigation. Watching, hoping, that the killer would be caught.

For the gardaí, the circumstances surrounding Patricia's death meant her murder investigation would be a mammoth task. It was estimated that a thousand people had attended the festival the previous night, and they all had to be interviewed. A team of over a hundred detectives and uniformed personnel was drafted in to help with the enquiries, while the Garda Press Office sent out numerous statements to the media, appealing to the public to contact Stepaside Garda Station if they had any information.

It was then that the 14-year-old witness came forward and informed gardaí about the man he had seen with Patricia, and how the two had walked away from the festival together. With 'the man in white' on top of their suspect list, detectives started wading through the stacks of quickly accumulating statements.

One of the first people to come forward was Vincent Connell. After hearing the news on the radio the day after the murder, Connell suggested to Mary Creedon that they should go immediately to the garda station to give a statement.

However, en route to the station, Connell turned the car in the direction of Johnny Fox's pub, saying he wanted to first check with the locals if there had been any developments in the case. This seems to have been a classic case of the killer returning to the scene of the crime.

From Glencullen, Connell and his fiancée went on to Stepaside. They were met by Garda James Broderick, to whom Connell announced that they had been at the festival the previous evening and wanted to help with the investigation. He and Mary Creedon proceeded to give an oral account of their night. Connell said that he had spent the entire evening with Mary in the beer tent, except for a few trips to the toilet, but that he was missing for no more than five minutes at any one time.

When her fiancé didn't mention that he had actually left her for forty-five minutes, Mary was too frightened to correct him. She confirmed his account of his movements. It was only years later that detectives realised what a crucial mistake it was to interview the pair at the same time.

Broderick then asked the couple if they would mind giving a written statement. Immediately Connell became extremely agitated. He refused, and ordered Mary not to do so either. He also refused to be photographed or fingerprinted, becoming increasingly hostile with each new request.

'He jumped up and got very aggressive,' Broderick later recalled. 'He said he had come to help and was being harassed, and demanded to see the superintendent in charge. I was not harassing him and explained I needed their movements and people they met that night. He got very aggressive and I told him he was not obliged to make a statement. I told him the superintendent was not there but the detective inspector would see him. He took Mary Creedon by the arm and left the building.'

Connell created such a fuss that other gardaí in the station emerged to see what was happening. Garda Broderick, who was completely taken aback by Connell's reaction, could only shrug helplessly in response to his colleagues' enquiring glances.

The bizarre behaviour of the young man was enough to raise the antennae of the gardaí, and Connell was placed on a list of possible suspects. Three weeks later, accompanied by Sergeant Bob Greene, Garda James Broderick went to Connell's home to try again to get a written statement from him.

'He invited us in and at first seemed relaxed and friendly,' said Broderick. 'But he would become agitated at the drop of a hat.'

On this occasion, Connell seemed content to have the gardaí write down an account of his movements. He was also shown a photograph of Patricia Furlong, and he said he didn't know her. However, when he was asked to sign the written account, Connell again became extremely annoyed. He ordered the gardaí out of his house and threatened to report them to the Garda Commissioner for hassling him.

But no matter how extraordinary his behaviour, Vincent Connell had a watertight alibi in the form of his fiancée Mary Creedon. In the absence of either motive or opportunity, detectives were forced to file away his statement and focus on their seemingly endless list of other possible suspects.

The description of the killer as 'the man in white' had been released to the public, and had sparked a fresh wave of interest in the case. Information poured into Stepaside Garda Station, and each statement had to be carefully read and checked. A file was opened on every man who had attended the festival on his own. The scene of the murder was combed for clues. But it all led to nothing.

One month after she was killed, the inquest opened into Patricia's death. The coroner, Dr Bartley Sheehan, said that Patricia had died as a result of asphyxia due to strangulation. This confirmed what everyone had already suspected. A few months later, the investigation began to wind down. But there was still a killer out there. The murder file remained open.

To Vincent Connell it seemed that was the end of his dealings with the Patricia Furlong investigation. He had successfully evaded arrest. It wasn't the first time, and it wasn't the last.

Born to an Irish mother in London on 30 March 1951, Connell was an only child who had received a very good education. He was an extremely articulate young man—a fact about which the judge at his trial would later comment—and an accomplished public speaker, having been awarded a Royal Society of Arts Advanced Certificate in Spoken English. He was also a talented musician, and when the urge took him he was capable of entertaining an entire room of people with his guitar and singing act.

However, hidden beneath his intelligent, civilised appearance there lurked a sadistically violent man who seemed to have a curious love/hate relationship with women. In the years before and after Patricia Furlong's murder, Connell left a string of ex-girlfriends in his wake, all of them traumatised, many of them scarred.

'He was no threat to men at all,' says (now retired) Detective Inspector Michael Canavan, who worked on the Furlong murder investigation. 'But he was lethal for women. He once poured boiling water over his mother and aunt. That was the type of brute he was.'

When he was 19, Connell moved to Ireland with his mother, and they settled in a house on Neagh Road in Terenure. For a few years, Connell worked for various insurance companies around Dublin city, but he was restless. He had always harboured a wish to join the police force, but was excluded from the Garda Síochána because he didn't speak Irish.

In 1977 he moved to Liverpool, where he joined the Merseyside Constabulary. However, after just six months he was asked to leave the force, amidst rumours that he had assaulted a sergeant.

He returned to Ireland in 1978, and took the next best option to joining the Garda by becoming a prison officer in Mountjoy. In the autumn of that year he was at a disco when he met a young woman called Gillian Kane, who worked as a dental nurse on Harcourt Street.

In the same pattern that Connell was later to display in his relationship with Mary Creedon, his relationship with Gillian Kane became very serious very quickly and on 24 December of that year they got engaged.

As soon as the engagement was made official, the abuse began— similar again to the experience of Mary Creedon. On 27 December 1978, the couple went to Kelly's Hotel in South Great George's Street. Connell had been drinking all day and at 1am Gillian began to get tired. She told Connell he could stay as long as he liked, but that she wanted to go home. A fierce argument ensued, with Connell insisting that Gillian stay out with him.

Before leaving the hotel, Gillian went to the women's toilets. Connell followed her into the restroom and punched her savagely in the head and face. 'He almost knocked the eyes out of her head,' says Detective Inspector Michael Canavan, shaking his head at the violence of the attack. 'It was a really vicious assault.'

When the couple emerged from the bathroom, it was obvious that something awful had happened. Gillian was bleeding profusely from an open wound in her head, and the right side of her face was already starting to swell. Connell told the hotel owner that his fiancée was suicidal, and that she had deliberately injured herself on a wash basin.

Also like Mary Creedon, Gillian found it very difficult to leave Connell, despite his abusive behaviour, and she was still engaged to him one year later. However, the relationship was heavily punctuated with arguments, and by January 1980 had hit a particularly rocky period.

It was at around 7.30pm one evening that month that Connell called over to Gillian's house at Daingean Park in Crumlin, where she lived with her mother, Phyllis. The couple had arranged to go out for the evening, but by the time Connell arrived Gillian was still upstairs getting ready.

Phyllis Kane invited him into the sitting room, and was going about her business when she heard a gurgling noise behind her. She turned around to see Connell with his hands around the neck of the family's terrier dog, throttling the life out of it. As he squeezed, he was shouting, 'Gillian loves this dog more than me.' Phyllis managed to rescue the dog from Connell, but four weeks later the animal disappeared forever.

Shortly after this incident, Gillian Kane finally summoned up the courage to end the relationship. Connell didn't take the rejection well. Twice over the next two years he set fire to Gillian's house in Crumlin by pouring petrol through the letter box and setting it alight while the family were inside. On the second occasion, they were lucky to escape with their lives.

However, this was mild in comparison to the horrific violence he attempted to inflict on Gillian's mother. For whatever reason—perhaps it was her refusal to let him strangle the dog—Connell had formed an inexplicable vendetta against Phyllis Kane. He contacted a hardened criminal and gave him specific instructions on how to rape and torture the elderly woman.

'After Connell was charged I was talking to this criminal from Cork who told me the most disturbing story,' says one detective. 'He said that Connell had paid him £2,000 to go to Gillian Kane's house and to attack her mother by putting a hot curling iron up her vagina. The criminal said that when Gillian's mother answered the door, standing there all silver-haired and innocent, that he couldn't do it. In fact, he said that he was so incensed that Connell would even ask him to do such a thing that he decided he was going to bring him up to the top of the Ballymun flats and throw him off. That never happened, in the end. But of course, he never gave Connell his money back either. He told me that he had never met someone who could appear so innocent and be so evil. As a result, he said he'd christened him "the man of a thousand faces".'

It was a nickname that was to stick, as detectives uncovered more of Connell's brutal history with women.

In the same year that his relationship with Gillian Kane ended, Connell also lost his job as a prison officer after it was discovered that he was playing music requests for the prisoners.

Moving away from working in law enforcement, Connell instead found a job as a presenter with the pirate radio station Radio Leinster. He also started working as an assistant manager in the Top Hat Ballroom in Dún Laoghaire, where he set up his own roller-skating team, called Vinnie's Wheels and Co. It is here that both detectives and the Furlong family believe that Vincent Connell met Patricia Furlong.

'Patricia used to go out there a good bit to go skating, so it makes sense that they would have met each other there,' says Angela. 'He had a roller-skating team and it would be very likely that she would have wanted to be on it. She loved the roller-skating. It was a bit of a laugh, even though you'd fall or get bruised. We couldn't get anyone who had actually seen them talking to each other, but he must have known her, if only to see. Dublin wasn't that big, you know.'

Whether or not he met Patricia in the Top Hat, Connell took advantage of his position to meet other women. It was while he was working in the ballroom that he met and started dating a girl called Barbara Wallace.

The relationship only lasted three months, but it was long enough for Barbara to determine that Connell had what she called 'a superior attitude' to people in authority.

During the eventual court trial, Barbara Wallace recalled how she was returning with Connell from a hotel one night. He was driving very fast and she advised him to slow down. He said if they were stopped by gardaí 'the best defence is to say you're being hassled and interfered with'. During cross-examination she refused to budge on what she had heard. 'I remember it clearly,' she said. This evidence was to become very pertinent during the trial.

By 1981, Connell had started going out with a girl called Agnes Long. Again, it wasn't long before he began showing his true colours.

On one occasion he wrapped his hands around her neck in what she firmly believed was an attempt to strangle her to death. Shortly afterwards, during a night out in Peekers Nightclub in Dún Laoghaire, Connell became extremely angry with Agnes and punched her in the face before extinguishing his cigarette on the side of her face, leaving her scarred for life.

Not long after that, the relationship ended, leaving Connell free to meet and woo Mary Creedon in January 1982. By the time the couple attended the Fraughan Festival together in July, Connell had already seriously assaulted Mary and put his hands around her neck in what she believed was an attempt to kill her.

In September 1982, just a few weeks after Patricia was killed, Connell made the decision to move to Liverpool to work as a presenter on Liverpool's Radio City. He pressured Mary Creedon to join him, which she did, despite her instincts warning her against the move.

In mid-October the couple came back to Ireland for a weekend visit, and during that time Mary noticed with dismay that Connell was now beginning to be hostile and aggressive towards her parents. The thought of her family suffering the sort of abuse that she was already enduring was too much for Mary, and she returned to Liverpool with Connell with the express intention of packing her bags and ending the relationship.

In their small rented house in Liverpool city, Mary told Vincent Connell that she was leaving him. He became completely deranged.

He beat her viciously and screamed that he wouldn't allow her to leave him. He was true to his word.

'He used to chain her to the radiator when he was going to work so she couldn't leave the house,' says Detective Inspector Michael Canavan, shaking his head again. 'This fellow was an animal really. There's no other way to describe him.'

Eventually, Mary succeeded in escaping just long enough to contact her parents. She pleaded with them to come quickly. They immediately set off for Liverpool, and managed to smuggle their daughter out of the house while Connell was at work.

Unfortunately for Mary Creedon—like Gillian Kane before her—Connell wouldn't leave her life that easily. Over the following years he bombarded her home with malicious phone calls, threatening to burn down her home and take revenge on her entire family.

Even eight years later, Connell's vendetta against the family had evidently not faded. Detective Inspector Michael Canavan recalls that during a search of Connell's house in 1990 he found a number of montages made from newspapers in a shed at the back of the premises. The cuttings referred to Mary Creedon and members of her family. Connell's fingerprints were all over the newspaper, and Canavan believes that even then he was contemplating a campaign of terror against the family.

After Mary left him, Vincent Connell's life in Liverpool took a turn for the worse. He had become very popular as a presenter on Radio City, and in January 1983 he was promoted from a night slot to the high-profile *City Extra* programme. However, by October of that year, Connell was regularly showing up late for work, looking tired and dishevelled. Eventually the station bosses gave him the sack.

Ironically, it was Connell's reaction to being fired that ultimately led to his arrest for the murder of Patricia Furlong. Instead of accepting the decision, Connell took an unfair dismissal action against the station.

In response, management at Radio City asked the station's chief investigative reporter, Kieran Devaney, to make some discreet inquiries into Connell's past. Within a very short time, Devaney had discovered that the DJ had given false references to Radio City. Then, when he contacted Connell's former colleagues in Ireland, he found them reluctant to talk about him because of his perceived links with the Patricia Furlong murder.

This led Devaney to make some further enquiries about the killing in Glencullen. He had met Mary Creedon during the time she was living in Liverpool, and he decided to go and visit her to ask her about that night at the Fraughan Festival. During the course of their conversation, Mary revealed that Connell had left her alone for forty-five minutes during the festival. She said that she had been too terrified to tell the truth until then, but felt safer now that she had finished the relationship. And, as simply as that, Connell's alibi was destroyed.

Devaney approached the gardaí, who in turn contacted Mary Creedon, who agreed to make a new statement containing the real version of events that night.

However, by the time Mary was being re-interviewed by detectives, Connell had once again moved out of the reach of the law. He had begun a new relationship with a young girl called Denise Raine, whom he had met in Liverpool. She was going to South Africa, and— maybe somehow sensing the approaching danger—Connell decided to go with her.

The relationship didn't last long, but before Denise could get away from Connell he had succeeded in crippling her for life.

'He attacked her with a hammer in Port Elizabeth,' says Detective Inspector Michael Canavan. 'He hit her on the head with the hammer, and left her paralysed for life down one side of her body. She was a beautiful young girl and he completely ruined her life. She never reported it either, because he told her at the time that if she went to the police he would kill her parents by burning them to death. And she believed him. He had that power, you see, to instil this God-awful fear into people, because they knew him and they knew what he was capable of.'

During the trial, Denise's parents came forward to the gardaí and revealed what Connell had done to their daughter. However, Denise was still too scared to officially report the attack, and there was little the gardaí could do to help.

Connell left Denise, her poor body destroyed, and continued his travels through South Africa. He did some freelance work for Radio Algoa and then spent some time in Namibia, where he worked on Radio South West Africa. At one stage, he was taken off the air in Namibia because he was drinking so heavily he was incoherent.

In 1985, Connell found a job with Radio 5, the nationwide South African state broadcasting corporation. It was there that the Irish DJ established himself as one of South Africa's top disc jockeys. He became a household name in the country, with millions of listeners tuning in for his popular Sunday Morning show *Sunday Braai* (or barbecue).

It was during his time with Radio 5 that Connell also became the driving force behind a major Live Aid-style fundraising campaign, which helped secure liver transplants for two young girls suffering from liver disease.

He then expanded his charity work to help the Society for the Prevention of Cruelty to Animals, using the *Sunday Braai* programme to find homes for hundreds of stray and injured dogs and cats and earning himself the SPCA's Reeve Forman Home Finding Award in 1986.

During this campaign, Connell worked closely with a council member from the SPCA called Barbara Nash. When she later heard he had been arrested, she declared herself 'stunned'. 'It is totally alien to the person I knew in the capacity of my work,' she said.

In a character reference given to Connell's lawyers, Nash said her personal perception was that he would react immediately to any animal needing help and that it would be totally uncharacteristic for him to act in a cruel or irresponsible way to animals.

To complete his apparent transformation, Vincent Connell also became a monk. 'I'll never forget watching that video of "Brother Vincent", dressed all in white, preaching to the congregation in South Africa,' says Michael Canavan, covering his eyes with one hand as if to block the memory. 'For a full hour that tape ran. I'll never forget it.'

All things considered, the man who presented himself to the people of South Africa could not have been more different from the violent, erratic individual who had lived in Ireland. However, as ever with Connell, appearances were deceptive.

Unsurprisingly, he had begun a new relationship when he settled in South Africa, with a woman called Felicity Louw. This love affair ended in marriage, and as soon as the wedding was over the beatings began. Felicity later claimed that Connell was a 'Jekyll and Hyde character' who, for the entire six months of their union, regularly beat her and her 18-year-old daughter. She said his charity work was nothing but a front.

'He played Mr Nice Guy on radio and in public but would laugh in private and say he only did it to further his career,' she said after he was arrested. 'The police approached me and told me he was facing a murder charge. They asked if I would go to Ireland and testify against him but I refused. I want to forget I ever knew him.'

Felicity's daughter, Sally, also spoke of her extremely negative experience of her former stepfather, describing him as 'a brutal man with an uncontrollable temper'. 'He twice beat me up badly for trying to convince my mum to leave him,' she said. 'He beat my mum with anything he could lay his hands on.'

In 1987, Connell returned to Dublin on a flying visit to his mother. Immediately detectives swooped in, and they interviewed him at Dundrum station. However, Connell steadfastly stuck to his original story and then flew back to South Africa the following day. From there, he bombarded the Garda Commissioner with complaints, on one occasion even ringing Dundrum Station and threatening to kill one of the gardaí who had interviewed him.

In 1989, Vincent Connell finally moved back to Ireland. He was immediately interviewed again, which prompted more heated exchanges and culminated in him storming out of the door. Unfortunately for gardaí, despite Mary Creedon's new statement, they still did not have sufficient evidence to arrest Connell for the murder of Patricia Furlong.

Matters rested for a while, and Connell found a job as a night news reporter with Capital Radio in Dublin. He proved an impressive and diligent worker, although some female staff members expressed unease about him. Station bosses were delighted when he secured an interview for the station with Archbishop Desmond Tutu during the South African elections.

However, relations with Capital deteriorated when Connell played a report from a British jail riot and claimed it was actually a recording of rioting in Mountjoy. In 1990, he was let go as part of a cost-cutting package.

In the meantime, he had also started a new relationship with a woman called Barbara Rooney, and by November 1989 the couple had moved into a flat in Fairview together.

On Monday, 20 November they went out for a drink in the local pub. As ever, the alcohol brought out the most aggressive side to Connell's nature, and when they returned to the flat he started an argument with Barbara and raised his hand, threatening to punch her.

Barbara tried to fight back. She told him that if he hit her she would scream for help and the man in the neighbouring flat would come to help her. Connell then took a sharp knife from the kitchen drawer and said he would stab the man before using the knife on

Barbara herself. He then put his hands around Barbara's neck, and squeezed so hard she was gasping for air. She later said she was sure she was going to die. And then she passed out.

When she woke up, she was lying in bed beside Connell, who was sleeping. She crept out of the flat and went to a local garda station. She returned with some uniformed officers, who escorted Connell out of the flat.

It was as a result of this serious assault that the name of Vincent Connell began circulating in Garda circles again. A number of meetings were held involving senior officers from the Patricia Furlong investigation, and it was decided to arrest Vincent Connell in connection with one of his arson attacks on Gillian Kane's home.

In May 1990, a team of gardaí went to Connell's home to carry out the arrest. To their dismay, they found he was gone. He had left Dublin for the day to attend a confirmation ceremony in Ashbourne, Co. Meath, where he was acting as a sponsor for the son of yet another female friend.

After the Mass, Connell decided to dress up as a priest for the celebrations in the house. He explained to his new girlfriend that he thought it would make a good show for the guests, and she doubtfully agreed. He was in excellent form, then, until word reached him that the gardaí had been at his home in Dublin looking for him. He went berserk. 'He got extremely drunk and starting shouting and screaming and getting sick and falling all over the place,' says Detective Inspector Michael Canavan. 'He created complete havoc.'

Eventually, other guests at the party managed to calm Connell down and he was put to bed for the rest of the night. The following morning, Connell called the gardaí demanding to know why they wanted to talk to him again. He was asked to meet detectives in Fleet Bar in D'Olier Street, where he was told it would all be explained. Connell agreed to the meeting. The trap was set.

By 5pm on 20 May 1990, the Garda team was in place. Almost an hour later, Connell walked into the Fleet Bar. Immediately, he was arrested for arson on Gillian Kane's house on 15 May 1982, and brought outside to where a patrol car was waiting to take him to Tallaght Garda Station.

'When we finally arrested him he didn't come with us easily,' says Michael Canavan. 'He was shouting out the window that he was being kidnapped by us, and screaming for someone to call the gardaí. Then when we got to the station he started playing the guitar, and singing "The Piano Man" by Billy Joel. He'd just switch that easily, from one personality to another.'

The events that took place over the next forty-eight hours at Tallaght Garda Station were the source of much dispute during the court case, and ultimately formed the cornerstone of Connell's defence.

As soon as he arrived at the station, Connell demanded to talk to his solicitor. Detectives allowed him access to the phone, but because it was a Sunday there was no reply from the solicitor's office. Numerous phone calls produced the same result—an answering machine.

Between the phone calls, detectives were talking to Connell about the fire they believed he had started at Gillian Kane's home. Connell flatly denied he knew anything about the fire, and then said he didn't even know a woman called Gillian Kane.

During the interview, Connell alternated between eerie calm and a state of extreme agitation and aggressiveness, pacing restlessly around the room and shouting abuse at the investigating officers.

At one point he approached one of the detectives, Sergeant Gerry O'Carroll, and sat on his knee. 'He sat on my lap and pretended to be homosexual,' O'Carroll later recalled. 'He was provoking me but I did not rise to that provocation.'

Later that night, Connell finally managed to make contact with his solicitor and a short conversation ensued. Shortly afterwards, he was put into a cell for the night.

The following day, determined to challenge Connell on his claim that he had never met Gillian Kane, detectives asked Gillian to come into the station to confront him. Gillian was initially and understand-ably reluctant to come into any further contact with her ex-fiancé, but agreed to help.

In the presence of Connell, Gillian answered a number of detec-tives' questions about their past relationship. After she left the station, Connell confessed to knowing her and admitted that it was he who had carried out the arson attack on her house. A statement was made to that effect, and John Courtney, then Chief Superintendent, served an extension order allowing Connell to be detained for a further twenty-four hours.

Now that he had confessed to the arson attack, detectives began to question Connell about the murder of Patricia Furlong. They put it to him that his ex-fiancée, Mary Creedon, had told them about his unexplained forty-five-minute absence from her company that night.

'He said that when he disappeared from Mary Creedon that he'd gone to meet a friend called Nella Allan from RTÉ,' says Michael Canavan. 'But we managed to track her down, and she told us that she wasn't even at the festival that night. We put this to Connell, and that was the first time he really faltered. He knew then that he was in serious trouble. It was shortly after that that he made his statement, and admitted that he knew Patricia Furlong, and that he had killed her.'

In the presence of Detective Sergeant Gerry Healy and Detective Jerry O'Connell, Vincent Connell told the story of what had happened when he left Mary Creedon that night. As he talked, Sergeant Gerry Healy took a written account of what he said.

'At one stage in the evening, I went to the toilet and met a lady that I knew,' Connell began. 'We were talking about roller-skating, probably because she was a customer of mine at the Top Hat in Dún Laoghaire, where I was assistant manager. Actually I know her name. It was Trish, from the Top Hat. She had aspirations to get on my roller-disco dancing team. When she would come to the Top Hat ballroom, she would always come over and acknowledge me. She did not come to me for roller-skating lessons.'

Connell went on to explain that after talking to Patricia for a few minutes, the two decided to go for a walk down the road. They left the festival grounds and soon came across a gate leading into a field. He described it as 'some form of farm iron gate', and said that the field inside was newly mown with a slope at the end of it.

They tried to open the gate but it was locked, so Connell helped Patricia climb over it before jumping over after her. They had walked together a few yards into the field when Connell put his arm around Patricia's shoulder.

'Then she slapped me in the face,' he said. 'This really incensed me and I hit her back. Then I lost my rag altogether and began to choke her with my hands. She began to scream, but I had to stop her. She fell to the ground.'

Connell fell on top of Patricia as she struggled desperately against him. He said that during the struggle the clothing from the top half of her body came up around her neck. At this stage, he said, she was starting to go quiet.

'I pulled her clothing up tight around her neck to stop her from shouting,' he said. 'I panicked and tied them around her neck and squeezed around her neck. During the struggle I . . . actually there was very little struggle.'

As Patricia's body went limp, her handbag fell to the ground, spilling its contents on the grass. 'There was a little make-up, door keys, perfume and a little diary,' said Connell. 'I can't recall any money, and there were some women's toiletries. I took the diary and some of the cosmetics away with me. I threw the bag down the field from where Trish was lying. Then I got onto the road over a nearby wall and walked back down towards Johnnie Fox's pub where I threw the diary and cosmetic items into a hedge. I then went back to the beer tent to Mary.'

Connell said he couldn't recall what he said to Mary when he returned, because he was very upset. 'We stayed on in the beer tent for a short while after that and went home at 3am,' he said. 'I heard the next day she had died. I did not know she was dead when I left her— she was breathing lightly. When I met Trish, I had no intention of killing her. I did not mean to do it.'

There was a brief silence in the room after Connell made his statement. While detectives were delighted that he had finally confessed to the crime, the reality of how Patricia had died, the pointlessness of it, was deeply upsetting.

Connell signed the statement then, the pen carefully scratching the signature 'V. Connell' onto the paper. Detectives heaved a sigh of relief. It looked as if the killer of Patricia Furlong might finally now be brought to justice. It was time to inform the family.

'We couldn't believe it, we were just so delighted,' says Angela. 'We thought everyone had forgotten us, you know? We got the word just a few weeks after my mother had died. She had spent the rest of her few years wondering who it was that took her daughter from her. We always said afterwards that she must have had a hand in it. That the first thing she did when she got to heaven was to make sure he was caught. But for my dad as well, it was especially wonderful to know that he'd been caught. And we were always thankful it wasn't someone we knew. But it was hard, too, because there was so much waiting after he was arrested, and then the trial itself went on for weeks. The waiting was hard.'

It took over a year for the court case to begin. Finally, in October 1991, the trial of Vincent Connell began. What followed was forty-two days of high drama, as Connell did everything in his power to avoid a conviction for murder.

It started with the allegations of abuse. Through his solicitor, Connell claimed that his arm had been twisted behind his back and that he had been head-butted and slapped across the face during questioning. He said that his beard was pulled and his head was pushed into a sink full of water in an effort to make him confess to the crime.

He claimed that the detectives had adopted a 'two nasty and two nice' approach to his interrogation. He also said he was assaulted by detectives while waiting for a court appearance in an interview room in the Bridewell Garda Station.

The defence team then called Dr Sean O'Cleary to the stand. O'Cleary said he had examined Connell at the request of his solicitor on 28 May the previous year and had found a number of minor injuries on his body. He said both Connell's wrists were sore, there was bruising on his right arm, his right shoulder was sore and he had tender spots on the back of his skull and neck. He also had bruising on the right thigh.

The doctor was then reminded by the prosecution that the day before he was arrested Vincent Connell had attended a barbecue in Ashbourne where he had tumbled down the stairs and fallen a number of times in the house and in the garden. O'Cleary was asked if Connell's injuries and bruises could have been inflicted on that occasion. The doctor agreed they could.

A stream of garda witnesses came forward then, all denying that they had seen or taken part in any abuse of Vincent Connell during his detention at Tallaght Garda Station. Detective Inspector Michael Canavan told the court that he believed the allegations were 'outrageous' and that he regretted there had not been a video recording made of the interrogation. 'It did not happen. Nobody laid a hand on Connell when I was present,' he said.

Following the allegations of abuse, Connell's defence team focused on the statement he had made in Tallaght, or, more specifically, on the writing itself. Taking the stand, Connell said that when he signed the statement he was in 'a state of virtual physical and mental collapse'.

A handwriting specialist called James Nash was then brought forward to testify that, unlike a normal signature, Connell's signature on the statement showed signs of tremor and hesitancy and 'lacked fluency'.

Nash also said that when Connell was first interviewed by gardaí in 1982, he had signed his statement 'Vincent A. Connell', but that the recent statement from Tallaght was signed 'V. Connell'.

Connell himself maintained that he had done this deliberately, so that when his case came to trial it would prove to the jury that he had signed his statement under duress. He said that he had never before signed his name 'V. Connell'.

However, when Detective Sergeant Gerard McDonnell heard this in court he believed he might be able to prove differently. He checked the Garda file on Connell, and found two letters that Connell had written from South Africa to the Garda Commissioner's office, both of which he had signed 'V. Connell'.

With that line of defence effectively stymied, Connell's solicitors then made legal history by being the first to use the controversial cumulative sum stylometry technique in an Irish court case.

The technique, also known as the cusum method, was supposed to be a scientific way of determining if a piece of text had been written by one or more authors.

By measuring the number of words in each sentence of a block of writing, the linguistics expert Dr Farrington was then able to plot a curved line on a graph, indicating the habitual way of writing that was specific to the author of the text.

Then he would apply the same method to another block of text that was supposedly written by the same author.

The theory behind the cusum method was that the graphs should match each other almost exactly. If they didn't, it indicated that more than one person had written the disputed text.

During the early 1990s this technique was used in many legal cases where there was disputed authorship, one notable example being the appeal of the Birmingham Six, but by the end of the decade the method fell into disrepute, after numerous bodies of research suggested it had serious flaws.

However, during Vincent Connell's court case the cusum method was still very much regarded as the latest in forensic linguistics. And Dr Farrington arrived into the courtroom armed with graphs that did not match. He took to the stand and said that in his opinion, more than one person had written Connell's confession in Tallaght Garda Station. It was a blow for the prosecution.

Sitting on the hard benches of the courtroom, the Furlong family watched the jury anxiously, wondering if they would be swayed by the science.

'We went every single day to the court case. We didn't want to miss any of it,' says Angela.

Pauline interrupts. 'Actually, I went every day until they showed the jury the photographs,' she says, quietly. 'I didn't like it, and I didn't go again after that. The photographs were very difficult to look at.' She puts her hand up against her throat in what seems to be an unconscious gesture.

On many occasions the Furlongs found themselves sitting close to Vincent Connell's mother and aunt, two families on different sides of the fence, both suffering. 'They were two little old ladies and we really wanted to go over to them and say, "Sorry for your troubles, we don't blame you", says Angela. 'But we weren't allowed to do that because they were on the opposing side. There were a few times when we found ourselves standing close to Vincent Connell too. And it was so tempting to talk to him and just ask him why he did it. Ask him if he realised all the devastation he had caused our family. But, again, we were afraid to damage the case.'

After nine weeks, the trial was finally coming to a close, but the drama continued right to the end. There was tremendous excitement in the prosecution camp when the gardaí managed to track down a witness who had seen Connell leaving the festival with Patricia Furlong—or a woman who looked very like her.

'One of the weaknesses of our case was that we didn't have anyone who could put Vincent Connell with Patricia Furlong,' says one detective. 'We had Patricia Furlong's friend, the young boy, who saw her with a man who looked like Vincent Connell. But we had no one who knew Vincent Connell who saw him with a strange woman. Then, during our second round of enquiries, we came across a friend of Vincent Connell's who was at the festival. This person knew both Connell and Mary Creedon. And he saw him outside the beer tent with a woman who matched the description of Patricia Furlong, who he said was definitely not Mary Creedon. The timing fit too. That really helped the case.'

After forty-two long days of evidence, the jury finally retired. Six hours and forty-five minutes later, they returned with a unanimous verdict: guilty.

Sitting in the dock, Vincent Connell looked stunned, and repeatedly whispered: 'I didn't kill her.' As the judge began handing down his life sentence, Connell continued to protest, getting louder and louder, saying: 'I did not commit this murder. I did not kill her.'

'He looked so grand, and so posh, and so innocent, you'd almost have believed him,' says Angela. 'You know, he certainly didn't look like the madman we had been hearing about. But then he could give you this sidelong look, and you'd see that he was just evil. He was an evil man. How he had not murdered before, I don't know.

In fact, one detective who watched Connell being led away believes it is entirely possible that he had killed more than one person. 'I've no doubt about it really,' he says. 'What he did to some of the women in his life was so violent, he went very close to killing some of them. And they're just the women that we know about. How many others are out there, and how many might not have survived him, we'll never know. It was a relief to see him taken off the streets.'

As he was escorted from the court, Vincent Connell turned to the spectators for mercy. 'Please believe me, I did not kill her,' he said, his voice rising now in hysteria. 'I swear to God. I never met her in my life.' He was escorted to the rear of the Four Courts, and driven away.

But that was not yet the end of Vincent Connell.

The appeal process started almost straight away. On Monday, 27 February 1995, the Court of Criminal Appeal began to review Connell's conviction.

The defence had brought forward a number of interesting grounds of appeal. Aside from the repeated allegations that Connell had made his statement under duress, the defence also claimed that he had been deprived of the right to a solicitor, that Patricia Furlong was not killed in the way Connell had claimed in his statement, and that they had new evidence from two witnesses that would prove that Patricia was seen alive at 2.15am—after Connell had left the festival.

Among the proposed new witnesses were Paul Dunne and Paul Regan. Dunne had been a DJ at the festival, and he had stated to gardaí that the disco had ended at 2.07am. The defence then claimed that Paul Regan had told gardaí that he had seen Patricia Furlong after the disco ended; which meant she must have been alive after 2.07.

In response, however, the prosecution said that the end time of the disco was never in question. It was accepted the disco ended at roughly 2am. A garda witness then said that at no time had Paul Regan stated that he had spoken to Patricia Furlong after the disco ended.

After consideration, Judge Egan decided that this evidence would not have affected the original trial in any way, and it could not be admitted.

The defence also proposed to bring forward a new expert, Dr Iain Eric West, a consultant forensic pathologist and head of the School of Forensic Medicine at Guy's Hospital, London. West had studied the post-mortem report, and concluded that Patricia Furlong had not been manually strangled in the way that Connell had suggested in his statement.

West believed that the top half of Patricia's clothing had been deliberately removed and carefully rolled into a ligature to strangle her, as opposed to Connell's description of pushing the clothing up around her face to stop her from shouting. West believed that a hand was placed around Patricia's neck in a deliberate act of strangulation, not as a spur of the moment assault to keep someone quiet. Fundamentally, West believed that Patricia had not been killed in the way Connell said she had. This backed up the defence team's theory that Connell had made his statement under duress.

Again, the judge decided that the proposed evidence did not differ materially from the evidence given at the trial, and Dr West's testimony was not admitted.

However, Judge Egan was swayed by two other points made by the defence. He decided that Vincent Connell had been interviewed for more than four hours at a time during his detention at Tallaght Garda Station, and that this was in breach of Garda regulations. He also pointed out that Connell had not slept at all during the entire forty-eight-hour period he was detained.

He ruled that Connell might very well have avoided making his statement of confession if he had received advice from his solicitor. He said that he believed there had been 'false information' between the gardaí that led to the solicitor not being present on the day Connell gave his statement.

As a result of that, Judge Egan said the appeal had succeeded 'on very narrow grounds' and that he was quashing the conviction for murder.

'The day that Vincent Connell got off in the Court of Criminal Appeal was the day that I decided to retire,' says Detective Inspector Michael Canavan. 'I just couldn't believe it. One of the reasons he got off was because it was ruled that he hadn't got any sleep. But how were we meant to make him go to sleep? We couldn't give him a sleeping tablet or we'd be accused of doping him. We followed the correct procedure, but he didn't sleep. That was not our fault. It was just so frustrating. We'd put so much work into the investigation, and he really was an evil man. Pure evil. But when you saw him in the witness box, you know, he could be very, very convincing. He'd just bring out one of his ten personalities. And it worked.'

Vincent Connell was a free man once again. But for the gardaí and the Furlong family, there was one remaining hope of putting him back behind bars—there were still ten outstanding charges against him in relation to his attacks on former girlfriends.

However, on the direction of the DPP, the charges of the attempted murder of three women were withdrawn, as were the two outstanding arson charges. Vincent Connell pleaded guilty to the four remaining charges of assault causing bodily harm to Gillian Kane, Mary Creedon, Agnes Long and Barbara Rooney.

Again, a small army of garda witnesses were called forward, this time to give evidence of the trauma caused to Connell's victims and their terror that he would be released back onto the streets.

Connell was given twelve years in total for the four assaults. However, the judge said that the maximum sentence for assault causing bodily harm was five years, and that Connell had already served this. Therefore, Justice Budd suspended the entire sentence, on condition that Connell be of good behaviour towards all the people of Ireland, particularly his four victims.

When making his decision to suspend the sentence, and effectively allow Connell to walk free, Justice Budd said he was taking into account that there was a lack of explanation for Connell's crimes. He said Connell had held down employment for most of his life, appeared very articulate and personable, dressed well and was well able to present himself.

He noted that Connell had had the education and intellect to be aware of the need to control his 'vicious propensities' after the first two assaults, but that he had nonetheless gone on to commit the third and fourth assaults. He now needed an opportunity to develop self-control and rehabilitate himself, said the judge.

He also pointed out that Connell had pleaded guilty to his crimes, had expressed remorse and had apologised to each of his victims.

The suspended sentence was handed down. Connell was a free man. As soon as the judge left the courtroom, Connell told the gathered press that he was entirely innocent of all the charges.

'I pleaded guilty to four crimes I did not commit under threat from the State of having to undergo a lengthy trial on further serious charges, including arson, which I firmly believe never took place and was a device used to arrest me and hold me for forty-eight hours under the Offences against the State Act,' he said.

'None of the incidents took place and I pleaded guilty to one incident at Peekers Hotel in Dún Laoghaire – a place I have never been to in my life.'

Connell then said he intended to leave the country entirely. 'What would you do after being through what I have been through?' he asked.

He said he would like to see the investigation into Patricia Furlong's murder reopened. While sympathetic to her family he said that they 'have been led to believe or were brainwashed into believing I was responsible for that murder'.

Back in the house in 30 Mulvey Park, the Furlong family cried. 'It was absolutely dreadful, we couldn't believe it,' says Angela. 'He had only done five years in prison. Nothing for taking a life. We were angry too, you know? We had been prepared for him to get out, but not so soon. We had this fear of walking down the street and bumping into him, so we were so relieved when we heard he had gone to England. But even then, if I saw a person that even looked similar to him, I'd get such a fright. A tightness in my chest. But we just had to keep laughing and keep joking. That's what gets us through tragedy, being able to smile about things. And we had each other, thank God. In the end Vincent Connell ended up a lonely man, on his own.'

On 21 March 1998 Hampshire Police broke down the door of a house on Eastern Road in Portsmouth. Inside, they found the body of Vincent Connell. He had been last seen alive on 11 March. Since then, he had suffered a major heart attack and died in his house, alone.

He had been studying legal science in Portsmouth University in the months before he died. He had also taken steps to have his blood samples compared with DNA evidence taken from the body of Patricia Furlong to prove his innocence.

Speaking in the aftermath of his death, Connell's solicitor, Greg O'Neill, said that Connell had made an awful lot of mistakes in his life.

'He was reviled most publicly for whatever wrong he did, but was demonised to an extent which was quite unprecedented and unjustified,' he said. 'I am absolutely satisfied having researched the circumstances of the murder of Patricia Furlong with great thoroughness that he did not commit her murder.'

Officially, the case of Patricia Furlong remains unsolved.

Chapter 5

The Unsolved Murders
of Antoinette Smith and
Patricia Doherty

They were found dead within a mile of each other. Both of them young mothers, both of them missing for months, both strangled, both buried on the same lonely stretch of the Dublin Mountains.

The murders of Antoinette Smith and Patricia Doherty filled the papers and shocked the nation. Their deaths added to the growing sense of unease in a country that still well remembered the murders of Patricia Furlong and Phyllis Murphy.

Although Antoinette Smith was murdered some years before Patricia Doherty, the close proximity of their burial grounds gave rise to fervent speculation that they may have been killed by the same person.

In the spotlight of increasing public pressure, gardaí sent out numerous appeals for information. They followed every lead, investigated every possible suspect. But to this day, the women have one more thing in common: their murderers remain at large.

It was a summer's evening in 1987 when Antoinette Smith left her home in Clondalkin and travelled with a friend out to Slane in Co. Meath for a David Bowie concert. The weather was warm and bright, and there was a great atmosphere at the concert. By the time it finished, Antoinette and her friend were in excellent form and looking forward to completing their day with a good night out in Dublin city.

At 27 years old, Antoinette had already been married for eight years and had two young children. However, the marriage was not going well and she and her husband, Karl, had separated and were no longer living together. As Antoinette left the concert and travelled back to the city centre, she resolved to enjoy her evening and not dwell on her marital difficulties.

When they got back to Dublin, the friends decided to go to the Harp Bar on O'Connell Bridge, before moving on to La Mirage night-club just off Parnell Square, a popular venue now known as Fibber McGee's. In the bar, Antoinette spotted a barman she knew. She waved him over, noticing that he was with another man. The barman and his companion ended up in conversation with Antoinette and her friend for the rest of the night, and when the nightclub finally closed at 2am, the four left the bar together.

As they walked down the street they discussed where to go next. After talking through a number of options, Antoinette and her friend realised they weren't going to agree on what to do, so instead they parted company. This left Antoinette and the barman to continue the rest of the journey down O'Connell Street together.

When they neared O'Connell Bridge, the barman too took his leave, and Antoinette was left alone in the city centre. She walked across the bridge, a lonely, vulnerable figure heading towards an appalling fate. She was never seen alive by her family again.

When Antoinette did not arrive to visit her children, Karl Smith became immediately concerned. It was out of character for Antoinette not to be in contact. He made a few enquiries and realised that no one knew where she was. Seriously alarmed, Karl contacted the police and reported his wife missing.

For nine months, nothing happened. Antoinette's name remained on the Garda Missing Persons list, but there was no indication where she might have gone after saying goodbye to her friend on O'Connell Street. She hadn't been home, and she hadn't been in contact with any of her family. While gardaí feared that something sinister may have happened to her, there was simply no information to go on.

Then on 3 April 1988 a young family went for a Sunday walk in the Dublin Mountains. Their outing took them in the direction of an area called the Feather Beds, in Killakee on the Glencullen Mountain. One detective who was working on the case describes how recent heavy rain in the area had washed away the top layer of soil, exposing a grue-some sight for the unsuspecting family.

'The kids were playing with a ball and it ran away from them towards a ditch,' said the detective. 'One of the young boys ran after it and he saw the remains of a human hand sticking up out of the bog. The body was decomposed. He got the shock of his life and ran back to tell his parents. They called the police straight away.'

The area was immediately cordoned off for technical examination, and with great care the body was removed from the shallow grave. Detectives saw that the remains of the dead woman had been somewhat preserved, due to the type of soil in which it had been buried. They also saw that the woman had a plastic bag over her head. And they knew they were dealing with a murder inquiry.

It didn't take long for the body of Antoinette Smith to be identified. The post-mortem results revealed that she had been strangled, but due to the level of decomposition that had taken place, the pathologist was unable to determine whether she had been sexually assaulted before her death.

An incident room was set up at Tallaght Garda Station, and Superintendent John Courtney took charge of the investigation. The Gardaí issued numerous appeals to the public for information, along with a photograph of the dead woman. For days, there was no news. Gardaí were conscious that because nine months had passed since Antoinette had gone missing, it was going to be much more difficult to find witnesses who might remember seeing her. They stepped up their appeals, desperate for some lead in the case.

Finally, a member of staff at the Abrakebabra branch on Westmoreland Street saw Antoinette's picture in the newspapers and contacted gardaí. He said that she had been in Abrakebabra on the night she disappeared, and that he had served her. He had watched as she walked outside the restaurant and noticed that she fell into conversation with two men. The next time he looked up, he saw her getting into the taxi with the two strangers.

'It seemed almost unbelievable that this man could have identified her, considering he just served her in a fast food restaurant nine months previously,' said one detective. 'However, the geography made sense. She was last seen walking towards O'Connell Bridge and that would have brought her onto Westmoreland Street. Also, this witness was particularly adamant that it was the same woman. So our next obvious move was to track down that taxi driver.'

Detectives trawled through every taxi company in Dublin, looking for the man who may have unwittingly driven Antoinette to her death. Eventually, they found a driver whose story seemed to match that of the Abrakebabra staff member.

He told gardaí that he was on Westmoreland Street when he was approached by two men. They told him they wanted to go to Rathfarnham, and asked him how much the fare would be. In the middle of the conversation, a young woman walked over to the car and started talking to the men. The taxi driver noticed that the young woman was somewhat drunk. After a short while, all three people got in the taxi and asked to be driven to Rathfarnham.

'The driver couldn't remember what the men looked like at all, but when we showed him the picture of Antoinette Smith he said he was very sure it was the same woman,' said one detective. 'That meant we had two witnesses with corroborating stories who together could put Antoinette in a car with two strange men on the night she disappeared. And the taxi driver was bringing them all to Rathfarnham, which is obviously very close to the Dublin Mountains. It seemed like a very promising lead.'

The taxi driver told detectives that on the journey out of the city he started to feel distinctly uncomfortable with the behaviour of his passengers. For no apparent reason, one of the men started talking about what would happen if they ambushed the driver and stole his taxi. While the man was posing the question in a joking manner, there was something about his demeanour that made the taxi driver feel very uneasy.

'One of the men was definitely a rough diamond,' said one detective. 'He was saying things like, "What would happen if we attacked you and took your car?" The other man seemed much more level-headed and he kept telling his friend to be quiet. But the taxi driver definitely felt that there was an air of menace about the men, and he said they had him on edge.'

As they approached the Yellow House pub on the outskirts of Rathfarnham village the men asked the taxi driver to stop the car. They paid him his fare, and the three passengers got out. The taxi driver started the journey back into the city centre, but as he drove away something prompted him to watch the two men and the woman in his rear-view mirror. He told detectives that they didn't turn into the driveways of any of the nearby houses, and they didn't walk towards a car. They seemed simply to be walking into the village. As the three figures faded into the darkness the taxi driver couldn't have known that he was now the last person to see Antoinette Smith alive.

'Our next obvious step was to search the whole of Rathfarnham,' said one detective. 'We did extensive house-to-house enquiries, but no one had seen anything or heard anything. We also made a list of all the cars that had been stolen in the area at that time, and all the cars that had been found abandoned. We traced them all and had them all examined for clues, but still we got nothing.'

Detectives also set up checkpoints on the road near the area where the taxi driver said he had dropped off Antoinette and the two men. They started the checkpoints at around 4am, the estimated time that the taxi had arrived in Rathfarnham. 'We wanted to target people who might normally go into town for a night out and be coming home at that sort of hour, so it made sense to set up the checkpoint at the same time,' said one detective. 'Again we talked to numerous people to see if they remembered anything, but again we got no new information.'

Weeks passed, and despite the best efforts of the detectives nothing new was emerging from the investigation. Gardaí made a fresh appeal to the public for help. Finally, a man came forward with what the investigating officers believe is very significant information.

He told detectives that he was in the habit of getting up very early and taking his dog for a walk in the mountains. He would drive to a car park near the Tibradden woods, and set off through the wild and rugged landscape. He enjoyed the peace and serenity of this early morning stroll, relishing the fact that the mountains were usually deserted.

Just a few short hours after Antoinette Smith disappeared, the man had driven to the car park. He estimated the time at somewhere between 6 and 7am on the morning of 12 July. He had started making his way up the path, his dog bounding ahead of him, when he noticed that there were two men standing at the top of the mountain. As he approached them, one of the men disappeared out of sight, while the other started down the lane towards him.

'As the man got close to him, the witness told us that he said "Hello" in the polite sort of way that you do if you meet someone in that situation,' said one detective. 'However, the other man just put his head down and seemed to be trying to hide his face. He didn't respond when the witness said hello. He just rushed by.'

The witness felt mildly discomfited by the encounter, but continued on his walk, idly wondering what it was the two men were doing in the area at such an early hour. When he reached the peak of the mountain, he turned around and looked back down the way he had come. He saw the two men, together again, at the bottom of the mountain. They were both urinating on the road. Then they turned and walked away from him.

'Something about them had made the man very suspicious at this stage, and it suddenly occurred to him that he hadn't seen any other car in the car park,' said one detective. 'The presence of the two men had affected him in such a way that he became convinced that the men were going to try to steal his car. He cut his walk short and hurried back down the mountain. But when he got to the car park, his car was still there and the two men were nowhere to be seen.'

Ruefully berating himself for what he viewed as an overreaction, the man had forgotten about the incident until almost eleven months later, when he heard the Garda appeal for anyone who had been in the area to come forward with information.

He gave gardaí a description of the man he had seen on the path, and based on that information an identikit picture was drawn up of the suspect and released to the public. The man was described as being in his mid-twenties, with dark hair and a dark complexion. He was estimated to be five-foot eight-inches tall and of an athletic build.

While the detectives were delighted to get a new lead in the case, ultimately the information didn't move the investigation forward. They had no luck in tracing the two men from the mountain, and no way of ascertaining if they were even remotely involved in the murder of Antoinette Smith.

'Firstly, we had no proof that those two men were the same two men who had taken the taxi with the victim,' said one detective. 'They could have been up in those mountains for any reason at all. It could have been to do with drugs, or some other crime, or it could have all been totally innocent. Secondly, even if they were the same two men, we still didn't have any proof that they had anything to do with the death.'

However, the detective said that the gut feeling of the investigating officers was that the two men were prime suspects for the murder.

'It's not that often that you'd come across two men walking around the Dublin Mountains in the early hours of the morning,' he said.

'Also, if you were to keep walking over that mountain where the two men were seen, you would get to the spot where Antoinette Smith's body was found. It was a fair distance to go, and it would take a while to cover by foot, but the fact remains that they were in the general area of a murder scene. And they were acting suspiciously. Ultimately, we made numerous appeals for those two men to come forward, and we never heard from them. That, in itself, suggests that they might have something to hide.'

Nothing else ever came of the investigation into the murder of the young mother. The file remained open, and in fact the case is now being officially reviewed by the new Garda Cold Case Unit.

But in the months and years afterwards, those detectives who worked on the case were always aware that there was still at least one murderer—possibly two—walking free among the public, maybe married, maybe with small children. This nagging knowledge was brought sharply back into focus four years later when another dead woman was found within a mile of Antoinette Smith's shallow grave.

It was Christmas time, and there was lots of last-minute shopping to be done. On 23 December 1991, Patricia Doherty set out from her home in Tallaght to pick up some vital items in the final Christmas rush.

It was just after 9pm when she shut the door of her three-bedroom terraced house in the small estate of Allenton Lawns, in Ballycragh in Tallaght. Her husband didn't ask where she was going. Since she had started her new job in Mountjoy Prison, Patricia's schedule had become somewhat unpredictable.

The 29-year-old mother of two was originally from Lisselton in Co. Kerry. She was living in Tallaght with her husband, Patrick, a former factory worker who was originally from Co. Donegal.

For the previous few years, Patricia had been working as a secretary in the primary school at Ballycragh in Tallaght, where her ten-year-old daughter and eight-year-old son attended. However, earlier that year she had started the fairly well-paid, if demanding, job as a prison officer in Mountjoy. The long hours and erratic schedule of her new post meant that Patricia's family had become used to not seeing her at regular intervals. This was to be a crucial factor in the time delay between Patricia going missing and her disappearance being reported to the gardaí.

As she set out from the small Tallaght estate at around 9.10pm, Patricia must have felt a little tired. She had already had a long and

Martin Conmey and Martin Kerrigan around the summer of 1970, before Una Lynskey disappeared.

A photofit of the middle-aged man seen by several witnesses driving the mysterious Zodiac down Porterstown Lane on the evening Una Lynskey disappeared.

23-year-old Phyllis Murphy, who was raped and murdered on 22 December 1979.
(© *Collins Photos*)

John Crerar, who was finally convicted of the murder of Phyllis Murphy, 20 years after he committed the crime.
(© *Collins Photos*)

Angry scenes outside Naas District Court as John Crerar is brought in to be charged with the murder of Phyllis Murphy.
(© *Collins Photos*)

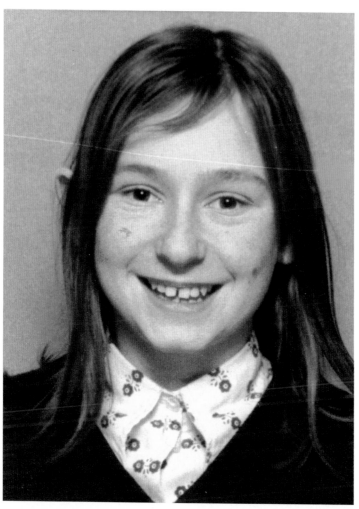

A younger Patricia Furlong, in a photo her family believe represents her best.

Vincent Connell, who was convicted of the murder of Patricia Furlong, and then controversially had his conviction overturned.
(© *Irish Times*)

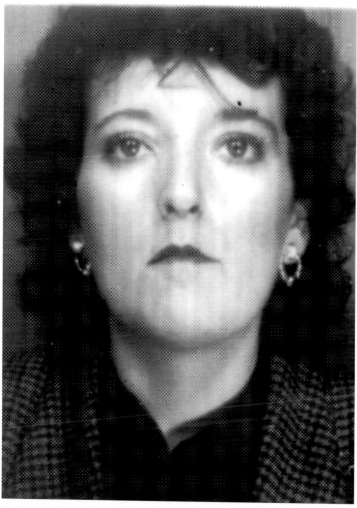

Mother-of-two, Patricia Doherty, who disappeared on 23 December 1991. Her body was discovered buried in the mountains six months later.

Patricia O'Toole, who was murdered in a frenzied attack in the mountains in 1991.

Private Sean Courtney, who was sentenced to life in prison for the murder of Patricia O'Toole.
(© *Derek Speirs*)

26-year-old American, Annie McCarrick, whose disappearance from the Dublin/Wicklow Mountains prompted one of the most high-profile missing person searches in the history of the State.

Gardaí search for any trace of
Annie McCarrick near Glencree
in Co. Wicklow.
(© *Collins Photos*)

Annie McCarrick
Age: 26   5' 8"   10 Stone

Square Jaw
Short Brown Hair
5' 8" to 5' 10"
Mid to Late 20's

Gardaí appeal to the public for information by releasing a picture of Annie McCarrick
along with a photofit of the last person to be seen in her company.
(© *Collins Photos*)

Eva Brennan, who went missing without a trace from Rathgar in South Dublin in 1993.
(© *Collins Photos*)

A man looks at a poster of missing women on a Garda car at the Square Shopping Centre in Tallaght in 2005.
Gardaí launched the poster campaign in a fresh appeal to the public for information on the unsolved cases of murdered and missing women, including those of Antoinette Smith, Patricia Doherty and Annie McCarrick.
(© *Collins Photos*)

21-year-old Jo Jo Dullard who went missing from a dark country road in Moone, Co. Kildare in 1995.
(© *Collins Photos*)

Jo Jo Dullard's sister, Mary Phelan, holds a picture of Jo Jo at a demonstration to highlight cases of missing people in Ireland.
(© *Photocall Ireland*)

27-year-old Philip Colgan, who was sentenced to life in prison for the murder of Layla Brennan.
(© *Collins Photos*)

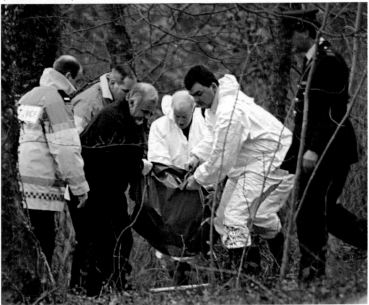

The body of Layla Brennan is removed from her lonely grave in the foothills of the Dublin Mountains.
(© *Collins Photos*)

Thomas 'The Burn' Stokes, who was given a life sentence for the rape of a woman in the Wicklow Mountains, leaves the courtroom smiling.
(© *Irish Times*)

Larry Murphy is photographed leaving the Central Criminal Court in 2001, where he pleaded guilty to the rape and attempted murder of a woman in the Wicklow Mountains.
(© *Collins Photos*)

Robert Quigley in Tralee Circuit Criminal Court, where he was sentenced to 12 years in prison for his attack on a young woman in the Dublin Mountains.

Convicted child killer Robert Howard, who was considered by Operation Trace during their investigation into missing women in Ireland.

busy day. That morning she had gone into a hairdressing salon to have her hair restyled into a new, much shorter cut. Then she had trawled through the toy shops, looking for presents for her young family.

At around 8.40pm that evening she had decided to leave the Old Bawn shopping centre near her home and go to the Square shopping centre in Tallaght. She was seen by a number of people, standing at the Londis shop in the Old Bawn shopping centre, where she told witnesses that she was waiting for the bus to the Square.

She was dressed quite distinctively in a full-length biscuit-coloured mackintosh coat, with a large gold and green patterned scarf over her shoulders. She was also wearing a multi-coloured but predominantly blue crochet jumper, a black skirt and black shoes. She wore gold earrings, and her wedding and engagement rings sparkled on her finger. Many people remembered seeing her, standing at five-foot five-inches tall, proudly displaying her new hairstyle to her neighbours.

It didn't take her long to pick up her messages in the Square shopping centre, and within minutes she was back at the bus stop, waiting to return to the Old Bawn shopping centre. When the 9.01 bus pulled up outside the Square, Patricia noticed a young woman struggling with a number of very small children and numerous shopping bags. She helped her get on the bus before boarding herself.

On arriving back to the Old Bawn, Patricia returned to her house in Ballycragh for a short time, before calling goodbye to her husband and setting off again. She left her used bus ticket behind her.

It is thought that Patricia left the house on one final trip to look for those special items that would complete the stack of Christmas presents already piling up at home. Former friends and colleagues later said they weren't surprised that she would be setting out so late on such a mission. They described the prison officer as a bright, hard-working woman who was simply devoted to her children.

If she had left to do some last-minute shopping, she would have had to walk along the poorly lit, though busy, Bohernabreena Road towards the Old Bawn shopping centre again. It appears that this is exactly what she did. The last definite sighting of Patricia Doherty was outside Brigid Burke's pub, opposite the Old Bawn shopping centre, at 9.22pm. From there she simply disappeared. She was never seen alive again.

When Patrick Doherty didn't see his wife the next day, Christmas Eve, he assumed that she must have gone to work. It was out of character for her not to make any contact whatsoever, but Patrick didn't become really concerned until Christmas Day. He then realised there was something seriously wrong when he arrived at Patricia's mother's house in Rathfarnham on Christmas morning, and Patricia was not there as had been arranged. After making a few phone calls he found that she also hadn't been in work, and her friends hadn't seen her. At 10am on 25 December 1991, Patrick Doherty went to Tallaght Garda Station and reported his wife missing.

Similar to the case of Antoinette Smith, Patricia's name was placed on the Garda Missing Persons list. Gardaí interviewed all of Patricia's relations, employers and friends, in an effort to find out if she had been in contact with them. Her bank account was checked for any evidence of recent activity. Her credit cards were monitored. Gardaí issued a missing persons notice giving a description of the young mother and her last known movements.

Patricia's family approached the media with her story, and early in 1992 an article about her disappearance was printed in the *Star* newspaper, along with details of other missing people.

But when all of this failed to throw up any clue as to where Patricia had gone, the gardaí were at a loss as to what else to do. As in the case of Antoinette Smith and so many other missing people, Patricia Doherty's file remained open, but dormant. The investigation was going nowhere.

For six months, nothing happened. Then, on 21 June 1992, a 46-year-old turf cutter called James Kelly started working his stretch of bog at Glassamucky Breaks in the Dublin Mountains.

It was one of Kelly's first days out on the bog that year, as it was common practice not to work with the peat during the winter months. He had started stacking turf about 100 yards from the county bog road when he noticed that one section of the bog appeared to have collapsed. It was then that he saw the white gleam of bones under the bog bank. Lying nearby, he saw a pair of women's shoes and some muddy clothing.

One detective who investigated the case remembers getting the phone call to say that another body had been discovered in the Dublin Mountains. 'It was a beautiful summer evening when the call came through,' he said. 'I was in the company of another detective, and we were told that a body had been discovered at the Feather Beds. We made our way to the crime scene as quickly as possible. There was considerable decomposition of the body. Visual identification was impossible.'

Gardaí were able to determine that the woman had had dark hair and was probably between 25 and 40 years of age. Even though it was impossible to immediately ascertain how she died, detectives felt certain that they were dealing with another murder inquiry.

Three days later, the body of the dead woman was formally identified through the comparison of dental records. It was Patricia Doherty.

A forensic examination was carried out on her remains in an effort to determine how she died. However, at an inquest into her death the State Pathologist, John Harbison, said that the decomposed state of the body meant he could not definitively rule on the cause of death. He was certain that Patricia had not died from a head injury or a gunshot wound but it was possible that she had been strangled. 'I cannot exclude strangulation as the deceased was young enough for her larynx to have flexed under pressure,' he said.

Harbison was also unable to say whether Patricia had been raped or sexually assaulted before she was killed. Detective Superintendent Pat King later confirmed that her body was fully clothed when it was found.

The inquest then heard from Detective Inspector Tony Sourke, who said that there was no evidence that Patricia had died of natural causes. This statement was backed up by Detective Inspector Edward Handcock of the Garda Ballistics Section, who said that an investigation of the bog had revealed it was very unlikely that Patricia had accidentally fallen into the hole. Her watch, a gold bracelet and a piece of her clothing had been found around eighty-nine feet away from the shallow grave, he said.

Ultimately, the Dublin County Coroner, Dr Bartley Sheehan, recorded Patricia's death as 'non-ascertainable'. However, all the evidence pointed to murder, and a full-scale murder inquiry was launched.

There was explosive media interest in the case. Almost immediately, people had started comparing the circumstances in which Patricia Doherty had gone missing to that of Antoinette Smith. Newspaper articles questioned whether two different murderers would coincidently choose to bury their victims within a mile of each other on the Dublin Mountains.

Female neighbours of Patricia Doherty told the press that news of her murder had caused them great concern. One woman commented that there was now a belief in the area that there were bodies of other missing women and young people in the mountains. It was only 1992, but already the mountains were gaining a sinister reputation.

With the spotlight of the media shining brightly upon them, a team of 20 detectives from Tallaght Garda Station set to work on the case. The results of the post-mortem had confirmed their suspicions that Patricia Doherty had died shortly after she disappeared on 23 December 1991, and that her body had been lying at the Feather Beds in the Dublin Mountains for the best part of six months.

They descended upon the last places Patricia was seen—her estate at Ballycragh, the Old Bawn shopping centre and the Square at Tallaght—and they began the first round of exhaustive enquiries.

The Garda Press Office also sent out an appeal for information. They asked for anyone who might have seen anything suspicious in the Dublin Mountains around Christmas time to come forward. They also said they were particularly keen to hear from anyone who might have seen Patricia between 6pm and 8.30pm on 23 December and after 9.22pm that evening.

Detective Superintendent Pat King, who was leading the investigation, pointed out that anyone who had seen Patricia with her new short hairstyle must have seen her on the day she died. He asked for these people to come forward. 'There are people out there who have some information they can give us,' he said.

The detectives also appealed to the young mother with small children whom Patricia had helped on to the bus. They said that it was very important that they trace this woman and asked her to contact them.

A few weeks after her body was found, gardaí staged a detailed reconstruction of Patricia's last known movements in a bid to jog the memories of people who may have seen her. They employed the help of a former colleague of Patricia's from Mountjoy Prison, who bore an uncanny resemblance to the murdered woman.

Wearing similar clothing—a long mackintosh and brightly coloured scarf—Patricia's colleague retraced all her last known movements. Photographs were taken of her and distributed to the media. But despite extensive press coverage of the reconstruction, no new information was forthcoming.

Detectives also put a Garda mobile information van near the site where Patricia's body was discovered, in the hope that it might spark people's memories and add impetus to the investigation. Again, the strategy failed to produce results.

Finally, four months after Patricia's body was found, her murder was covered in the first ever episode of *Crimeline*. The programme was broadcast on Monday, 21 September 1991, and it led to a large public response, with over sixty calls flooding in from around the country. Detectives followed up each call, hopeful that they might finally get a break in the case. But the appeal turned up no new information. One detective described the frustration of the investigating officers.

'We never really got a lead on it,' he said. 'Anyone we talked to, we just hit a stone wall. There was one witness who said that he saw her getting into a red car on the night she disappeared, but that witness had a criminal record and therefore there was obviously a reliability issue. I believed him, actually, but some of the other detectives didn't. It didn't matter really, in the end, because it didn't get us anywhere. We knew that she was all dressed up as if she was going somewhere on the night she went missing. We did have one possible suspect in the case, but no real evidence to tie him to the murder. We also considered her job as a prison officer—whether she might have come across someone who would be holding a vendetta against her—but again, that didn't come to anything. It was really one of those cases where she just seemed to vanish into thin air.'

As the investigation started winding down, people continued to wonder at the coincidence of the location of the women's burial sites. Detectives, too, were uncomfortably aware that they now had two unsolved murders of similar victims who had disappeared in somewhat similar circumstances and been found within a mile of each other.

However, it was only ten years later, when many more women had disappeared or been attacked or murdered in the vicinity of the mountains, that an official Garda operation, Operation Trace, was set up in an effort to find out if there was any common thread between the murders of Antoinette Smith, Patricia Doherty and many more women.

To this day, no link has been found. And the murderers still run free.

Chapter 6

The Murder of Patricia O'Toole

The brick that was used to kill Patricia O'Toole weighed five and a half pounds. A heavy, dense lump of stone. Not easily lifted, again and again. After the attack, the 32-year-old woman's face was left bloodied, broken and unrecognisable. She died on the roadside, in the Dublin Mountains.

Her crime had been to joke, unwisely, with a man she didn't know. A man who for weeks and months had been exhibiting severe mood swings and violent, erratic behaviour. A man who was deemed not safe to be left alone with his own children. A soldier trained in combat and scarred from fighting.

Sean Courtney claimed that a fuse went off in his head that night. That he was not in control of his actions. Only he knows the truth of this. What is undisputed is that the slight, polite soldier from Dublin carried out one of the most frenzied, brutal, unprovoked murders in recent history.

It was a sunny morning on Friday, 30 August 1991. Patricia O'Toole woke up in her house in south Dublin, opened her wardrobe and looked for an outfit that would be suitable both for the office and for socialising afterwards—Patricia was planning to go out that night with friends, and she wanted to look good. Both she and her husband Brian were well known on the social scene in Dublin for their flamboyant lifestyles and committed party-going ways.

Patricia was particularly looking forward to this night out as just one week previously she had finally finished her thesis for the fitness instructor's course she had been attending in Thomond College. She remarked to her older sister, Anne Scannell, that she felt like the hostage John McCarthy being released from prison in the Lebanon now that she had finally finished the course.

After some thought, she decided to wear a sleeveless beige and brown top and a pair of navy Bermuda shorts. It was a simple outfit, but with her long blonde hair, blue eyes and fit, toned figure, Patricia needed little to complement her looks.

Born Patricia Madden on 12 April 1959 in Baldoyle, Co. Dublin, Patricia was the younger of two sisters. She was always interested in her health and keeping fit, and had trained with the under 18s team at Seapoint Rugby Club.

She was bright and ambitious and enjoyed school, completing her Leaving Certificate in 1976 with four honours. Afterwards she took a secretarial course in Dublin, and worked in a number of different offices before going abroad to work in Greece for a year.

When she returned to Ireland she found a job as a clerk in the pensions department of Consolidated Insurance Brokers in Mount Street. It was while she was working there in 1984 that she met her future husband, Brian O'Toole. Two years later they bought a house together in Killiney, and in 1990 they were married in a registry office in London— Brian O'Toole having been divorced.

By the morning of 30 August 1991 the couple had been married just over a year, but financial difficulties were already putting a strain on the marriage. They had taken to frequently socialising separately, a situation not helped by Brian O'Toole's new job working late hours as a doorman at a nightclub in the city.

Brian was scheduled to work that evening, so Patricia was already resigned to not seeing him that day. She left her home at 8 Watson Avenue in Killiney for the last time, and drove her little white Peugeot 205 to where she worked on Mount Street in the city centre.

There was an excited atmosphere in work that day, as everyone was going out afterwards to mark the departure of one of the members of staff. Festivities started immediately after work, as the merry group from Consolidated Insurance Brokers travelled the short distance to Scruffy Murphy's pub.

As always, Patricia was in the centre of the crowd, cracking jokes and chatting to everybody. She was hugely outgoing and entertaining, and very popular with her work colleagues. The group remained drinking in the pub until about 9.50pm, at which point everyone began to get hungry.

Patricia and some of her friends made their way up towards Abrakebabra on Baggot Street, and quickly refuelled with some piping hot kebabs, before continuing on to Russell's pub in Ranelagh.

There they bumped into another work colleague, Evelyn Cooper, who had become very good friends with Patricia since she joined the company in 1985. She thought Patricia to be in excellent form and considered her to be unaffected by the amount of drink she had consumed.

Cooper and her husband joined the party and they all decided to move on again, this time to O'Brien's pub in Ranelagh. There, Patricia had two pints of beer before the group proceeded to the Pronto Grill down the street, where they shared a bottle of wine. Patricia was talking to Cooper about her father and her family, and her friend later recalled that while Patricia was in high spirits, she appeared to be unaffected by the alcohol.

At about 1.30am on 31 August 1991, the party finally began to wind down and everyone headed their separate ways. Conscious that Patricia had had a substantial amount to drink, Evelyn Cooper was a little anxious when her friend announced her intention to drive home. She offered her a lift, but Patricia refused, insisting that she was fine. As she walked towards where her car was parked at the Triangle in Ranelagh, Patricia told the Coopers that she was going to meet a friend in Sachs nightclub. 'It's down here,' she said, indicating towards her car as she waved goodbye. It was the last time her friends saw her alive.

Across the city, in the West County Hotel, Sean Courtney was also preparing to head home after his night out. He had spent the evening with his girlfriend, Rosaleen Holland, at a disco in the hotel. They had arrived at 8.20pm and had been drinking steadily for hours. When the bar closed at 12.30am, Courtney had four full pints stacked up in front of him. He drank all four, bringing the total to around twelve or thirteen pints of Carlsberg that night.

Courtney and Holland were companionable, happy and drunk as they made their way from the hotel to a friend's house at around 2am. They had been going out with each other for a year and a half, and had been living together for just a few weeks. It was still early in the relationship, and they were deeply in love.

The blossoming new romance represented a fresh chance at happiness for the 25-year-old soldier. Life for him recently had not been so good.

He had had a happy childhood; he was raised in Drimnagh in Dublin by loving, hard-working parents. His father was a bus driver with CIE and his mother worked part-time as a cleaner.

When he was 12, Courtney shocked his family when he responded to problems at school by taking an overdose of his mother's nerve tablets. While the medication did not appear to create any long-term difficulties for Courtney, it was perhaps an early indication of his inability to deal with stress and life's difficulties.

Two years later, the then 14-year-old had a run-in with the gardaí when he was arrested for burglary. He got off with a warning and escaped the court without a criminal conviction.

All his young life, Sean Courtney dreamed of joining the army. He tried to enlist when he was 16, but was rejected on account of his age. For two years he worked as a signwriter, biding the time until he was old enough to become a soldier.

In 1983 he met his future wife, Amanda. They were seeing each other for a year and a half before they had their first child, and got married in 1985. The young couple moved into their own house in Fettercairn in Tallaght and a few months later Courtney finally enlisted in the army.

The following Christmas, he went on his first peace-keeping mission to the Lebanon. It was an uneventful trip, and he enjoyed it. He later described it as 'a different experience, a different way of life'. It also gave him an opportunity to save some money, and when he returned to Ireland in October 1987, it was to a new house in Leighlin Road in Crumlin.

His relationship with his wife continued to go well, and he doted on his son Michael, who was then three years old. Amanda was pregnant with their second child when Courtney decided to go back to the Lebanon on a second tour of duty. Unbeknownst to himself, this trip was to mark a new, turbulent period in his life.

The young solider was stationed with other Irish troops in the village of Ittazutt in southern Lebanon. The tour was proceeding without incident until 13 June, when an Israeli tank opened fire in the area. To Courtney's horror, he suddenly felt rounds of ammunition whizzing over his head. He took cover in a bunker, and watched as a wounded dog came limping from a nearby field, a bloodied stump where his leg should be. The dog was followed by a group of locals, armed with rifles and a rocket launcher, and furious at the disruption to their village.

One of the Arabs pressed his gun into the back of Courtney's head and demanded to see the camp commander. After some discussion, the commander managed to restore some calm, but the barracks remained surrounded by armed Arabs. Courtney regarded them fearfully and exchanged last messages for his family with another private.

Later that day, he saw one of the villagers walk towards an armoured car full of Irish soldiers. He saw the man take out a grenade, and believing the Arab meant to kill the soldiers, he shot in his direction. The bullet ricocheted and hit the man in the leg.

After that incident, Courtney began receiving threats from the locals. About a week later, Private Paul Reilly asked his commanding officer to take Courtney off duty. He said he thought that he was unstable and that the shooting incident had seriously affected him. 'He wasn't the Sean I knew,' Reilly said later.

Courtney was moved to another posting, which also came under regular fire and was at least as dangerous as the last. In mid-July he returned home for the birth of his second child. It was then that the cracks began to show.

His family noticed he was drinking more than usual, that he was snappy and preoccupied, and clearly unhappy. When the time came to return to duty, Courtney strained against it. He made various excuses and managed to delay the trip for a few days.

However, eventually he had to leave and in August 1988 he flew to London to get a plane to Tel Aviv. When he arrived at Heathrow Airport he became very nervous and started sweating uncontrollably. He looked at the gangplank onto the plane and abruptly turned away. He couldn't bring himself to board the El Al flight.

The following day he returned to Dublin and spent another two weeks in Ireland, telling the army that he wanted to spend more time with his wife and newborn child. Later that month, he set out again for Lebanon. He completed the journey this time, but he cried all the way to the border.

Two days after his arrival, another private reported Courtney unfit for duty because he was complaining of feeling ill. He was briefly admitted to the medical centre, a respite from reality.

But there was no escaping the violence. Shortly after returning to his post Courtney heard shouting outside the barracks, followed by a deafening bang. The door of one of the toilet cubicles swung open and the body of his friend, Paddy Wright, fell to the ground, a gaping shotgun wound in his stomach. Wright had shot himself at close range with his own rifle. The blood was everywhere.

Courtney ran away. He ran and ran, feeling as if he was going in slow motion, feeling as if he wasn't moving at all. The following day he told officers that he couldn't stay in the Lebanon. In October 1988 he returned home, his dream of life as a soldier shattered, his pride in tatters, his mind in turmoil.

Immediately, Amanda noticed a marked change in her husband's demeanour. He was extremely irritable and erratic, and began to have regular nightmares about being executed. He would wake up in the middle of the night with his eyes open, his brain still flashing images of himself being shot. He began drinking more heavily.

While he had never been violent towards her before, when he returned from his second tour of duty Courtney started shouting at Amanda and the children, and regularly smacked his son for minor offences. He no longer seemed to have any interest in or time for his family.

While he had been away, Amanda had slept with an axe handle beside her bed for protection. One night after he returned, Courtney woke up screaming and grabbed the axe handle. He waved it frantically at someone he believed was in the room and began running around after them. Amanda watched in terror as her husband swung the handle at thin air, shouting at his hallucination.

The young soldier developed a deep aversion to enclosed spaces, and began to shake and sweat profusely when he went into banks and other claustrophobic areas. On one occasion he started shaking uncontrollably when he saw a street lamp light up outside the house because he thought it was a flare in the Lebanon. Another time, Amanda watched as her husband leapt for cover behind the coffee table in their sitting room when he heard a car backfire outside. Again, he was shaking.

Courtney's parents also noticed the change. James Courtney found his son to be very upset upon his return from the second tour. He no longer had any interest in renovating his new home, and snapped at his father over minor issues.

'He was a different chap altogether,' James Courtney said later. 'He would try to shout you down. He was restless in himself.'

Mary Courtney was also distraught at the change in her son's behaviour. Every time she visited his house she found he was constantly shouting at his children, screaming at them to shut up. It upset her to the extent that, after a while, she stopped visiting.

By June 1989, the situation had become untenable, and Amanda announced she was leaving Courtney and taking the children with her. He said later that he wasn't upset at her decision, he was glad. 'I couldn't stand them in the house,' he said.

After the marriage broke down, Mary Courtney tried to convince her son to get psychiatric help, but he refused. He didn't think there was anything wrong with him. But Mary Courtney was so concerned about his behaviour that she became afraid to leave him alone with his children. Mary made sure her own daughter was with Sean when his children came to visit him. 'I was afraid he'd lose his temper with them,' she said later.

The following April, Sean Courtney made one last attempt to overcome his fears. He returned to the Lebanon, believing it might be better because he would be in a different area. But everything was a reminder of the previous trip. He started having crying bouts again and regular panic attacks.

Private George Flynn, who had trained with Courtney as a cadet, was with him on the third tour. After a few days, Courtney asked to speak to him, saying it was important. He then quietly told Flynn that he was contemplating sending off some rounds of ammunition if he was not sent home. Flynn thought he was joking until Courtney broke down and started crying. It was clear he was desperate to leave.

Around the same time, Mary Courtney was getting hysterical phone calls from her son, in fits of tears and begging for someone to get him home.

Just over a week after arriving in the Lebanon, Sean Courtney was returned to Ireland for the last time, on medical grounds. He was admitted to St Bricin's military hospital for treatment. Amanda went to visit him with his parents and found him heavily sedated, crying uncontrollably and walking around in a daze.

Courtney was assessed by a psychiatrist and, at his own request, was released after a few days.

Sean and Amanda lived together for about a month in one last-ditch attempt to save their marriage. But, ultimately, Courtney was not interested in making the relationship work. The union ended for good during the World Cup in 1990, when Amanda returned home and saw Courtney driving away from their house with another woman in the car beside him.

The other woman was Rosaleen Holland. Two days after meeting her at a disco, Courtney left his unhappy marriage behind him. He also set about trying to leave the army and applied for a driver's job in CIE. Within a few weeks, the two had fallen in love, and in July 1991 they moved into a flat together.

However, the nightmares continued, and sometimes Holland woke up to find Courtney crying loudly in his sleep. She urged him to see a psychiatrist, but still he refused. While she maintains that he treated her very well, she admits there were some times when Courtney violently overreacted to a situation.

Occasionally, when he lost his temper, he would shout and scream at her. In June 1991, during a trip to Tramore, he punched a man who said something derogatory about her.

And in August 1991, just a few weeks before he murdered Patricia O'Toole, Courtney became completely irrational during a row with Holland. They were on holiday in Westport, and during the argument Courtney grabbed Holland's bag of chips and flung them over a wall. He stormed off, later emerging from his room saying that he was going to go back to Dublin. The couple's friend, Stephen Stack, who was with them, tried to persuade him to change his mind. Courtney asked him to get in the car before driving off at a speed that left Stack clinging to his seat in terror. He later said that Courtney was behaving totally abnormally and appeared not to be in control of his actions. It took about ten minutes for him to calm down from his rage.

They had been back from Westport for just over a fortnight by the evening of 30 August. After the disco they made their way to Stephen Stack's house along the Grand Canal at Inchicore to watch a film and have some tea. Courtney promptly fell asleep.

Soon his fatigue began infecting the rest of the party. They turned off the video machine and Holland declined an invitation to stay overnight, saying that they weren't far from home. Stack helped her wake Courtney, and walked with them some way towards their flat. He left the couple outside Hyland's shop on the Suir Road. Holland and Courtney were making their way slowly down the street when a little white Peugeot 205 pulled up beside them.

After leaving her friends in Ranelagh, the evening had taken a dramatic turn for the worse for Patricia O'Toole. She had decided against going to Sachs nightclub, and instead turned the car towards

Inchicore, to where her former boyfriend, Christopher Hoctor, lived at the junction of Connolly Avenue and Goldenbridge Avenue.

Hoctor and Patricia had first begun dating in 1978. They broke up before rekindling the relationship for a short time in 1980. They had remained friends afterwards, but had not seen each other since the September of the previous year, when Patricia had dropped in unexpectedly and the two had had a lengthy conversation about the direction their lives had taken.

That evening, Hoctor was alone in his home and already in bed, having made no arrangement for Patricia to call in to see him.

Driving around in her little car, Patricia soon realised that she didn't know exactly how to get to Inchicore. She had only ever travelled there by taxi or bus. The combination of the dark unfamiliar streets and the alcohol in her system quickly led to her becoming confused and scared. Despite not having appeared drunk to her friends, analysis of her blood later showed she had 150 milligrams of alcohol per 100 millilitres.

Fifteen minutes after leaving Ranelagh, Patricia pulled up in Dolphin's Barn on the South Circular Road where two men were parked outside Windsor Motors. She asked for help, and they told her to continue in the direction she was going.

By 2am, she had made it to the junction of Goldenbridge Avenue with Southern Cross Avenue, but still didn't have her bearings. There were two men standing at the junction and they pointed her in the right direction. However, she didn't follow the route they gave her, and continued instead towards the Grand Canal.

Two barmen, Conor O'Leary and Joe Fitzgerald, were cycling home near the Suir Bridge at about 2.30am, when the little white car pulled out of Goldenbridge Avenue and came towards them on the wrong side of the road. Patricia O'Toole rolled down the window and asked again for directions to Connolly Avenue. At this stage she was visibly upset, mumbling and crying. The men saw that she was tense and panicky and was rocking back and forth while holding the steering wheel.

As the men were giving her directions, a red Fiat came down the road towards them, driven by a man called John Coloe. He saw the white car was on the wrong side of the road and, believing it was dangerous, decided to reprimand the driver. However, as he pulled up alongside the Peugeot he saw the blonde woman at the wheel was very distressed, and appeared to be quite drunk.

The two barmen cycled away as Patricia asked John Coloe the best way to Connolly Avenue. He told her that it was very close by, and said she could follow him in the car there. However, after driving a few hundred yards down the road to the address she was seeking, Coloe looked in his rear-view mirror to find the blonde woman had some-how not managed to stay with him. He drove back to where he had met her, but couldn't find the Peugeot anywhere. The next time John Coloe saw the blonde woman, he was identifying her from photo-graphs given to him by the gardaí.

Patricia O'Toole was so close. A few hundred yards from her des-tination. But it was late and it was dark and she was completely disorientated. Sometime between 3.45am and 4am, she spotted a young couple walking down the Suir Road. The man was slight, with dark hair and a dark, neat moustache. For the last time, she pulled in to ask for directions.

Courtney and Holland were just fifty yards away from their flat when the white Peugeot pulled up, and Patricia O'Toole rolled down the window. Courtney started giving her directions, gesturing at the turns she should take. But Patricia was tired and confused, and she didn't understand where she should go. She asked them if they'd get in the car and show her.

Rosaleen Holland sat in the back seat, Courtney in the front. Later, when asked why he thought it was necessary to drop Holland home first—considering how close they were to home—Courtney replied: 'It was late at night. You wouldn't know who would be out.'

Patricia offered the couple a cigarette and asked them if they had a lighter. She pulled up outside the flat on the South Circular Road, and Holland got out. Courtney called after her and said he wouldn't be long. Holland looked at her watch after she entered the house. It was 4.10am.

In the little white car, an amiable conversation had developed between Patricia O'Toole and Sean Courtney. He told her a little bit about his life as a soldier, and about how he had been married but was now separated. In reply she told him some snippets of her own life and relationships.

They came to a stop at a junction of five roads. Connolly Avenue now stretched out in front of them. Patricia O'Toole was within a stone's throw of her destination. And then it all went wrong.

According to Sean Courtney, Patricia turned to him and 'for no reason at all' said: 'You never know who you are picking up at this time of the night. I could get you done for attacking me. If I went to the police, it would be your word against mine.'

She laughed then at the joke she had made. She found the suggestion funny. But in Courtney's head, something snapped. He later maintained that a friend of his in the army had been jailed for attacking a girl, even though all his colleagues believed the man was not guilty. This was why, said Courtney, he did what he did.

He hit her. With his fists. Several times. The punches landed hard and fast on her face and head. She was so shocked that she didn't react, didn't even try to defend herself. And then, suddenly, she was unconscious, slumped against the steering wheel. Blood dripped from cuts on her face.

Courtney had a number of options then. He could have left her there and counted on the fact that she wouldn't be able to identify him. He could have driven her to the hospital, and tried to explain what he had done, or tried to revive her himself. But, he claims, he panicked. He says he didn't really know what he was doing.

He moved Patricia's limp frame into the passenger seat and started the car. He headed towards the Dublin Mountains. It was at least a fifteen-minute drive, but Courtney claims not to remember any of it. He says he has a flash of driving past the Creek pitch-and-putt club, but that is all.

As he drove the city lights faded into a dim glow in his rear-view mirror, and soon he was surrounded by inky blackness. At some point, Courtney says, it just 'kind of dawned' on him that he was sitting in the car with an unconscious woman, heading up the mountains. He says he then decided to park the car somewhere and leave it, and get home as quickly as possible. He took the next right turn, which would bring him back to the city. But then Patricia came to. And she started to scream.

Courtney screeched to a halt, pulled the car into the entrance of the Frank Kelly GAA pitch. His hands lashed out at her, trying to stop her screaming. He grabbed her by the throat. The passenger door flew open, and Patricia tumbled out of the car, scrambling to get away. Courtney fell out on top of her, and the two of them engaged in a fierce struggle on the ground. Patricia kicked and scratched and screamed again.

She managed to almost break free, and began pushing herself backwards away from Courtney, still screaming for help. The soldier's hands fell on a rock. A five and a half-pound lump of dense brick. Using both hands, he brought it down with terrible force on Patricia's head. Again and again he hit her.

During the post-mortem, John Harbison found injuries on Patricia's arms and hands that suggested she had fought desperately to defend herself. He also noted eighteen severe injuries to her head and neck. Her nose had been flattened. Her skull fractured. Both her cheekbones broken. Her upper jaw was separated completely from the base of her skull.

As blood rushed into her lungs, suffocating her, Patricia gasped her final words. 'Don't ruin your life,' she said.

Finally Courtney dropped the rock. He knelt, gasping, beside Patricia's body. A pool of blood radiated from her head, crimson splashes fanning six feet to the right, nine feet to the left.

But Courtney could only focus on the silence. He saw the woman lying beside him. And then he heard her breathing stop. 'The sound was so quiet that time of the morning,' he said. 'I was half sick.'

He said he panicked then, and decided to make it look like a sexual assault. With difficulty, he removed Patricia's brown and beige top and her navy shorts, both ripped now and covered in blood and mud and sand. He threw them away, not noticing where they landed.

He dragged her naked body in from the side of the road before getting back in the car. As he reversed he felt a bump as the rear wheel went over something. He suspected he had just run over Patricia's body, but didn't get out to make sure.

He drove back into the city, his own clothes saturated with blood. One of his hands left a bloody palm mark on the steering wheel of the car. When he reached Dolphin's Barn, he pulled up just as a police car went driving by. 'As I looked at my hands they were red with blood,' he said later. 'I wanted to get the blood off my hands. It was everywhere, on my arms, all over me.'

Courtney threw the keys of the car into the canal, and then knelt at the water's edge to wash the blood from his body.

He walked back to his flat, but realised he had no keys to get in. He slumped on the doorstep, leaning his head against the wood, crying as he waited.

At 9am, Holland woke up and saw Courtney outside. Muddled with sleep, she didn't notice the bloodstains on his clothes as she let him in. Courtney carefully undressed and stored his clothes under his bed. The couple fell asleep.

Minutes after Sean Courtney drove away from the murder scene in the white Peugeot, a cyclist came pedalling up the road. It was 5.30am and he was on his way to work. Just as he reached the top of the hill, he noticed a shape at the side of the road. It looked to him like a large doll. Or a body.

He tried to brake, but the bike was already submitting to gravity on the other side of the hill. As he sped down the road, he wondered at what he had seen.

An hour later, mechanic Aidan Cullen approached the entrance to the GAA pitch on his way to work. His headlights fell on an inert shape at the side of the road. Cullen thought maybe it was a discarded mannequin. But as he slowed the car, he saw vivid splashes of red against white skin. It was a woman, covered in blood.

'I got a call early in the morning of the 31st that a body had been found on Mount Venus Road,' says now retired Detective Inspector Tony Sourke. 'I went to the scene as quickly as I could and met there with the then Superintendent Pat King.

We found the body of a young woman. She had obviously been the victim of a savage assault. Her face had been very badly battered, to the point where it was difficult to identify her. When I saw the photograph of her later, it was clear that she was strikingly beautiful.' He grimaces, shakes his head. 'It was hard to relate that photograph to the badly distorted face of the woman we found.'

The scene was immediately preserved and a full-scale murder investigation was launched. 'All the forensic experts were called in,' says Sourke. 'Technical teams, fingerprint teams, photographers. The State pathologist was informed. We had the area sealed off. We had to endeavour as best as possible to protect the body from the elements.'

There was nothing on the body to identify the woman, so gardaí drafted the most accurate description they could, and sent out a press release to the media, informing them that a woman had been found dead in the mountains. By Saturday evening, the story had hit the papers.

Unaware of the activity taking place in the mountains, Sean Courtney slept until three o'clock that afternoon. When he finally got up, he put his bloodstained clothes in the washing machine, a task he normally left to Holland. He claims he felt sick that day, and was unable to do much. He managed to watch a football game on the television, before—despite his nausea—going out to get a takeaway. On the way home he picked up a copy of the *Evening Herald*. The woman's body had been found.

That evening, Holland exclaimed angrily as she emptied the washing machine. 'I saw that the dye had run from his navy trousers and that everything was blue,' she said. 'There was a pink shirt belonging to me which was now navy.'

The next day, Courtney played a football match, but claims he continued to feel sick about what he had done. He says he rang the special telephone line in Tallaght Garda Station that day but that the line was engaged. 'I wanted to say sorry,' he said. 'I didn't know who to tell.'

While the solider agonised over making a confession, the murder inquiry was continuing apace. On Sunday morning, the white Peugeot 205 had been discovered at Dolphin Road. Gardaí soon established that the owner of the car had been recently reported missing by her husband at Cabinteely station. Two officers peered inside the windows of the car. They saw blood smeared around both doors, and near the boot. The scene was immediately preserved.

Brian O'Toole, who had reported his wife missing, was called back to Cabinteely Garda Station. He brought with him photographs of Patricia. He was shown the wedding ring and another ring that was found on the dead woman. Brian O'Toole identified the body of his dead wife that evening. However, such was the damage done to her face that dental records were necessary to confirm the identification.

Now that they had a name, gardaí quickly began trying to piece together the last known movements of Patricia O'Toole.

Early in the proceedings, Brian O'Toole was ruled out as a suspect in the murder. The net was cast wide then, over everyone who had had contact with the dead woman on the night of her death.

'You don't assume anything in a murder inquiry, you just can't,' says Tony Sourke. 'You can't guess at what happened because you cannot conceive what is in the mind of a person who commits such a crime as this. So you have to look at everything. You start with a large circle and you move in towards the core.'

On Monday, gardaí sent photos of Patricia O'Toole to the press, appealing to the public for information. The murder captured the attention of the Irish people, and there was a massive media interest in the case. It dominated conversations around the country.

Rosaleen Holland was in work early in the week when a colleague told her about the dead woman in the mountains. She didn't really pay any attention to it. 'At that stage it had nothing to do with me,' she said. Holland was more worried about her boyfriend, who had been very quiet all weekend and didn't seem well.

For Sean Courtney, the publicity surrounding the case was an unforeseen nightmare. As scheduled, he worked his shift in the Cathal Brugha army barracks on Monday, and tried not to listen to the speculation about the killing. He kept his head down, and forced himself to go to work again on Tuesday. But the pressure was building, the talk was too much. Rumours abounded that the gardaí had a number of fresh leads, that they were narrowing their enquiries. Courtney called in sick for the rest of the week.

The rumours about the Garda investigation were true. 'A large number of people came forward about the night in question,' says Tony Sourke. 'We were working in ever-decreasing circles. And then, as a result of a little bit of intelligence, we changed the focus of our investigation to Inchicore. And we started door-to-door enquiries there.'

The weekend came and went. The speculation grew. The murder investigation was splashed across the front of every Sunday newspaper. And it all got too much for Sean Courtney. On Monday, 9 September he rang Rosaleen Holland at her workplace and said he had something to tell her. At 3pm he collected her and her colleague, Elizabeth Abbey, from work.

Sitting in the back seat, Abbey noticed that Courtney seemed very upset. She saw tears shining in his eyes. The car radio was on, and a news bulletin announced that gardaí believed Patricia O'Toole had given two people a lift on the night she was killed. Abbey watched as Courtney abruptly turned off the radio.

Back at the flat, after dropping off Abbey, Courtney started crying. He told Rosaleen Holland to look under the driver's seat of the car. He told her there was a newspaper there, that she should fetch it, but not look at it. Confused and frightened by his tone of voice, Holland did as her boyfriend asked. She returned to the flat with the newspaper, and then let her eyes drop to the front page.

Smiling back at her was the female driver who had asked directions of herself and Courtney the previous weekend. Holland stared at the photograph. 'I just kept looking at it,' she said. 'I couldn't believe what he was saying to me, that he'd killed the girl.'

Courtney started shaking and rocking back and forth, sobbing that he hadn't meant to do it. He had 'no intentions', he said. Holland asked if he'd raped the woman. He said he hadn't. The couple hugged and cried together. Then Courtney said he had to return to work.

He left Holland alone in the flat, staring at the smiling face of Patricia O'Toole. She went out and bought another paper and read more about the killing, the details of the brutality sinking in. At 6.50pm Courtney called in and told her not to worry, that he would 'do the worrying'. He asked her to call him at work. Holland didn't make that call.

Instead, she phoned her friend, Elizabeth Abbey, who—having watched Courtney curiously in the car earlier—already suspected what was wrong. Holland left the flat and met a group of her close friends. She told them what had happened. It was decided they would have to tell the gardaí.

In Inchicore, gardaí were continuing the painstaking work of door-to-door enquiries. 'It takes time and effort, but on an international basis there has been no more important system of inquiry ever devised,' says Tony Sourke. 'It is the most effective for establishing what happened in relation to serious crime.'

'As a result of the door-to-door inquiries in the Inchicore area, one of our officers, John Maunsell, received some important intelligence. He was told the name of someone who knew something about the murder. As a result of that information, he talked to another person, and then another person. Eventually, Maunsell tracked down a final bit of intelligence that led us directly to believe the suspect was Sean Courtney. He rang Tallaght Garda Station, and we began setting up the arrest.'

At 12.55am, Detective Superintendent Gerry McCarrick, Detective Superintendent Pat King and Detective Inspector Tony Sourke went to Cathal Brugha barracks.

'Courtney wasn't expecting us, but having said that he was open enough in what he said at the time,' says Sourke. 'He seemed shocked and remorseful.'

Courtney was arrested and brought to Tallaght Garda Station where he waived his right to silence and made a full confession to the killing. He told gardaí that it was something Patricia O'Toole had said that prompted him to hit her, and it was panic that led him to kill her.

'What he said in his statement was borne out by the sequential order of events,' says Sourke. 'The following day, he brought us on the route from where he had first met Patricia O'Toole to where he murdered her. He was very polite, very mannerly, not aggressive at all. He was mostly quiet, except for when we were turning the car at Mount Venus road, the murder scene. Then he repeated the words he had told us about the night before: "Don't ruin your life," he said.'

It took two years for the case to come to court. Finally, in January 1993, Sean Courtney appeared in the stand, wearing full military uniform. He replied 'not guilty' when the murder charge was read to him.

His defence counsel said that at the time of the killing Courtney was 'for all practical purposes insane'. Thus began a lengthy legal drama, with Courtney's defence team trying desperately to convince the jury that he was not in control of his actions when he killed Patricia O'Toole, and that he was therefore not capable of forming an intent to murder. Intent was key.

A number of psychologists testified to the court that Sean Courtney displayed all the classic symptoms of post-traumatic stress disorder (PTSD), brought on by his time served in the army. The court heard that people with PTSD were hypersensitive to threat and that they reacted to any threat as if it were 'a life-threatening' one. One of the well-recognised features of PTSD is uncontrollable outbursts of anger or rage.

While none of the experts agreed that Courtney was insane at the time of the murder, they all agreed that he would not have been fully in control of his actions at the time.

In his closing speech, Courtney's defence counsel told the jury that they could legally conclude that Courtney was insane at the time of the murder in the sense that he was debarred from refraining from doing what he did.

The prosecution pointed out that while there might be some validity that Courtney simply lost control when he first hit O'Toole, it was what happened next that really mattered. The prosecution asked the jury if they believed that Courtney could have driven a long distance up the mountains, with an unconscious woman at his side, without forming some intent.

For five hours and forty-six minutes, the jury deliberated. Then, at 1.10am on 22 January 1993, the verdict came in. Guilty.

Courtney sat, his thin white face showing no emotion, as cries of joy and grief filled the packed courtroom. He was sentenced to life in prison. The judge got up and left the court.

In the midst of the cheers and hugs, Courtney stood up, and the humble, polite man disappeared. 'She was only a fucking tramp,' he shouted, his voice echoing above the celebrations. He bowed his head then. A man who had dreamed of the honour of serving his country. A failed soldier. A convicted killer. A prisoner of the state.

Chapter 7
The Disappearance of Annie McCarrick

I t is the most high-profile missing person case in the history of the state. And it's not over yet. Fifteen years after the American student Annie McCarrick disappeared without a trace, detectives still believe they can solve the mystery. Their investigation continues. Their determination remains strong. New leads are emerging.

As they sift through the stacks of statements and evidence, it seems only one thing in this case is certain: Annie McCarrick didn't go missing. She was taken. She was killed. And she was hidden. From the very beginning, detectives were looking for a murderer.

For her family, it started with a phone call. On Monday, 29 March 1993, Nancy McCarrick was in the family home in Long Island, New York busily preparing for her trip to Ireland the following Thursday. Nancy cherished any opportunity to spend time with her daughter and was very excited about the trip.

At 4.30pm, the phone rang. The slight crackle on the line indicated that it was a long-distance call. For the McCarricks, that usually meant Annie.

However, it was Hilary Brady's voice that spoke from Dublin. He was a close friend of Annie's and he had often spoken to Nancy in the past. He didn't want to worry her unnecessarily, he said, and he didn't want her to get upset. But he was concerned because no one had seen Annie for three days. She hadn't been to work. She hadn't been in her flat. No one had spoken to her.

Nancy's stomach dropped, and she immediately started fighting stabs of panic. 'Annie was never out of touch for hours, let alone days,' she said. 'I just knew something was wrong.'

Struggling to remain calm, Nancy packed her bags and went directly to JFK Airport in New York City, where she took the first flight to

Dublin. When she arrived, Hilary Brady met her in the arrivals lounge. She looked at him enquiringly, but he shook his head. Still no news from Annie.

Nancy called her husband John and broke the news. He, too, left their home in Long Island, and began the trip to Ireland.

Together, Nancy and Hilary went directly to the Garda station in Irishtown, where Nancy McCarrick formally reported her daughter missing. Hilary explained to gardaí that Annie had missed a pre-arranged dinner on Saturday night, which was very unlike her. He said that she hadn't turned up to work, and that no one had seen her since 9am on Friday.

No one knew then that Annie had, in fact, been seen since Friday morning. That she was spotted getting the bus to Enniskerry. And that she was seen on Friday night, in the Dublin Mountains. In the company of a strange man. A man who probably killed her.

Gardaí opened a new file—not knowing that soon it would be filled with hundreds of statements—and told Nancy that they needed to know everything about 26-year-old Annie McCarrick.

Annie's childhood, by all accounts, was idyllic. Living by the sea in Bayport in Long Island, Annie was sheltered and safe and surrounded by love. Her upbringing resulted in a happy, confident, outgoing woman who expected to see good in everyone. Ironically, it was this inclination to trust that may have ultimately led to her death.

Annie's interest in Ireland began when she was 20 years old, during the Christmas holidays of her first year in Skidmore College in upstate New York. Her cousin was organising a group of people to travel to Ireland for a week, and Annie's parents encouraged her to go. 'I remember her saying to me that she couldn't go, because it was Christmas and she wanted to spend it at home with her family,' said John McCarrick later. 'But she went over there, and after two weeks she called us and said she didn't want to come home because she loved it so much.'

Thus began Annie McCarrick's love affair with the Emerald Isle. The people, the culture and the history all appealed to her sense of romance and her sense of self. When she finished her year in Skidmore, she enrolled in St Patrick's College in Drumcondra and moved her life to Ireland. 'She found it difficult because you had to know Gaelic and even though Annie was great with foreign languages, she wasn't about to take that up,' said John.

But Annie stuck with it, and after a year she was eventually accepted into St Patrick's College in Maynooth, from which she graduated in 1990 with a BA in English Literature, German and Sociology.

Afterwards she decided to move back to New York, where she enrolled in a master's programme at Stony Brook University. Within ten months she had completed a master's degree in English. But the young woman was restless. She missed Ireland, and the friends she had made there. During Christmas 1992 she announced that she wanted to return to Dublin, to try to make a life for herself there.

Her parents tried to hide their disappointment at the thought of their daughter moving so far away. But they knew that Annie was happy with her decision, and they had to support her. On 6 January 1993, they waved goodbye at JFK Airport. Nancy reminded her that she'd be over to visit soon. The tall, striking figure of their daughter disappeared through the departure gates. They never saw her again.

True to her sense of romance, Annie had hoped to find work in a bookstore in Dublin, but employment was not that plentiful and instead she had to settle for various waitressing jobs. She spent some time working in the Courtyard Restaurant in Donnybrook, before moving on to Café Java on Leeson Street. She had settled in well there during the weeks before she disappeared, and had also found a lovely apartment nearby in Sandymount.

She got on well with her two flatmates, Jill Twomey and Ida Walsh. They soon developed an easy comradeship with each other. On the Friday she disappeared, the girls wished her a nice weekend before they left the apartment at 9am.

Hilary told gardaí that the last he heard from Annie was later that morning. She called to arrange for him and his fiancée to come over to her place for dinner the following evening.

However, said Hilary, when they arrived at the arranged time on Saturday, they found the apartment in darkness. It was so unlike Annie not to keep plans that Hilary was immediately concerned. He didn't have the phone number of the apartment so he rang Nancy in Long Island and told her his predicament. She gave him Annie's phone number, but there was no answer. It seemed clear that there was no one home. The couple went for a drink in a nearby pub, and then returned to the apartment to try again. But there was still no response. Worried, but unable to do anything, Hilary went home.

The next morning, he went into Café Java and was told that they had not seen Annie since 3pm on Thursday afternoon. They had expected her to drop in to collect her wages on Friday evening, but there was no sign of her. And then the following day Annie had not turned up for work, even though she was pencilled in on the roster. She hadn't even dropped in homemade apple tarts to the café, as promised, and at no point had she phoned to explain her absence. All of this behaviour was extremely uncharacteristic of Annie, who had already established herself as a reliable employee in the café.

Seriously concerned now, Hilary rang Annie's apartment again, and one of her flatmates answered. They said Annie wasn't there, but that she had left a shopping bag of groceries on the kitchen table. They said they hadn't seen her since Friday morning. Hilary hung up the phone and, after only a second's hesitation, he dialled the international code for Long Island, New York.

Then their story came to an end. Sitting with gardaí, Nancy McCarrick and Hilary Brady said they had little more information to offer. Both admitted that Annie was extremely trusting, and that she felt there was no threat to her safety in Ireland. It was also totally out of character for her not to be in contact with her family and friends. Something bad had happened, they said. Annie was in trouble. They knew it.

Among the gardaí who were involved with the case from the beginning was the then Detective Inspector (now Assistant Commissioner) Martin Donnellan. He had arranged to go away that weekend, when Annie was reported missing. But after reviewing the details surrounding her disappearance, Donnellan cancelled his plans.

'I stayed because I felt there was something very unusual about the case, something different,' he said. 'From the offset, it didn't seem to be an ordinary missing persons case. It didn't feel right to leave.'

Donnellan and a team of gardaí began the painstaking process of trying to piece together Annie's last movements. They had no crime scene. No body. No reports of an attack or witnesses who might have heard a scream. Detectives made a public appeal for information, and started working from the point when Annie said goodbye to her flatmates on Friday morning. What did she do next?

From all over the country, information flooded in from people who were sure that they had seen Annie. As detectives sifted through the mass of alleged sightings, and talked to her close friends and colleagues, vital information began to seep through. Slowly, a picture began to emerge of Annie McCarrick's movements in the hours before her disappearance.

In an interview with Annie's flatmates, it emerged that they had had a short conversation with her on the morning of Friday, 26 March. Before they left the apartment they had popped their heads round her bedroom door to tell her they were going to the country for the weekend. Annie, who was sitting up in bed knitting, said she had no great plans for herself, but that she was considering going for a walk in Enniskerry later that afternoon.

After her flatmates left, the 26-year-old pottered around the house, having breakfast and doing some laundry. She put a fresh load of clothes into the washing machines in the basement of her apartment building and washed a few more delicate items by hand in the sink.

She didn't bother with too much housework, however, as she was planning a big clean-up of the apartment on Sunday, in preparation for her mother's arrival that week. Annie was really excited about showing Nancy around her new home, and had big plans for their time together. During a search of her room, detectives found two theatre tickets that Annie had bought in anticipation of her mother's visit.

With her washing done, Annie prepared to go to the shop to pick up some groceries. She wore brown cowboy boots over tights, and a tweed thigh-length jacket that had been made for her by a friend in New York. Around her neck hung a thirty-inch gold chain with a pink gold locket in the shape of a heart and a crucifix. On her hands, she wore a plain wedding band that had belonged to her grandmother and a gold signet ring. She also donned a small gold Rolex watch with a brown leather strap. Standing at five foot eight inches, with an impressive mop of brown hair, Annie cut a striking figure as she left her apartment to walk to Quinnsworth in Sandymount.

In the shop, Annie bought ingredients for the apple tarts she was planning to bake for Café Java. Detectives later got the receipt and compared it with all the items found in the shopping bag in her apartment. Everything was accounted for.

From there, Annie went to the AIB in Sandymount. She had a large amount of money in a Visa account, cash in a bank account and an American Express Card, but Annie didn't make any withdrawals. She was only interested in transferring her account to that branch. This money was never touched after she disappeared.

While reviewing CCTV footage from the bank, gardaí spotted Annie McCarrick on the grainy footage, standing tall among the crowd. The date on the film was 15 March, one week before she went missing. Because Annie was wearing the same coat and carrying the same bag as the day she disappeared, detectives decided to publicly release the recording in the hope that it might jog someone's memory. More calls came flooding in, but they led to nothing.

With her various messages done, Annie returned to her apartment, left her groceries on the table and started planning the rest of her day. It was at this point she phoned Hilary Brady and arranged for him to come to dinner the following evening. Then she phoned her friend Anne O'Dwyer, and told her that she was thinking of going for a walk in Enniskerry, Co. Wicklow, that afternoon. Annie asked her if she'd like to come along.

Her friend regretfully declined, saying she was still recovering from an operation on her foot. Annie wished her the best before saying goodbye. She grabbed her coat and handbag and left the apartment again.

A man cutting grass in Annie's apartment block noticed the tall woman striding confidently down the road towards the bus stop. From across the street, Bruno Borza, who worked in the local chip shop, also saw her walking in the same direction, towards the stop for the number 18 bus to Ranelagh.

'The best sighting we have of her is in Ranelagh,' said one detective. 'Apparently, it was like the two witnesses said— she had taken a bus from Sandymount to get there. Then we know that she got a bus that was destined for Enniskerry, because she was spotted by a woman who used to work with her.'

Eimear O'Grady had worked with Annie in the Courtyard Restaurant in Donnybrook. When the 44 bus to Enniskerry arrived in Ranelagh, Eimear got on and then spotted Annie getting on after her. The American woman went upstairs, so the two didn't speak. Eimear got off at her stop shortly afterwards, unaware that she had just made the last positive sighting of Annie McCarrick.

'This woman is really our principal witness,' said one detective. 'She knew Annie, so when she says that she is certain that she saw her, we can take it that that's true. But unfortunately she got off the bus in Milltown, and the bus continued on to Enniskerry. We know that Annie had said earlier that she intended going to Enniskerry, but the bus driver didn't remember her get on or off. And there were no cameras on the buses at that time. Therefore we cannot be sure that Annie stayed on the bus until the final stop. Having said that, all indications are that she was going to Enniskerry that day for a walk.'

Gardaí decided to focus their enquiries on that area. They searched all the local land, expanding their investigation some distance outside the town. However, they came up with nothing. None of the passengers who got off the bus in Enniskerry remembered seeing her, and none of the local people recalled a tall young American woman being in the area. Frustrated and worried that they were focusing on the wrong area, gardaí made further appeals for information.

Eventually a woman from the local post office came forward and said she had served someone matching Annie's description on Friday evening. The customer had bought three stamps for postcards. This was to be the only possible sighting of Annie in Enniskerry. All leads were running cold. Then gardaí received a phone call that was once again to change the focus of the investigation.

A man called Sam Doran contacted detectives to say that on the night of Friday, 26 March he was working as a doorman at Johnnie Fox's pub in Glencullen in the Wicklow Mountains. He said that he recognised the woman in the missing person posters because she had been in the pub that night. He was sure of it.

Another doorman, Paul O'Reilly, backed up Doran's claim that a woman who looked very similar to Annie was in the pub that evening.

Sam Doran told gardaí that the Jolly Ploughmen band was playing in the pub, in the cabaret section at the back of the bar. He remembered that at about 10pm he was approached by a couple who wanted to go into the lounge to watch the band. Doran informed the couple that there was a £2 cover charge for entry, and the man paid for both of them.

He said the woman was tall, American and looked very similar to Annie McCarrick. She was in the company of a respectable, athletic-looking man aged between 24 and 28, who was about five-foot nine-or ten-inches tall. The man had square shoulders, dark brown hair cut neatly and a clean-shaven square face. He was wearing a green three-quarter-length wax jacket which may have had brown trimmings on it. He was not familiar to any of the staff.

After being given a detailed description of the man, gardaí were able to draw a sketch of what he looked like. Shown a photo mock-up of his image, none of Annie's friends was able to identify him. They said that if he had been an acquaintance of Annie's, they would almost certainly have known him.

Two years later, the gardaí produced a new computer drawing of the man, and released it to the public along with an appeal for information. Again, while a number of calls came through, nothing of note resulted from this appeal.

Determined not to see another avenue of investigation hit a dead end, detectives heaped huge resources into investigating the lead. They organised a carefully coordinated search of the area, an operation that reached its peak when 500 volunteers turned out to help the gardaí and mountain rescue personnel. They also interviewed all the staff in the bar and circulated questionnaires at Johnny Fox's exactly three weeks after Annie disappeared. But there had been no more sightings of Annie in the area, and not one item belonging to her was ever found. She had literally disappeared without a trace.

Once again, the investigating officers had to consider the possibility that that they were searching in the wrong locality. From all over the country, people continued to report sightings of Annie. She could have been anywhere.

'The problem from the very beginning was that we couldn't be sure that it was Annie in the bar,' says one detective. 'We knew that she had been to Johnny Fox's before with her friends from Sandymount and that she liked Irish music. We knew she was planning on going to Enniskerry that day for a walk. And to this day, those two witnesses remain adamant that it was Annie in the bar that night and that she was with a man. Sam Doran came forward in the very early stages of the investigation to tell us this. But the weakness of it is that no matter how sure he is, he can't be positive. It wasn't like the witness who saw her on the bus. Doran didn't know Annie, so he could only be so sure.'

However, paradoxically, detectives believe that the fact that they have not heard from the couple who were seen by Sam Doran lends credence to the theory that Doran was most likely the last person to see Annie McCarrick and the man who killed her.

'No man came forward to say he was in Johnny Fox's with a woman from the United States on that night,' says one detective. 'No man came forward to rule himself out. Why not? If he was innocent there would be no reason not to come forward. And the campaign at the time was so public, he must have been aware of the appeal for information. Also, very significantly, no woman came forward either, to say that she was the American lady who had been in the bar that night with a man. So that would mean there are two people out there, keeping quiet for no reason. It doesn't prove anything, but it is suspicious.'

Detectives also had to consider the question of how Annie managed to get from Enniskerry—if indeed she was ever there—to Johnny Fox's pub, over four miles away. Gardaí knew that she was an enthusiastic walker, and could easily have covered the distance on foot. There was also the possibility that she met someone in Enniskerry, or on the road in the area where she was walking, and that she agreed to go with him to the pub.

'Annie saw no harm in any Irish people,' said one detective 'Her friends were always telling her not to be so trusting, but she just never thought herself to be in danger here. If the sighting of her in Johnny Fox's is correct, our suspicion would be that she met someone, maybe in the Enniskerry area, and that she agreed to go with him to the pub. That man, whoever he is, would certainly be the suspect in this investigation.'

The theory that Annie accepted a lift from a strange man, who later killed and perhaps buried her in the Wicklow Mountains, was one that rang uncomfortably familiar with detectives.

They still well remembered the case in 1987 of Antoinette Smith, the young mother of two from Clondalkin who disappeared from the streets of Dublin. They remembered how, six months later, her body was found in a bog at Killakee.

They were also conscious that just two years previously, Patricia Doherty from Tallaght in Dublin was also abducted and murdered. And her body, too, was found in the Dublin Mountains, within a mile of where Antoinette Smith had been buried. Both women had been strangled.

No one had ever been arrested for either murder—and no one has to this day. While investigating Annie's case, detectives had to bear in mind that those killers were still out there.

There were also a number of outstanding missing women cases in Dublin at that time, including those of Patricia McGauley, a mother of two who disappeared from Clondalkin in 1991, and 39-year-old Mary Cummins, who went missing in Dublin in 1992. Viewed through a wide-angle lens it became apparent that a significant number of Irish women had been killed or had gone missing within a relatively short period of time. Speculation exploded in the media and the public domain: could there be a serial killer in Ireland?

As part of the investigation into Annie's disappearance, gardaí therefore decided to survey all the cases of missing women from the greater Dublin area in an attempt to establish if there was any common link between them.

While reviewing the stacks of paperwork, a young female garda noticed that the same man's name appeared in the case files of Patricia McGauley and Mary Cummins. Even though this had nothing to do with the disappearance of Annie McCarrick, it nonetheless required further investigation. Thus came about the discovery of two of the most gruesome murders in the history of the state.

On 12 September 1991, Patricia McGauley was reported missing by her common law husband, Michael Bambrick. The couple had two young daughters and lived together at 57, St Ronan's Park, Clondalkin. Bambrick told gardaí that Patricia had left the house to visit her mother in Smithfield and had simply never returned.

Despite this claim, there was considerable circumstantial evidence to indicate that Bambrick had had some hand in his partner's disappearance. However, in the absence of a body or any hard proof the gardaí had no basis upon which to arrest him and Patricia McGauley's disappearance remained classed as a missing persons case.

Reluctantly, gardaí left Bambrick to get back to his life, where he was left in charge of his two young daughters, Adrienne and Louise.

Almost one year later, on 23 July 1992, single mother Mary Cummins went out for the day with her young daughter Samantha. They left their house at Nicholas Street in the Liberties in Dublin, and went to Carr's pub on Francis Street, where Cummins met some friends for drinks. It seems that by sheer coincidence, Michael Bambrick was also in the pub that day with his daughter. While their children played together outside, Bambrick and Cummins started chatting with each other in the bar. They got on well, and Cummins arranged for one of her friends to take Samantha home while she stayed in the bar with Bambrick. The 39-year-old woman was never seen again.

During the initial investigation into her disappearance, Bambrick told gardaí that he and Cummins had gone their separate ways after leaving Carr's pub.

However, now that he was a definite link between the cases of the two missing women, it became clear that Michael Bambrick needed to be questioned again.

He was arrested in January 1995, but denied any knowledge of what had happened to the two women. In April 1995 gardaí obtained permission from Dublin Corporation and began excavating Bambrick's back garden on the twelfth of that month.

For days, they dug up the garden with a miniature excavator, searching for the bodies of the two women. But nothing was found. They then used radar equipment to see if the interior floor space of the house had been disturbed. Finally, forensic experts found a positive reaction for blood on the floorboards.

This was sufficient evidence to warrant an upgrading of the investigation and specialist gardaí with experience in difficult murder investigations were brought in to help.

A number of people close to Bambrick were asked for statements, including his daughter Adrienne. Then, during an interview with Bambrick's former girlfriend, Stella Mooney, gardaí gleaned some significant information.

Mooney, who had had a child with Bambrick, revealed that he used to enjoy tying her up during sex, as well as dressing in women's clothing, and engaging in other unusual sexual practices. At one stage during their relationship, Bambrick had also told her he killed a girl in Clondalkin, but didn't want to remember it because it was 'too disgusting'.

Gardaí received other, unrelated allegations against their prime suspect from another source. All the information together provided them with a sufficient lever in the interrogation process to convince Michael Bambrick to confess. In a statement made on 24 June 1995, Bambrick related to gardaí the full details of his crimes.

He said in September 1991 he and Patricia McGauley went out for a few drinks. They returned to their home after collecting their children and had a brief argument over cigarettes before things quietened down.

When they went to bed, Bambrick initiated sexual intercourse with McGauley just as she was dozing off. He pinned her underneath him and tied her arms behind her back, ignoring what he said was 'a small bit of a struggle' and McGauley's shouts at him to stop.

He then stuffed a pair of tights in her mouth, and tied them around her head. He claimed that McGauley had sometimes let him do this because it gave him a thrill. He explained that he enjoyed tying women up because then, he said, 'I knew I could do what I wanted.'

However, on this occasion Bambrick said he heard McGauley gasping for air and then realised that she was dead. He said he panicked. The tights were wound so tightly around her head that he couldn't untie them and had to use a scissors to cut them off.

Then he carried his partner's body to the box room and left it there while he contemplated his next move.

Eventually he returned and, using a paper knife and a junior hacksaw, he cut off her arms, legs and head and put the dismembered body parts into plastic bags. He buried the remains in a corporation dump at Balgaddy in west Dublin.

Bambrick said it was a similar sex session that had led to the death of Mary Cummins. He admitted that they had in fact left Carr's pub together, and had gone to a number of other bars before returning to his house in St Ronan's Park.

He said they were in the sitting room together when he started touching her, before tying her hands behind her back with a belt and putting tights in her mouth. He admitted that Cummins had tried to 'push him off' during the encounter but added 'I just knew at the time I couldn't stop.' He heard her say something like: 'You're choking me.'

Cummins, too, gasped for breath before she died. Again, Bambrick dismembered her body and the following day he buried it in a field at Kishogue, within a mile of where his former partner lay.

On the morning he made his confession, Bambrick brought detectives to the site at Lynch's Lane, Balgaddy, and identified the two burial areas. The following day the excavation began. Mary Cummins's remains were the first to be found, but it took another week before Patricia McGauley's body was recovered. Dental records and DNA were used to positively identify the women, and Michael Bambrick was brought before Kilmainham Court and charged with murder.

Bambrick pleaded not guilty to murder but guilty to manslaughter of the two women. In the absence of definitive evidence as to how the two women died—the only account that the State had was from Bambrick himself—the plea of manslaughter was accepted and Bambrick was sentenced to eighteen years in prison.

The investigation into Annie McCarrick's disappearance had succeeded in finding a killer. But for the McCarrick's, this provided little comfort.

The review of other missing women files didn't turn up any other relevant links between the cases. However, the suspicion that a serial killer might be operating in Ireland only increased in the years following Annie's disappearance, as women continued to disappear around the country. In Leinster alone, three more women disappeared in highly suspicious circumstances within five years of the last sighting of Annie McCarrick.

Then, in 2000, one extremely violent man came to the attention of gardaí following a brutal attack on a young woman in Carlow. His modus operandi immediately sparked the interest of detectives. Larry Murphy from Baltinglass in Co. Wicklow was a quiet family man who had never been in trouble with the law until he abducted, beat and viciously raped an innocent woman, before driving her to the mountains, where he attempted to kill her by putting a plastic bag over her head. By a stroke of extraordinary luck, she managed to escape. And Murphy was caught.

Conscious that his crime bore the hallmarks of someone who was practised in what he was doing, detectives investigated Murphy's history at length. He worked as a contractor carpenter, and rumours began to circulate that he been working on the roof of Johnny Fox's around the time Annie disappeared. The name of every contractor who had ever been at the pub was checked, but no leads emerged. Murphy had no history of work with the pub.

'There were many meetings about Murphy, to see if there was any link at all between him and Annie McCarrick,' said one detective. 'But you know, he went into that courtroom and pleaded guilty to his crime, and he said nothing else, ever. We were never able to establish any link between him and any of the other missing women.'

However, another source close to the investigation points out that Murphy was a perfect fit for the description of the man seen by Sam Doran in the bar. 'He's the right age, the right height, the right hair colour,' said the source. 'He lived close to the area. He knew the mountains well. Of course, it could all be a coincidence. But since he has gone to prison, there have been no other disappearances of women in the area. I think that's an interesting aspect of the case. Also, even though the vast majority of homicides are committed by someone the victim knows, Murphy's victim seems to have been chosen at random. That makes him a very different, very specific type of attacker.'

But for Annie McCarrick's family and for the detectives investigating the case there was little comfort to be taken from these suspicions. The fact remained that Annie was still missing, and the identity of her killer was still unknown.

In the weeks after she disappeared, John and Nancy McCarrick set up base in a bed and breakfast in Rathgar in Dublin, and developed a system whereby one of them stayed by the phone while the other went out on the streets looking for information. They pasted hundreds of posters of their missing daughter all over the city, and combed the college campuses for any sign of her.

They sought the help of a clairvoyant to try to pinpoint the spot where Annie might now lie, and—when the Garda investigation eventually began to wind down—they employed a private detective to continue the search for their daughter.

As days stretched into weeks, through a haze of grief and trauma, John and Nancy found that they could no longer talk to each other about Annie. While Nancy found it therapeutic to surround herself with her daughter's belongings, John couldn't look at pictures of Annie or go near her bedroom. They had entirely different ways of dealing with their pain, and the devastation of losing their only child placed a massive strain on their relationship. After two months of campaigning and searching for their daughter, they were forced to make one of the most heartbreaking decisions of their lives. They returned to New York without their daughter.

Information continued to pour in from different counties around Ireland. 'There were sightings of her all over the country, and we chased up all of them,' said one detective. 'For example, she was supposed to have been seen down in Kilkenny, after a truck driver came forward and said he gave her a lift from Mount Juliet to Waterford, but we tracked down that girl and it wasn't Annie. It just shows how, even with the best of intentions, witnesses can give us wrong information. There was a lot of that in this investigation. We never really got any lead on it.'

There was another possible development when gardaí were contacted by a young nurse who said she had been walking in an area of the Dublin Mountains with her dog about a month after Annie disappeared. She didn't have the dog on a leash, and he ran ahead to a clearing in the trees. Then she heard something fall. She went to investigate and saw that her dog had knocked over a long item wrapped in black plastic bags that had been standing against a tree trunk. It was a spade. It was then that the nurse got a very bad feeling about the clear-ing. She noticed there was a bad smell in the air, and she had enough experience in the medical profession to recognise it as the stench of decaying flesh. The woman contacted gardaí as soon as she got home.

Immediately, they launched a search of the area. Soon they discov-ered a sports bag in a ditch which held the remains of a large dog. The smell was attributed to the animal, and it was assumed the spade was used to dig his grave. The search ended. However, to this day the nurse still has questions about why the spade was wrapped in plastic and left behind in the woodland. She believes that the area should have been searched more thoroughly, that perhaps there might be more to be found.

Another very promising lead emerged in June 1997, when detectives received information that two men were seen burying a very large box in a pet cemetery in Dublin on the day Annie disappeared. The men had claimed they had a dog in the oversized wooden container, and refused the offer of assistance from the owner of the cemetery, adamant that they would do the job themselves.

After initial investigations it was decided to dig up the cemetery. There followed a huge operation involving twenty gardaí from the Forensic Science and Ballistics sections of the force. Annie's parents were told about the dig and were kept informed of developments.

The media got wind of the activity at the cemetery, and soon the public were hearing reports that Annie McCarrick might be buried in the graveyard. After hearing one such report on the radio, two men contacted gardaí and said they had buried a very large greyhound in the cemetery in late March. A friend of theirs had made the coffin for them, and had overestimated the size of their dog, which was why the box was so big. Their story was confirmed when the remains of the animal were discovered shortly later. Another lead, another dead end.

In the us, the McCarricks were still desperately trying not to give up hope. John McCarrick arranged for a retired police officer from Scotland Yard to travel to Dublin to review the Garda investigation. After careful inspection of the files, the British officer told the McCarricks that gardaí had exhausted every possible avenue. The investigation could not have been more thorough. Nothing had been overlooked.

'He was a ranking officer and he was very factual with me,' said John McCarrick. 'And he said, "If this was a very intelligent person, assuming a male, who was working by himself, and if he kept his mouth shut, you'll never know." He said he could do it repeatedly, and no one would ever know.'

The same sentiments were expressed by another source close to the investigation, when asked what profile they would put on the murderer. 'It was a loner, who never spoke about it to anyone,' said the source. 'He probably buried her, or put her in a slurry pit or a quarry. If he ever divulged it to anyone it would have come out by now. But he's a loner, he definitely kept it very much to himself.'

Fifteen years later, the investigation into Annie McCarrick's disappearance is being reviewed once again. Detectives, such as Assistant Commissioner Martin Donnellan, who were involved in the case admit that it is one they would passionately like to solve. Recently, new leads have emerged, and gardaí are once again on the trail of the killer. They haven't given up hope, they say. They might find him yet.

But for the McCarricks, now, it almost doesn't matter anymore. Their marriage has ended and John McCarrick has been beset with ill health. A bomb imploded in their lives the day that Nancy McCarrick answered the phone in Long Island, and that damage has never come close to being repaired. Time has helped, though, says Nancy.

'She's still in my thoughts, every day, but time helps a tremendous amount,' she says, her voice gentle and softly accented. 'One day you wake up and realise that a moment went by when you didn't think of her. Then as years go by, there are more moments like that, so slowly you find that you're not thinking of her every moment of every day. And that helps a little. I think you grow around it, rather than away from it.'

Asked if it would help her now if Annie was found, Nancy McCarrick stays silent for a long time.

'I honestly don't know,' she says with a sigh. Then, more forcefully, she adds: 'Yes, it would be better. It definitely would. One of my greatest fears for the longest time was that something had happened to her and we just weren't looking in the right place. We looked for her so hard, but what if we weren't looking in the right place? At least if she was found I could bring her home. And that, at least, would be something.'

Chapter 8

The Disappearance of Eva Brennan

Collette McCann stands at the door of her spotless bungalow, watching the car pull up to the gate. She's a very good-looking woman. Friendly, relaxed and impeccably dressed. There's an expression of tired concern on her face, as if everything she sees worries her, and she's a little weary of caring so much.

She has agreed to talk this morning about the sudden, shocking disappearance of her sister Eva Brennan in 1993. In an earlier phone conversation, she has already told me that she believes Eva was murdered, and that her body is buried in the vast and lonely expanse of the Dublin Mountains. For fifteen years she has never stopped searching for her sister. It is perhaps not so surprising that Collette McCann looks weary.

We walk into the kitchen, which overlooks a blanket of green fields and little white houses in the valley below. The McCann household is situated about thirty minutes' drive outside Dublin, a little haven of serenity despite its proximity to the capital city. I comment on this, and Collette smiles. 'All the family live close to Dublin,' she says. 'We're like the Indians, circling the wagon. We're very close that way. It's one of the reasons I'm so sure that something bad happened to Eva. She'd never have just left. She wouldn't have done that to Mam and Dad and the rest of us. She couldn't have hurt us like that. She wouldn't have been able.'

Eva Brennan was 39 years old when she went missing. It was Sunday, 25 July 1993, the afternoon of a bank holiday weekend. A summer's day. A mild, calm day. A day for doing very little, and eating a lot.

Eva woke up in her little one-bedroom apartment in Madison House on the Rathgar Road. The view from her window was the local church across the road, looming tall and comforting at the 'V' intersection leading into Rathgar. It was a quiet, settled and safe area of Dublin. In fact, Eva's apartment, which sat over an archway on the first floor, had been carefully chosen by her parents specifically because it would be difficult to access—for a burglar or any other unwanted visitors.

'When Eva decided to move out, Mam and Dad helped her to find a place and they put a lot of thought into it,' says Collette. 'They found her an apartment in this gorgeous spot opposite the church and also opposite Dad's pub, the 108. It had to be on the first floor, because they were thinking all the time of what would be safest for her. We were always very conscious of keeping safe, as a family.'

That day, Eva planned to do the same thing she and her siblings did every Sunday—go to her parents' house in Terenure for Sunday lunch. She donned a pink tracksuit and ran a brush through her short brown hair. With her slim, five-foot seven-inch frame, her bright blue eyes and fair, unlined complexion, Eva Brennan looked ten years younger than she was. She grabbed her raincoat and her bag, which held her keys and purse, and headed down the stairs.

Although her family can't be certain, they think that Eva went to Mass that morning, because she normally went to Mass every day. She was a very religious woman. 'She always had this thing of going to Mass,' says Collette McCann, spooning some coffee into two large mugs and stirring vigorously. 'She went to Mass every day. She'd always laugh at my sister Eileen and myself, and say that God had put her on this earth to pray for us heathens.'

Even though there was a church right beside her apartment, Eva normally went to Mass in St Joseph's in Terenure, where she had been going for years. 'She knew Monsignor Greehy there,' says Collette. 'She knew all the priests around. She used to go to prayer groups there in the evenings as well. That was what she enjoyed doing.'

After Mass, Eva strolled up the road in Terenure towards her parents' house. As she walked she may have glanced up at the Dublin Mountains, stretching into the sky in the near distance, and thought about the American girl Annie McCarrick who had been last seen there three months previously. There had been huge media coverage of McCarrick's disappearance, and the Brennan family had had conversations about how traumatic it must be to lose a loved one in such a way.

At around 1pm, Eva arrived at the family home to find a number of her siblings were already there, reading the paper, chatting and generally relaxing before their meal. There were seven children in the Brennan family, so the house was always alive and buzzing with people. Eva sniffed the air and concluded that the Sunday roast was already in the oven, so she went to investigate.

'She wasn't in the best of form anyway that day, the same way everyone can wake up feeling annoyed,' says Collette. 'She went into the kitchen to see what was in the cooker. She took a look and said, "Not feckin' lamb again". I think we might have had lamb twice that month, or something.'

Eva stomped into the sitting room, looking for somewhere to vent her bad humour. She started giving out about the choice of roast, and one of her brothers pointed out that if she didn't want to eat the lamb she could go elsewhere for food. Eva decided she'd do just that. 'Out the door she went, and that was the last time any of us saw our sister,' says Collette.

It was the most innocuous of arguments. An everyday spat between relations, a familiar occurrence in a large, close family. As Eva shut the door behind her, the rest of the Brennans didn't give it another thought. No one ever suspected that all their lives were about to change for ever.

For two days, no one heard from her. While most families might consider it normal not to be in daily contact with each other, in the Brennan clan this counted as highly unusual.

'Eva had a set routine,' says Collette. 'Going to Mass, going to her prayer group, going to meet her friends. And part of that routine was going to Mum and Dad's most days for lunch. She didn't really cook for herself, she was like a big kid. So when she left the house on Sunday we just figured she'd be back when she was hungry.'

All day Monday, there was no news from Eva. 'Daddy thought that this was very strange on Monday, when there was no sign from her or phone call from her or anything,' says Collette. 'But you know, she was an adult and she didn't have half a temper on her. He just figured she was still annoyed about what had happened the previous day.'

Finally, on Tuesday, Eva's father, Davy Brennan, gave in to his worry and went to look for her. He called over to her apartment in Rathgar and rang the doorbell repeatedly. There was no response, no crackling of the intercom, no indication at all to suggest that Eva was inside. Immediately Davy felt there was something wrong. He knew his daughter and knew that she was a creature of habit. He called out her name, but was greeted with silence.

Trying to control his growing sense of panic, Davy Brennan ran across the road to the 108 pub and asked a barman there for help in breaking into the flat.

Between them, they managed to smash a window in the apartment. The barman climbed in and then opened the door from inside for Eva's father. As he walked into the hallway, he knew at once that his instinct had been correct. There was something seriously amiss. The apartment was spotless, nothing had been touched, there was no sign of a struggle or anything untoward. But Eva wasn't there.

Davy Brennan took a quick look around the flat and saw that Eva's keys and money were gone, along with the bag she had been wearing on Sunday. There was no sign of her pink tracksuit, but the jacket she had been wearing at the weekend was hanging over the back of a chair. It seemed Eva had returned home after visiting her parents' house on Sunday, before leaving the house again with her bag, but not her jacket.

Deeply worried, Davy Brennan went back to Terenure to break the news to his wife that Eva wasn't at home. While this may not have been a cause of alarm for other families, both Eva's parents knew immediately that something was very wrong. They decided that they better go to the Garda station to report Eva missing.

'Poor dad,' says Collette, staring into her swirling cup of coffee. For the first time in recounting the story, her voice breaks with the emotion of it and she bites her lip to stem the tears. 'He was the quietest man, the best gentleman there ever was. He loved us so much and he tried so hard to make us happy and keep us safe. And for him to have to go down to the gardaí and say his daughter was gone . . .'

She breaks off, and a heartbreaking silence falls over the kitchen. After a short pause, Collette shakes her head, and starts speaking again, her voice stronger now as she tells of the phone call from her father that changed her life.

'I had been away for the weekend anyway,' she says. 'Dad rang here and said, "Eva's missing." I just said, "How do you mean 'missing'?" He said, "She's not around. She's not in her apartment. We haven't seen her since Sunday."'

'So I said that I was on my way over. I went straight over to the house and didn't leave it again for three or four weeks. I went in the door and everybody was just sitting around, looking at each other, crying. No one knew what to do. A few people were going out and about with the dogs, looking and walking. Daddy had reported her missing down in the police station, did an interview with the police. But that was it. That was how easily it happened. Our Eva was gone.'

Collette pauses again and shakes her head a few times, as if trying to clear her mind. 'It's still just so strange,' she says, looking up and almost smiling at the strangeness. 'I had a person, a sister who was so close to me. And all of a sudden that sister is gone, disappeared, wiped off the face of the earth. In one afternoon, all our lives changed forever. It leaves you with all these questions, questions that can't be answered. But whoever did something to her, I suppose they'll eventually come in front of a higher being, if there is one.'

In the hours and days after Eva went missing, the Brennan family fought the urge to give in to panic, and tried to organise themselves to search for her. 'There was no one around to help us or tell us what to do, we didn't even know where to start,' says Collette. 'We had figured out that she had gone back to her apartment from Mum's house because her coat was there. And obviously she went out again. There was no sign that there'd been any sort of a break-in or anyone in the apartment who shouldn't have been. She just seems to have left the house of her own accord: whether it was afternoon, evening or night-time, we don't know.'

The family considered the possibility that Eva had gone for a walk in the evening and had come to harm along the way, but almost as quickly rejected the theory. 'She wouldn't go for a walk unless she was going somewhere,' says Collette. 'She wasn't the type to just head out for a stroll for the sake of it. The problem was, she was living at a crossroads. She could have gone any number of directions. The only thing we're pretty sure about is that she didn't head towards Terenure, because my brother Paul's was on the way and Mum's was on the way. And if she was in bad humour with Mum, she would have called into Paul's. That's the way it worked. I suppose there could have been a prayer meeting or there could have been a Mass. We don't know.'

The Brennans found two of Eva's address books and systematically started calling everyone on the list. But no one had seen her, no one had heard from her, no one could tell the family anything that they didn't already know. The gardaí tracked down a man from Donegal, who used to go to a prayer group with her, but he could contribute nothing to the investigation. They also found an ex-boyfriend of Eva's who had moved to Liverpool. He had nothing new to tell them.

'She didn't have a boyfriend at the time,' says Collette. 'She'd had a couple of boyfriends in the past and at one stage one of the men gave her a ring, but I don't think it was an engagement ring, I think it was more of a friendship ring. She was going out with one man for a while. But for the most part, she wasn't really interested in romance. She was very busy, going to her prayer meetings, or going dancing, or meeting with friends.'

Asked about what Eva did to earn a living, Collette gives a short, embarrassed little laugh. 'Nothing at all,' she says. 'No, I'm only joking. But the truth of the matter was we were spoilt brats, we didn't really have to work. I did some beautician work for a while, Eileen did a little bit of typing, and Eva would just doss around. The boys in the family worked with Dad in the pub and the girls just didn't do an awful lot. We were spoilt,' she smiles sadly. 'Daddy's little princesses.'

No clothes or other belongings were missing from Eva's house, but this is not the only reason the family believe she didn't go on an unplanned holiday or trip.

'The way it is in our family, the rest of them all think that I live in the sticks because I'm a little bit outside of Dublin,' says Collette. 'They think you need a passport to come to this house. The rest of them all live in Dartry, Bushypark, Clonskeagh. It's like the covered wagon and the Indians going round. Nobody moved too far away from Mum and Dad and the Terenure area. The point is, if Eva had gone away on a trip, it would have been a big thing that Eva was going away on a trip. Do you know what I mean? She would have got new clothes and everybody would have known that she was going. We all know who's doing what, where and when, and especially with Eva because she suffered from depression.'

A slightly uncomfortable silence falls in the room when Collette mentions Eva's struggle with depression. At the time of her disappearance it was widely reported in the media that Eva was depressed, and rarely would an article be written about the 39-year-old woman without a reference to this. The inference, never said but always implied, was that Eva Brennan was mentally ill and quite possibly committed suicide on that Sunday afternoon when she walked out of her apartment and out of her family's life.

It is not at all surprising, therefore, that Collette's expression becomes slightly defensive now. She gazes calmly across the table, immediately challenging any unspoken suggestion that depression had something to do with Eva's disappearance.

'You know, she had it bad sometimes, she had it good sometimes,' she says. 'But in the few weeks before she went missing she was fine. It's one of the hardest parts of it, people assuming that she killed herself. But if you look at it logically, if she had killed herself, where is her body? She couldn't have buried herself. We had the Liffey searched by the Garda Sub Aqua Unit. She wasn't there. So where is she, if she killed herself?'

Suddenly her shoulders droop and it's as if the fight visibly seeps out of her. It's difficult to imagine how traumatic it must have been for the Brennan family—frantically searching for their lost sister and daughter while constantly battling with the raised eyebrows, pitiful glances and the whispers that no one but Eva herself had anything to do with her disappearance.

'She started suffering from depression when she was sixteen, and we didn't know what was going on, or at least I certainly didn't,' says Collette. 'We knew she was a pain in the ass sometimes, but that was about it. I think in those days that she was given medication to shut her up. It affected her weight; she would blow up like a balloon and then go back to being skinny. Mostly, I noticed it in her weight. I suppose it did impact on her life. She'd sometimes be difficult, or be bad-humoured, or have a bad day. But everyone has bad days. And in the weeks before she went missing, she really had been fine.'

The Brennans felt that they had to inform the gardaí of Eva's depression, even though they knew that both the police force and the public would automatically take a different view of the circumstances in which she disappeared. 'We didn't want it to come out a few weeks later and then it would seem like we were hiding it for some reason,' says Collette. 'But I do think it made a difference to how the case was investigated. And that was so frustrating. It was the thing that upset me more than anything at the time. Eva had depression and therefore everyone assumed she had killed herself. But if you were to apply that logic, then half of Ireland should have killed themselves by now, because half of Ireland suffer from depression. It's just too easy to write her off like that.'

The Brennan family have thought about whether there might be any truth in the theory that Eva took her own life, but they have rejected this explanation for a number of reasons.

First, and fundamentally for the family, they simply don't believe Eva would have done it. 'She wouldn't have done it to Dad, she wouldn't have hurt him like that,' says Collette. 'And I know some people might think I'm being naive, but you know your own. No one else knows your family like you do. And I know Eva didn't kill herself, because she wouldn't hurt the rest of us like that. Not even in a fit of temper would she do that.'

Aside from the family's gut instinct, the timing and location of Eva's disappearance cannot be ignored. She went missing in south Dublin city in the early 1990s, at a time when other young women in the Leinster area were also vanishing. The murders of Patricia Furlong, Antoinette Smith and Patricia Doherty had all taken place in the previous years. And, of course, Annie McCarrick had only recently gone missing within a relatively short driving distance from Eva's home.

Also, although no one knew it at the time, more young women were fated to disappear in highly suspicious circumstances in the Leinster area in the years after Eva vanished.

When Operation Trace was eventually set up to examine the links between these cases, Eva Brennan's disappearance was not officially included. However, privately, detectives recognised that the circumstances surrounding her disappearance were too coincidental, too suspect to be ignored. They carried out discreet enquiries into Eva's case, and ran her details through the ovid computer system to compare her disappearance with that of the other missing women. All their efforts came to nothing. There were no leads at all. Eva, quite simply, had vanished.

While they were happy that private enquiries were being made, the Brennan family still question why Eva's case wasn't officially part of Operation Trace. 'Eight women went missing at that time,' says Collette. 'Our Eva was one of them. I don't know, maybe it was because she had depression or because she was thirty-nine and didn't fit the age profile. But it broke my heart every time those six women were mentioned and Eva wasn't. It was one of the most hurtful things that happened since she went missing. I really did think there was a serial killer at the time. It had to be something like that. There were so many women going missing. They were there, and next thing they were gone. I know that each one had a different story, but for each of them to just vanish off the face of the earth, it was too peculiar. When that man, Larry Murphy, was arrested, it made me wonder. I know he was a carpenter, and I do know at the time Eva went missing the 108 was being done up. I asked the garda to find out where Murphy was working at that time, but I never got an answer. I suppose I suspected everybody.'

In the days and weeks after Eva disappeared, the Brennan family began to resign themselves to the horrible reality that she could very possibly be dead. For Collette, her sister's fate has played vividly in her mind many times. 'When she first went missing my imagination ran riot,' she says. 'I could actually see her being hammered to death. In my mind's eye, I could see her being raped and killed, and I could feel every drop of earth that fell over her when she was buried. But I had to stop thinking like that. You have to make yourself stop, or you just go under. I think she was dragged up the Dublin Mountains and killed and buried. That's where I see her now, when I think of her. I think of her in the mountains.'

Every day, at least one member of the Brennan family made the trip to the police station to see if there was any news of Eva. 'It got to the point where she had been missing for six months or so, and I went into the station and one of the garda just looked at me as if to say, "Oh no, here she is again",' says Collette. 'And that was the first time I cried. I had held it in up to that point because I felt I needed to be strong, and I thought that if I started to cry I'd sit in a corner and I'd cry for the rest of my days.'

The Brennans hired a private investigator to look into the case and paid him for four months. At the end of every week, they waited hopefully for news. Despite his efforts, he never came up with any new information. After a considerable sum of money led only to weeks of disappointment and silence on their sister's whereabouts, they terminated the contract. Another avenue exhausted.

Twelve months passed in a flurry of searching, interviews and grief. Finally, one year after Eva disappeared, her siblings unlocked her apartment and went inside to clean it. 'We dusted and hoovered and washed everything in sight. And it was after that that the police went in and took fingerprints,' says Collette. 'Everything just seemed to be done backwards. I blamed them at the time, but I don't think I can now, because I don't think they knew what to do. We were always told that if you have a problem the police will fix it. So we thought when we went to the police, they'd find Eva. But of course, it wasn't as simple as that.'

It's fifteen years now since Eva walked out of her family home, never to return. The family still talk about her often. And they still cry. They replay that fateful afternoon in their minds and explore again and again various scenarios that could have led to their sister's disappearance.

'I often speak to Eileen and Paul, and we've wondered if she would have been naive enough to take a lift from someone or do something stupid like that,' says Collette, shaking her head. 'But then we remember: if Eva was standing at a bus stop and if a man stood beside her, she'd walk to the next bus stop. Even if that meant she would miss the bus. And that was back when the world was not like it is now. She was very aware of danger, very aware of safety. She wouldn't have gone anywhere willingly with a stranger.'

I ask when the family finally made the heartbreaking decision to stop searching. 'We haven't,' says Collette. 'We never will.'

There's very little else to say. An almost visible grief has settled over Collette as she offers to drop me to the town to get the bus. The air is heavy with defeat.

It's still bright outside, but there's no one on the street near the bus stop. Collette barely slows down, before shifting gears resolutely. 'I'll bring you to the one on the other side of town,' she says. 'There'll be lots of people around there. It'll be safer.'

Chapter 9
Double Rape, Double Conviction

There were two days left in 1994. But for the woman standing on the gloomy corner of Fitzwilliam Place in Dublin, 31 December would be nothing to celebrate. It was cold and it was dark and she was miserable. She was on the streets again, after months of being clean. Only 20 years old, and back to rock bottom. Back on the gear.

A silver car pulled up beside her, a Ford Escort estate with a Northern registration. She began the slow walk over to the rolled-down window, where the driver was waiting expectantly. Her steps echoed faintly in the night. She just wanted this to be over. To have the money, have the drugs, have some peace.

She tried not to think of her boyfriend, waiting angrily at home. They'd had a huge argument before she left the house that night. He wanted her to give up heroin. He'd reminded her that she'd been free from the drug for eighteen months. She had only been using again for seven weeks. It wasn't ever too late to give up. If she could do it once, she could do it again. But she told him she needed it to 'feel normal'. She'd cried, and pleaded with him to understand. She told him she loved him as she shut the door on the warmth inside.

On the corner of Fitzwilliam Place, she leaned from the waist, resting her arms on the window sill and peering inside. Her heart sank. There were two men in the car. With one man it was always a risk. But two left her terrifyingly vulnerable. She voiced her concern. The driver, a well-dressed man in his mid-thirties, shook his head reassuringly, almost kindly. He looked her in the eye as he told her that he was dropping 'his brother' off around the corner. Soon they would be alone, he said.

They discussed a price—£30 for oral sex. She didn't have full inter-course with any of her clients. It was her way of showing loyalty to her boyfriend. Her testament to her love. No matter how desperate, how gnawing the need, she wouldn't betray him in that way. The sum of £30 brought her closer to her target of £120. Three or four such contracts and she would be free to go home. She agreed.

She sat into the car and directed the driver to a car park in Ranelagh, a spot she'd used before where they were unlikely to be disturbed. The driver jammed the car into gear, and drove around the corner. His 'brother' didn't get out of the car. They passed the entrance to the car park, the driver deaf to her cries of warning, followed by cries of alarm. The silver car sped through the suburbs, heading for the mountains now. The woman screamed and screamed until it was clear that it was making no difference. She stared at the dark streets, flashing by in a haze of terror. And she knew she was in serious trouble.

Thomas Stokes was driving, and the man beside him was not his brother. Adrian Power was only 22 years old, but in his short life he had already been arrested for violence against women. Originally from Maddenstown in Co. Kildare, he was callous and savage and not that smart. Three years earlier he had been convicted of indecently assaulting a tourist in London. Now he was back on the streets, looking for more trouble and more victims.

Power was easily influenced by stronger male characters, and for all his dangerous tendencies he was no match for Thomas Stokes of Piercetown, Newbridge, Co. Kildare. Stokes was a Traveller. Or, in his preferred words, an 'Irish tinker'.

Ten years older than Power, and infinitely more calculating and intelligent, Stokes was calling the shots that night. He too had a criminal record, much longer and more varied than his companion's. In fact, one garda later described him as a 'versatile' criminal. 'He has every type of conviction, which is unusual because burglars usually don't branch out,' said the garda.

Thomas Stokes's life had started with grief and become dominated by hatred and violence. When he was 13 years old his parents and brother were killed in a car crash on the Naas Road. The young boy watched as the flames engulfed the tangled metal, burning his family and leaving him orphaned and alone. The image became imprinted on his memory, and he developed a morbid fascination with fire.

He went to live with an aunt, with whom he travelled around the country. His education was haphazard and unorganised, with Stokes spending only a few weeks in any place before moving on. He left school with only a skeleton knowledge of how to read or write.

Like many young Travellers, Stokes was self-employed, making money by collecting scrap metal, selling goods at markets and labouring on farms. In 1982 he married his cousin Christina Stokes, and they lived in Waterford for some time.

Shortly afterwards, during a visit to Athy in Kildare, Stokes showed his capacity for sexual assault. It was a dark winter evening when he picked up a teenage schoolgirl just outside Athy town. He took her down a narrow laneway, and had begun his assault when he was disturbed by a passing farmer. In 1984, at Dungarvan Circuit Court, he was convicted of the offence and sentenced to four years in prison.

Three years later he was released, and he and his family moved to Britain to make a new start. There, Stokes took up night classes, effectively teaching himself to read and write. He became actively involved in the 'Gypsy' community in the UK, and started working for an offshoot of the *Big Issue* magazine.

Through the magazine, Stokes started exposing what he said was the 'brutality inflicted on Travellers, including women and children, by the gardaí'. He became obsessed with inequality and prejudice against Travellers by the authorities, and developed a deep-rooted hatred for the police force.

During the late 1980s Stokes's marriage began to break down and the couple started to have lengthy, violent rows. Eventually, Christina moved out of the house and away from her husband, taking their child with her. In retaliation Stokes started making menacing phone calls to his wife, threatening to kill her. He tracked her down to where she was staying with relations in a house at Notting Hill in London. He carefully poured petrol through the letterbox and then set it alight. The blaze very nearly burned his family alive. He also set fire to a nearby lorry. His trademark use of fire earned him the nickname Thomas 'The Burn' Stokes.

In 1989, a jury at Knightsbridge Crown Court listened with horror to police tape recordings of the threatening phone calls that Stokes had made to his wife. That year he was convicted of three counts of threatening to kill, arson endangering life and criminal damage to property by fire. He was sentenced to eight years in prison for his crimes.

However, three years later, Stokes managed to convince the parole board that he was a 'person of reformed and changed ways'. He was released back into the community, four years early. For both the gardaí and the British police, who knew the violent individual who lay behind Stokes's innocent appearance, it was deeply frustrating.

One Garda describes how Stokes had an uncanny knack of appearing harmless and unthreatening, when he so desired. 'If you were talking to him, he's a sweet as pie,' said the Garda. 'He dresses pretty well. He's slick. But when he was around, you had to watch your home and yourself.'

It was 1993 when Stokes was allowed back onto the streets. He officially separated from his wife, and in September he returned to Ireland where he settled into a halting site in Clondalkin in Dublin.

The following summer he moved to another site in Bray, Co. Wicklow. However, that Travelling community was forced to leave by the gardaí when a developer obtained a High Court Order to have them removed from the land. On 4 May 1994, Stokes displayed his growing hatred of the police when he rammed a Garda patrol car near Monasterevin in County Kildare.

He was arrested and charged, and the case was still working its way slowly through the legal system by the night of 29 December 1994, when Stokes and his eager companion pulled up to Fitzwilliam Place in Dublin, looking for a victim.

As they drove, they argued. Adrian Power wanted to stop off and buy some cannabis from a dealer in the area. Stokes, on the other hand, was eager to get to the mountains and begin raping and abusing the woman in the car.

During the argument, Power referred repeatedly to Stokes as 'Tom', much to the disgust of the older man. He snapped at him to be quiet, and ordered him to use a different Christian name.

The Ford Escort pulled in to the side of the road, where a caravan was parked in the darkness. The internal light bulb flooded the interior of the car with a murky yellow gleam, and the woman looked carefully at the two faces of her abductors as they negotiated over the purchase of the cannabis. Power turned around in his seat and offered some of the drug to the woman. She declined, tears making wet tracks through her makeup.

Her panic increased as Stokes restarted the car, and drove further out of the city, finally stopping on a lonely bog road on Powerscourt Mountain.

Over the next two and a half hours, the men systematically subjected the woman to violent and degrading sexual abuse. They started by forcing her to give both of them oral sex, ignoring her cries and pleas to be set free.

'They were rough and kept calling me a tramp,' the woman said later. 'I was crying and screaming. They told me to shut up or they would bury me. I told them I wanted to get home to my kids and my mother. It went on for some hours but it seemed like forever. I thought they were going to kill me.'

After receiving oral sex from the woman, both men decided to take a break. They each calmly lit up a cigarette, blowing the grey smoke into the night, ignoring the shivering, whimpering woman beside them.

Then Stokes announced that he wanted to have sex with the woman. Sick with the knowledge that she was helpless to stop him, the woman made one last-ditch attempt to protect herself. She told Stokes she had AIDS and asked him to use a condom. He did so, raping her with a detached brutality. At one point he turned to Power and said: 'Look at her. She loves it.'

Power waited his turn, and then also raped the woman. At some point during the attack he bit her chest, his teeth digging into her skin. In a final, degrading and painful act of violence, the men then had anal sex with their victim.

Sated at last, they dressed and threw away any rubbish from the car, including the used condoms, tissues, cigarette and condom boxes. Before they left, Stokes walked around to the back of the car and produced a car jack. In her beaten, broken state, the woman was sure it was a gun, and that the men were now going to kill her. But Stokes just kept the car jack by his side as he drove back down the mountain. It was never clear what he intended to do with it, but gardaí later agreed that the woman may well have had a lucky escape.

When they reached Rathfarnham, Stokes dragged the woman out of the car and ordered her not to look at the registration before speeding off into the darkness. She lay there, hugging her knees, rocking back and forth. Gratitude at being alive struggled with the images of what had just happened, which replayed in her mind with gut-wrenching clarity. There she stayed, gently swaying, until a couple came across her shaking form. When she saw them, she could only say one thing:

'I never thought I'd see a face again.' The couple quickly wrapped her up and took her to the Garda station.

The next day, on the eve of the New Year, gardaí accompanied the woman to the scene of the crime. There, among the flattened weeds and grass, they recovered the items she had described being thrown from the car, including a used condom.

On 1 January 1995, gardaí launched a nationwide alert for Stokes and his car. A fax was sent to all garda stations, warning officers to be on the lookout for the rapist and describing him as 'extremely dangerous and possibly armed'.

That same day, Garda Des Quinn was driving his patrol car through Cork city centre when he noticed a silver Ford Escort parked outside a guesthouse on Glanmire Road. Minutes later, Stokes set off in the car and headed towards Tivoli Bridge. It was at this point that Quinn pulled him over and asked for his name and licence.

Calm and collected—despite his hope of avoiding all contact with the gardaí—Stokes identified himself as 'Anthony Maguire of Newry'. He seemed earnest and open, and Quinn later said he was 'very convincing'. However, Stokes's driver's licence had a Dundalk address on it, despite his claim to be from the North. Quinn followed his instincts and arrested Stokes for a traffic offence.

Immediately, the rapist knew he was in trouble. His mind began racing over the events of the last few days, looking for possible alibis and ways of defending his case. In his head, a fantastic new version of the story began to emerge.

When it was established that he had used a false name, Stokes received a fourteen-day prison sentence in Portlaoise. In the meantime, the word was sent to Dublin that the rapist had been caught. When he was released from Portlaoise on 23 January, a new team of gardaí was waiting for him. Stokes was rearrested for false imprisonment, sexual assault and rape of a woman in the Dublin Mountains.

In the meantime, forensic officers had been combing the crime scene for further evidence to link Stokes to the attack. On 4 January, a second used condom was found among the weeds in the spot where the rape had taken place. Gardaí handed the condom over to the Forensic Science Laboratory for DNA analysis.

Stokes didn't say anything when he was brought to Harcourt Terrace Garda Station in Dublin, where his victim immediately identified him from a parade of seventeen people. He declined to answer any questions, and ignored his own legal advice by refusing to provide forensic samples to the Gardaí. However, when asked for a hair sample he grabbed a handful of his hair and ripped it out at the roots. The unnecessary violence was one of the only physical indications of the anger simmering within him.

In the Forensic Science Laboratory, Dr Maureen Smyth had been able to extract DNA from the semen found in the second condom. She then compared this with DNA taken from the hair sample provided by Thomas Stokes. It was a match.

Stokes's clothes were also subjected to microscopic examination, and a second forensic scientist, Dr Sheila Willis, found that fibre evidence 'very strongly supported' contact between the victim and Stokes's jacket.

After the woman positively identified Stokes's car, the silver Ford Escort estate was also combed for clues. A hair belonging to the victim was found on the seat and Dr Willis found that there was fibre evidence linking the woman to the car.

Semen had also been found on the woman's blouse, and a DNA sample had been taken. However, this was not a match for Thomas Stokes. Gardaí knew that they were looking for a second attacker, but Adrian Power had thus far been successful in avoiding detection. Despite repeated questioning, Stokes refused to say anything to identify his comrade.

The search for the younger man lasted two years. In 1996, Power was finally apprehended and charged with false imprisonment, oral rape, rape and buggery of the woman in the mountains.

In October of the same year the case against Stokes finally came to court. In the months since his arrest the self-styled champion of the 'Irish tinkers' had focused all his considerable intelligence into preparing quite a show for the jury.

He was impeccably dressed when he arrived into the courtroom, wearing silver-framed glasses and a look of earnest concentration. Only those sitting close to Stokes could see that the left arm of his glasses was carefully sellotaped in place.

On each day of the unusually long sixteen-day trial, Stokes carried with him a brown cardboard folder containing biros, papers and official-looking documents. As each witness took to the stand, Stokes would open a soft brown pencil case, pop the cap off a biro, and start taking detailed notes of the testimony being given. By the end of the trial he had filled hundreds of pages with his neat, self-taught script. When he was not writing, he sat with his hands in his lap, occasionally unfolding a tissue from his folder and polishing his glasses. His entire appearance and demeanour was closer to that of a diligent court clerk than a savage, calculating rapist.

When it came time for him to defend himself, Stokes came into his own with a carefully prepared and entirely fictional version of events. It was based around his own passion—the prejudicial actions of gardaí against Travellers. He was being framed, he said, the victim of a conspiracy involving gardaí, prison officers, a doctor, the forensic scientists and, of course, the victim herself.

Before taking to the stand, Stokes instructed his counsel, Blaise O'Carroll SC, to give the jury an introduction of sorts. O'Carroll informed the court that Stokes had spent his time in prison working on a book about his life, beginning with the death of his parents and then going on to detail the various negative encounters he had had with the gardaí. His client was a member of the Travelling community, said O'Carroll, and he felt 'a certain pressure coming from that'.

The groundwork laid, Stokes then began giving six hours of evidence about what he insisted had really happened around the dawn of the year 1995. He started by telling the jury that when he returned from Britain to live in Ireland he knew there would be some sort of reprisal from gardaí for his previous crimes.

As he had expected, his life as part of the Irish Travelling community was marred by 'much intimidation and gun pointing'. At one point, he said, gardaí raided his caravan and stole hundreds of pages of his proposed book, a camera, a typewriter and photographs.

'I thought we had all grown up over the last twenty years,' he said. 'It is very hard to stop telling truths.' He said he was writing his book in order to 'send a message to his own people' of the Travelling community: 'I am being accepted. You can be too, by changing a little.' He told the jury about being evicted from the halting site in Bray, Co. Wicklow, in what he said was a contravention of various High Court orders. He painted a picture of a war zone, with gardaí and developers on one side and Travellers on the other.

'I saw earthmovers coming from all directions, mothers grabbing children, tears in their eyes,' he said. 'It looked like a war to me. It looked like Soweto, South Africa.' He said his pregnant common-law wife was so badly injured during the eviction that she had had to be hospitalised.

Stokes claimed that the rape investigation team from Rathfarnham Garda Station were all present at the Bray eviction, including the head of the investigation, Detective Sergeant James Costello. He named Costello as one of the 'main conspirators' who 'stalked and followed [him] everywhere', along with Sergeant Patrick Tully and Garda Mary Walsh, who were also part of the rape investigation team. Stokes said that he had made a complaint to Travellers' representatives and newspapers at the time.

Having established his belief that he was living in a climate of fear and intimidation, Stokes moved on to the night of the attack. That evening, he told the jury, he had been taken ill with piles and had stayed in a house in Kildare. Evidently he had used his considerable ability to charm the female owner of the house, a health worker, into officially backing up his story.

She took to the stand and swore to the jury that she had let Stokes use her bed that night while she slept in a chair. She said she had noted this in her diary.

However, the prosecuting team, led by Maureen Clark SC, announced that they had had Garda handwriting experts examine the diary as part of the investigation. Under the entry that was made on 29 December, the gardaí discovered an obliterated line of script that read: 'I let Tom stay in my room last night . . . I am looking forward to my own bed tonight.'

The prosecution pointed out that this indicated Stokes had slept in the house in Kildare on the previous night, 28 December, not on 29 December. But the health worker loyally stuck to her part of the fabrication and said that Stokes did not leave her house until after 9am on 30 December.

Undeterred by this blip of truth, Stokes continued his narrative. After spending the night in Kildare, he said, he left the house on 30 December and spent the night with his brother in Tallaght. The next day he decided to visit his estranged wife and children for the New Year, but en route he took an impulsive detour and ended up in Cork city.

There, he said, he went to look for an old girlfriend, but couldn't find her. During his search, he met another woman outside a pub and they started talking. They walked together back to his car, he said, where they engaged in gentle consensual sexual intercourse. 'We were chatting, talking,' he told the jury softly. 'We were both, I suppose, interested in some friendship for the night. We made love.' He said he took out the duvet he kept in the car, and after having sex the couple 'slept in each other's arms and woke when it was light'.

In tortuous detail, Stokes described how the following morning he put two used condoms, some tissues and a Benson and Hedges cigarette box into a plastic bag. He said he booked into a bed and breakfast on the Glanmire Road and left the bag in his room. That evening he went out to get food, and it was then that he was arrested on the Tivoli Bridge by Garda Des Quinn.

After he was arrested, Stokes said, the gardaí searched his room, found the bag of condoms and rubbish, and then planted it all at the scene of the rape in the Wicklow Mountains. It was one of his more outrageous allegations in a string of ludicrous claims.

While the police were busy framing him for the crime, Stokes said, he was being intimidated in his cell in Mayfield Garda Station in Cork city. He said the only explanation he had been given for his arrest was that gardaí from Portarlington, Co. Laois, were investigating some matter. He claimed he was also questioned in relation to the North of Ireland and interrogated about any political connections he might have.

He painted a picture of himself, confused and scared, as gardaí kicked at the door of his cell and assaulted him in an attempt to frighten him into signing a false confession. He said that at one point Sergeant Patrick Tully from the Rathfarnham rape investigation team slipped a copy of a Sunday newspaper under the door. A circle had been drawn in pencil around an article entitled: 'What should we do with Travellers – Should we put them in Spike Island or Timbuktu?'

Finally, his tale came to an end and the defence rested his case. But not for a minute did Stokes drop his act. On Saturday morning, as Maureen Clark SC summed up the prosecution case against him, his note-taking became even more furious.

When Clark was reminding the jury about the Benson and Hedges cigarette box found at the scene, Stokes carefully placed a box of Major cigarettes on the bench beside him.

There was more frenzied scribbling as Justice Moriarty charged the jury, and the writing didn't end until they retired at four o'clock that afternoon. Four hours later they returned with a majority verdict on all three counts. Guilty, guilty and guilty.

Stokes sat with his hands crossed and his head down as the foreman told the court the decision. Then he began to tidy up. He tapped all his papers neatly together, bound them with elastic and placed them back into the folder, followed by his soft brown pencil case.

Then, as the judge thanked the jury, Stokes crossed himself quickly and put his hands together in prayer, before standing up to talk to his legal team. He had reason to be continuing his performance—sentencing was yet to come.

Unfortunately for him, his efforts were not appreciated by the judge. Thomas Stokes was given one of the heaviest sentences ever handed down for a single sexual crime in the history of the State. The judge imposed a life sentence upon him for the rape of the woman in the mountains, and concurrent terms of twelve years for kidnapping and the maximum five years for sexual assault.

Standing between two prison officers, Stokes took occasional notes as Justice Moriarty described him as 'cynical', 'unscrupulous', 'devious', 'dangerous', and 'criminal'.

'Far from being a spokesman or apologist for Travelling people, it seems to me that in this unhappy case you have brought considerable discredit to any persons who might wish to associate with you,' said Moriarty. 'Your conduct during the trial has shown a callous and cynical disregard for the truth. I cannot think of any person in my ten years as a judge here who has shown to be so devious, dangerous and unscrupulous.'

Blaise O'Carroll said that after the sentence was handed down, he was instructed to appeal against the verdict. As he spoke, Stokes put his hand to his mouth and seemed to be yawning. He also appeared to be smiling faintly as he stretched out his arm to allow the prison officer to handcuff him in preparation for his lengthy return to prison.

As he was led away from the courtroom, Stokes decided there was no longer any point in his pretence. He grinned lazily at his victim as he left, before raising his hand in a two-fingered salute. Few people mourned as the cell door was shut once more on Thomas Stokes.

Two years later, the trial of Adrian Power also came to court. The charges of rape and buggery had been withdrawn by the prosecution, but those of false imprisonment and oral rape remained.

In direct contrast to his older accomplice, Power admitted to everything the victim had said, and his defence argued only over the issue of consent. The jury of seven women and five men took just under ninety minutes to decide that the victim had fought the two men throughout the attack. It was rape.

However, both the prosecution and the judge accepted that Stokes had played the leading role in the attack and Power was jailed for ten years for his crime—considerably less than Stokes, but another heavy sentence in relative terms.

With Power finally convicted, and Stokes already serving a life sentence, the gardaí were hoping not to have any more dealings with the two brutal rapists. However, even from behind bars, Thomas Stokes could not resist causing mischief and pain for innocent people.

When an 18-year-old woman disappeared in broad daylight in Newbridge, Co. Kildare in 1998, Stokes followed the case with interest. The teenager had gone missing near his home town, and all the indications pointed towards her having been abducted.

For six months Stokes read about the investigation. He watched as the woman's family issued increasingly desperate pleas for information.

Perhaps it was a crime that Stokes himself would have liked to commit. Perhaps he took a special interest in the case because it was close to Newbridge. Maybe it was just bored cruelty that prompted Stokes to contact the gardaí claiming he had vital new information about the disappearance.

Two detectives travelled to Arbour Hill prison and interviewed him at length. After some time it became clear that he was wasting their time. For the grief-stricken family, another hope would be dashed, another lead run cold. Swallowing their frustration, the detectives left Arbour Hill, trying not to look back at where Thomas Stokes sat grinning in his cell.

Chapter 10

The Murder of Layla Brennan

H e was, and still is, the most dangerous type of killer. Charming, good-looking and devastatingly attractive to the opposite sex. His power over women is mesmeric and undisputed. At the turn of this century it was very nearly strong enough to traverse the courtroom and convince two young female jurors that he was innocent of his crime. Very nearly. But on 1 November 2000, Philip Colgan was unanimously found guilty of the savage murder of a 24-year-old woman called Layla Brennan.

Ultimately, the jury believed he had enticed Layla into his car, strangled her with her bra, and then beaten her unconscious body with a car jack after hiding her in the Dublin Mountains. When he was sentenced to life in prison, his mask of innocence slipped a little, and onlookers later described their horror at the man they then saw. One detective said that to look into his eyes was like looking into a black hole. No feeling, no emotion, no humanity. As cries of grief and celebration exploded in the courtroom, Colgan was handcuffed and led towards the door. He was used to prison. He'd been there before.

The young man from Laragh Close in Donaghmede in Dublin didn't come on the Garda radar until he was 19 years old. Until that point Philip Colgan had led a normal life. He came from a hard-working, decent family. He had no previous convictions. Then, in November 1991, the teenager decided to rape a 79-year-old woman.

Colgan has never explained what drove him to such indiscriminate, savage violence. He had spent the evening with his girlfriend, and at 1.30am he saw that she got safely into a taxi home. After watching the car drive away, instead of heading back to his house, Colgan chose to take a late-night stroll around his neighbourhood, padding softly through the dark streets of North Dublin.

After about half and hour, he spotted a block of old folks' homes. In what seems to have been an entirely impulsive decision, the young man picked one of the houses at random and quietly forced his way inside.

At around 2am, the sole resident of the home, a 79-year-old widow, woke up to find Philip Colgan lying on top of her, holding a knife against the thin skin of her throat. He calmly informed her that if she screamed he would kill her.

The woman was terrified, and in her panic her breathing started to shorten and her lungs began to close. She was an asthmatic, and fear had brought on an attack. She gulped for air and promised Colgan whatever he wished if he would allow her to use her inhaler. He refused, only permitting her to get up to fetch £120 that she told him she had in the wardrobe. The savings of a pensioner.

After stuffing the cash into his pocket, Colgan raped the old woman, and subjected her to what detectives were later to describe as 'other degrading sexual acts'. He then tied her up, using the straps of her handbag and a sheet he tore into strips. At some stage during all the activity, Colgan snagged his expensive silk shirt. It ripped and left a small diamond-shaped piece of thread at the scene.

Unaware that he had left vital evidence behind, Colgan told the old lady not to struggle and that he would call the gardaí to come and release her. He then left the apartment. He never called the gardaí. When he arrived back to his house in Donaghmede he took off his expensive shirt and hid it in a box in the attic.

The old woman was left, bruised and humiliated, strung up in her soiled, ripped sheets. As the minutes and hours ticked by and no one came, she began to bang her head on the wall, hoping the sound would alert her neighbours. She was lucky. She was found.

A few days later, as gardaí were combing the scene for clues and interviewing everyone in the vicinity, Colgan went into the city centre, still buzzing from the triumph of the previous attack, and now looking for more entertainment.

He entered a nightclub, his eyes scanning the room for a suitably susceptible target. His gaze settled on a young Spanish woman, and he walked over to her, his long stride oozing confidence, his face open and attractive. After a short conversation he had convinced her to go with him to his home in Donaghmede, where he said he was throwing a party.

When they arrived at the quiet, empty house, Colgan convinced the young woman to come inside, making various excuses about the obvious absence of any party. He brought her into his bedroom, turned the radio on full volume, and sexually assaulted her. As the young woman struggled and fought, gardaí called to the house, knocked on the door and asked Colgan to turn down the music. The noise had woken the neighbours.

Shortly later, more gardaí—who were making enquiries in the area in relation to the attack on the elderly woman—knocked on Colgan's door. He closely fitted the description given to them by the victim, and after interviewing Colgan they arrested him for the crime. Afterwards, detectives from Raheny led by Detective Sergeant John Shanahan, searched his house and found the silk shirt hidden after the attack. He was now forensically linked with the rape, and he admitted his crime.

When asked by detectives how he felt when he returned home after attacking the old woman, Colgan showed no hint of regret. 'We expected him to show some remorse,' said one garda who was close to the investigation. 'But all he said was, "I was thinking of my shirt being ripped and I was really pissed off about that. It was a good shirt."'

Almost eight months later Colgan appeared in the Central Criminal Court, charged with both crimes. His defence counsel, Gregory Murphy sc, appealed for leniency in the sentencing for the assault on the Spanish woman, referring to reports by a psychiatrist which noted that Colgan had taken an Ecstasy tablet and had had a lot to drink in the pub before the attack.

Murphy also drew attention to Colgan's age, pointed out that he had no previous convictions, and said that at an early stage in the investigation he said he was willing to plead guilty for the crimes.

Judge Paul Carney was presiding over the case. He listened to Gregory Murphy's pleas for leniency and then refused an application from him to backdate the terms of detention to the previous November, when Colgan had been taken into custody. He sentenced the young rapist to eight years for the rape of the elderly woman and a concurrent six-year prison sentence for the sexual assault of the Spanish woman. In giving his sentence, Carney pointed out that the State could well appeal the sentence on the grounds of leniency.

The State did not appeal. Worse, Philip Colgan got out on early release. And because of that, Layla Brennan lost her life.

Layla Brennan came from a loving, happy home in West Dublin. Until she was 12 years old she was the only child in the family. For her parents and her grandparents she was, quite simply, the light around which all their worlds revolved.

Since she was killed, the Brennan family have publicly spoken very little about Layla. For the most part, they have regarded the media with suspicion and bewilderment. They have good reason.

Philip Colgan was a double rapist and a brutal murderer. But during his trial, it was Layla's character that was sullied and besmirched, Layla's life that the jury were asked to judge. From the outset, every newspaper article written about the trial carried two descriptions of Layla Brennan, designed to denigrate her to the point where it really didn't matter what Philip Colgan had done. Those words were 'heroin addict' and 'prostitute'.

The Brennans were forced to watch, helpless and grieving, as their daughter's dignity was legally and methodically ripped to shreds. Now, almost a decade after her death, the Brennans have cautiously decided to try talking again, to make another hopeful and fearful attempt to do justice to their daughter's memory.

Mags Brennan, Layla's mother, arrives at our agreed meeting point – a half-empty pub in Crumlin, full of men and pints and racing scores flashing on TV screens. She smiles shyly, warily. Although the Brennans now live in Kildare, having moved out of Dublin to get away from the memories, Mags is in Crumlin on this day to tend to her sick father. She explains that we wouldn't have been able to talk properly in his house. 'He has never accepted Layla's death,' she says. 'He can't talk about it at all. I just didn't want to be upsetting him.'

The barman places two mugs of coffee peremptorily on the table, and Mags picks hers up immediately, both hands wrapped around it protectively. She blows on the steamy surface and starts to talk quietly about Layla's childhood.

The family of three moved to Neilstown in Clondalkin when Layla was still young. The little girl quickly made friends, and soon had a tightly-knit group of close companions, with whom she did every-thing and shared everything. When she was 12 years old, her baby brother was born, followed the next year by a baby sister.

I mention that Layla must have been very treasured, having been an only child for twelve years. Mags nods and swallows and suddenly her eyes blur with tears. 'Never mind me,' she says, smiling her exasperation. 'I fill up, and then I get over it and I stop. Don't take any notice.' She waves a hand in the air, frustrated at how quickly and easily the memory of Layla affects her. Her hand reaches into her bag.

'Here,' she says. 'Before I forget.'

She hands over a picture of Layla, dressed in a light pink dress, a bridesmaid at a wedding. She's five-foot five-inches tall, with sparkling blue eyes. Her long curly blonde hair is pulled loosely away from her face. She's not looking at the camera, but she's smiling, and the light is reflecting off her cheeks. As if Layla herself is glowing. She looks happy, healthy, loved.

After primary school, Layla progressed to Coláiste Bríd in Clondalkin village. When she was in fourth year she took up an offer from a friend of the family to start working on Saturdays as a receptionist in a dental clinic in the city centre.

Layla loved her job. She was a very social individual, and thrived from interacting with the clients. She also took huge pride in being employed and having an income—however small—and she regularly stayed on in the clinic after her shift, preparing things for the following day. The owner of the surgery was very impressed with her ability and her maturity. He soon gave her the responsibility of opening up the premises in the morning. After a year working weekends at the clinic, Layla decided that instead of going back to school to complete her Leaving Cert she would start work there full-time.

By the time she was 19, Layla was happily cushioned in between her family life, social life and working life. Things were good. It was then she met her boyfriend and fell in love for the first time. It was perhaps the most clichéd of pitfalls – her boyfriend was a drug addict, and Layla decided to save him from himself.

'She was just besotted with him,' says Mags. 'She tried to convince me he wasn't on drugs, but I just knew he was. And that's how Layla fell in. At first she wanted to try to help him, she thought she could make him better. That's the type of person she was. But then she started dabbling herself. It all went wrong for her.'

As her relationship with her boyfriend grew more serious, Layla gradually stopped hanging out with her friends and family, and started spending every minute with him. 'Over the two years that she was going out with her boyfriend she really only saw her friends every now and again,' says Mags. 'She became completely separated from them really.'

On her twenty-first birthday, Layla spent the evening alone with her boyfriend. 'There was a party all organised with her friends,' says Mags. 'And then all of a sudden she didn't go. That's when I remember clearly registering the negative influence that he was having on her. I also noticed it in her mood. She became cranky and easily annoyed, and that wasn't her at all. She was always so happy and pleasant.'

As the months went by, her family began to notice other changes in her behaviour. Layla began staying out late during the week, and soon Mags started getting regular phone calls from Layla's boss, saying that she hadn't turned up for work. 'She had such a great relationship with him, and I knew that he wasn't just ringing to find out where she was,' says Mags. 'He was worried about her, like the rest of us.'

A year and a half before she was killed, Layla announced that she was moving out of the family home and into the city centre, where she and her boyfriend had found an apartment together. She packed her belongings, deaf to the protests and pleas of her parents, and took the bus into town. The next six months were the lowest period of Layla's young life.

'It was like she just disappeared off the face of the earth,' says Mags. 'She never found any apartment. I know sometimes she stayed in the Oliver Bond [a social housing project in the inner city] with her boyfriend, and sometimes she stayed somewhere else. We left messages for her everywhere, trying to track her down. But she didn't want to be found. She was on drugs at the time.'

There's a lot that the Brennans don't know about what Layla did to survive during those months. She had lost her job at the clinic, so she had no income. And now she was feeding a heroin habit, sleeping where she could find a bed. Maybe she did resort to prostitution during this time, but there's no evidence to suggest that she did. Whatever happened, and however she survived, after six months of living with her boyfriend and using heroin, Layla had finally had enough. In September 1997, she moved back home to Clondalkin, her head bowed with shame.

'The way we saw it, we were just so relieved and delighted to have her home,' says Mags. 'She had made mistakes, but everyone makes mistakes, and that's what we told her. The problem was, no matter what we said, Layla was so embarrassed and ashamed of herself. She went into counselling to help her get over the drug habit, and her counsellor said it was the strangest thing he'd ever seen. He said even though she had used heroin, she wasn't addicted; the problem was with her head. She actually didn't need any programme to get off drugs, but she did need to get her head sorted. She was totally emotionally strung out. She had come to believe she didn't deserve anything.'

Shortly after moving back home, Layla started going out with a young man called John, a gentle and caring person who was totally besotted with her. On Christmas Eve, when they came back from Mass, John gave Layla her Christmas present—a sparkling new watch. 'I was talking to her afterwards and she was just so upset,' says Mags. 'She was crying and saying that she wasn't good enough for John. Because she had no job, she hadn't been able to buy him a present. She just hated not having money, not having her independence.'

After the holidays, Layla became determined to get her life back on track. She enrolled in a FÁS course to get retrained and qualified for a new job. At the beginning of February she told her parents that she had decided she was going to move in with a friend of hers who was living in the city. Her friend had small children, and Layla thought she could help her take care of them. She was also still finding it difficult to face her family and her friends, and wanted to rebuild her life and regain some pride in herself before returning home.

Once again, her family tried to convince her not to leave. While they knew she was no longer using drugs, and that her new flatmate was totally separate from the drugs scene, they were also conscious that she was emotionally fragile. They wanted to look after her, to help her be happy again. But Layla was unmovable. She had got herself into this situation, and she was determined to be the one to fix it. She packed her bags for the last time.

One month later she was dead.

In Wheatfield Prison, Philip Colgan hadn't stopped using his charms. After years of staring at the walls of his dreary dark cell, he met a new prison employee, a music teacher called Mary Gleeson. He carefully gauged her initial reactions to him, and recognised the female susceptibility to him to which he had grown accustomed. He focused all his considerable charms on winning her over.

Mary Gleeson was a secondary school teacher who had lived her life carefully abiding by the law. She had a good, steady job. She owned her own home at Crannagh Castle in Rathfarnham. When she met

Colgan, she was made aware of his convictions. She knew that he had raped a 79-year-old woman. And yet, when Colgan began initiating a relationship between them, she didn't resist. And when he asked her to marry him from behind the bars of his cell, she said yes.

Gleeson may have been swayed by the fact that Colgan was attending—and eventually completed—a sex offender rehabilitation programme. She may have decided that he had paid for his crime. That he was young and thoughtless and cruel when he raped his previous victims. That the man she knew would never now be capable of such a crime.

Whatever her reasoning, Mary Gleeson was totally, hopelessly smitten with her new fiancé. Colgan's power over women had evidently not waned during his time inside. Gleeson rejoiced with him when he was released from prison eighteen months early, having officially been rehabilitated. Five months later, in September 1998, they were married. Colgan moved into Mary Gleeson's house in Rathfarnham, in South Dublin—a whole new anonymous side of the city, where no one knew about 27-year-old Colgan's past.

It wasn't long before the rows started. 'He had a temper, shouting, slamming doors and giving her general emotional abuse, and she had to live with this,' said one detective after the trial. 'He went through a succession of jobs and, when he did have work, he would stay out late at night, saying he had to work late or he had to see friends. She had her suspicions that he was seeing other women.'

Gleeson's unease was well-founded. During the course of the investigation into Layla's death, detectives unearthed evidence that Colgan had started being unfaithful shortly after he was married. Sitting in his office in Rathfarnham Garda Station, Detective Sergeant Tom Doyle, who led the Layla Brennan murder inquiry, tells me about an incident which really proved to gardaí the extent of Colgan's influence over women.

'Philip Colgan is a big, tall, broad fellow, about six-foot-two,' says Doyle, raising his arms in the air to indicate the height and breadth of a well-built man. 'He was very good-looking, with sallow skin and jet black hair pushed back from his face. All the girls fancied him. He was suave, clean-cut, just really attractive to women. In the course of the investigation we were talking to a young female who lives locally who had a very lucky escape from Colgan. She told us a story that just demonstrated the impact this guy has on girls.'

Leaning back in his chair, Doyle tells me how the girl in question was driving home one night when she passed a car that she thought belonged to her friend. She flashed her lights to say hello, and then turned into her apartment complex.

'Within a minute, the car was pulling in behind her,' says Doyle. 'Colgan was the driver. He got out, and when she saw him she apologised and explained that she thought he was somebody else. He said, "Well, who did you think I was?" He started a conversation with her and within the space of about two or three minutes she had invited him into the apartment, where she spent the night with him.'

Doyle leans back in his chair, shaking his head in astonishment. 'That's the kind of charisma that this guy was in a position to produce on a given night, at a given moment. He had that power. He charmed this girl and got into her house. Within the space of a few minutes, he was in bed with her. When I was talking to him, there was nothing in his eyes. But women? Women would just fall for him like that.'

He clicks his fingers. The sharp noise accentuates the silence that follows.

On the night of 1 March 1999, through to the early hours of the following morning, a year after being released from prison, Philip Colgan began prowling the streets of Dublin once again.

He met with a friend whom he knew from prison, Stephen Curdy, and together the men went from pub to pub, drinking and looking for women. In a bar close to St Stephen's Green, the pair began chatting to two women who seemed to be promising prospects. When the women announced that they were moving to another bar, Colgan and Curdy went with them.

However, on arriving at Eamonn Doran's pub in Temple Bar it emerged that the boyfriend of one of the girls was working as a doorman there, and the other girl's boyfriend was waiting inside. As the two women made their excuses and disappeared into the pub, Colgan and Curdy were left standing on the street, their efforts thwarted, their pride stung.

'I would say that those two girls who knew the bouncers and stayed in the club were very lucky, because it could have been one of them that he ended up with,' says Detective Sergeant Tom Doyle. 'Certainly that night Colgan was out to do damage.'

The two men returned to where Colgan's car was parked on St Stephen's Green, at which point Stephen Curdy announced he had had enough. He was going home. Alone now, Colgan turned the car around and began driving slowly in the direction of Nassau Street. He is the only living person who truly knows exactly what happened next.

'What we feel from the investigation is that he was out on the street that night looking for some female companionship and he wasn't having any luck in the bars,' says Detective Tom Doyle. 'So we think he started driving around, looking for women on the street, maybe a prostitute. And we think he saw Layla.'

Doyle points out that there was no evidence at the time—and there is still no evidence—that Layla was walking on the street in the capacity of a prostitute. 'It implies prostitution maybe, but there's no clear-cut evidence,' he says. 'She wasn't known to the regular prostitutes in town. The vice squad, who would be familiar with all the prostitutes, didn't know her. She certainly wasn't well-known on the streets. Maybe on occasion, if things got very bad for her, she did go out. But there is no evidence to prove it.'

During the court case, the public and the media readily accepted the contention that Layla was a prostitute. After all, it had already been said that she was a heroin addict, and heroin addicts are notorious for resorting to any means possible to earn money for drugs.

However, in her post-mortem report, State Pathologist Marie Cassidy found that all of Layla's organs were healthy, her teeth were healthy and she was somewhat overweight—unusual for a heroin addict. Both Detective Sergeant Tom Doyle and Mags Brennan also point out that when Marie Cassidy was on the stand, she explicitly said that there was no trace of drugs in Layla's system, and nothing to suggest she was a drug addict. This was not recorded by the media at the time.

If, as the evidence suggests, Layla was no longer using heroin, it raises questions over the contention that she was a prostitute. She wouldn't have had the same desperate need for money to feed her habit.

Doyle points out that it is equally likely that Layla was simply walking down the street when Colgan spotted her. 'Maybe he pulled in and asked her if she wanted a lift somewhere, or asked for directions, or somehow struck up a conversation with her that convinced her to get in the car,' says Doyle.

'He could have been talking to her for twenty minutes, longer, before she decided to get in the car with him. The point is, we don't know. He's the only person who can tell us that. But we have to bear in mind the incident with the local woman in Rathfarnham, where Colgan had charmed himself inside her house in a few minutes. It might not have been at all unusual for him to pull up at the side of the road and charm a girl into his car in the same manner—any girl, not necessarily a prostitute.'

There is one other explanation, proffered by Mags Brennan. 'I think that he knew Layla,' she says. 'At one stage during the trial, one of Layla's friends was in the house and she noticed a newspaper on the table. It was one of the first times a picture of Colgan was printed, and she looked at it and said, "Is that not the man that we met at the christening?" She was convinced that she and Layla had seen him at a christening. That Colgan knew Layla already.'

Whatever conversation took place between them on the dark street in Dublin, it convinced Layla to get into the car. With the 24-year-old girl at his side, Colgan pulled away from the kerb, and set off towards Donnybrook, on the south side of the city.

Philip Colgan later told gardaí a myriad of different versions of what exactly happened next. Of these, gardaí believe that his first account of events is probably the closest to what actually took place, although they are aware that even this story is almost certainly slanted to show Colgan in the best possible light.

Colgan said Layla Brennan was a prostitute and that he had picked her up to have sex with her, having agreed on a sum of £60. He said that he parked outside the Belvedere Rugby Club in Simmonscourt in Ballsbridge, and both he and Layla had a cigarette. Then, he said, Layla began to take off her clothes. Suddenly Colgan decided he didn't want to have sex with her any more, and told her to get dressed again. Layla was insistent that he still pay her £60, and warned him that she had noted his registration number and would tell the police if he didn't pay her. The mention of the gardaí made Colgan panic. He was determined not to go back to prison. When Layla made a movement to get out of the car Colgan pulled her back, and hit her twice, two quick hard punches in the face. The second blow was vicious enough to knock Layla unconscious. In his statement to gardaí, Colgan said: 'Once I hit her, I knew I had to kill her.'

Detective Sergeant Tom Doyle believes there are aspects of this account that make sense. 'For whatever reason Layla was in that car, she might have got uncomfortable with him,' he says. 'Maybe she had just decided to go for a few drinks with him, and suddenly he tried to mess around with her. Either way, she wasn't having any of it, and she started to fight back. Maybe, when he made a move on her and she resisted, he knew that he was in trouble. He simply could not afford to have another rape allegation made against him, given his history. I think he might not have set out to kill her. I'd say he set out to rape her, and things didn't go as well as he'd hoped. So he did the only thing he believed he could do. He killed her.'

The post-mortem report by State Pathologist Marie Cassidy did find evidence of attempted rape, although there was no semen found at the scene. In her conclusions, Cassidy noted: 'There was bruising to the outside of the vaginal area, indicating forceful attempted vaginal penetration. There were no internal injuries to indicate whether or not there had been complete penetration.'

Battered and bruised, Layla soon began to regain consciousness. She realised the danger she was in, the violence that the man beside her was capable of inflicting. And she began to scream.

Nearby, an overnight home-help nurse, Margot Dukes, was working close to the rugby grounds. She heard what she later described as growling sounds which alarmed her considerably. She said the sounds were of two men or a man and a woman and she was frightened because the ferocity was such that it might damage that person's vocal cords.

Colgan was panicking. Layla was fighting him and screaming and scratching at his face, struggling desperately to be free. 'I couldn't stop her,' he said later. 'So I grabbed her by the throat and squeezed and squeezed.'

Marie Cassidy found injuries around Layla's mouth and chin which she believed could have been caused by Layla's killer placing his hand over her mouth to prevent her making any noise. She also found fingernail markings around Layla's neck, which she believed could have been made by Layla herself, as she clawed at Colgan's hands, trying frantically to relieve the pressure on her windpipe.

As her air supply was cut off, and her strength was rapidly diminishing, Layla fought Colgan with everything she had. She left half-moon nail imprints on his neck, and cuts and scratches on his face and hands.

Then she weakened and began to go limp, her struggle for life failing. Colgan took off her bra and wrapped it around her throat, tying it so tightly in a knot at the nape of her neck that it left a deep red indentation in her skin. Finally, Layla fell unconscious for the last time. In a statement to the police, Colgan said: 'I knew if I let go I'd be going back to prison. I took off her bra and tightened it around her neck. I tightened it as tight as I could for ten, fifteen, twenty seconds. I knew she was dead.'

But Layla did not die then. Not immediately.

Colgan lifted her body from the car seat, perhaps unaware that drops of her blood and strands of her curly blonde hair were left behind. He put her in the boot. He drove towards the Dublin Mountains, and finally stopped at the side of the Killakee road, beside a crudely surfaced car park. The lights of his car illuminated a stretch of remote woodland, exposing a cold scraggy landscape, devoid of any human life. The night air was totally still.

As Colgan got out of his car, the silence was broken by the sound of another vehicle, rumbling through the mountains. Suddenly, the darkness was lit up by white headlights, and Colgan squinted his eyes against their glare. The car drove by without slowing down, and the driver never came forward to gardaí. But Detective Sergeant Tom Doyle believes that the unexpected appearance of this car had a lot to do with Colgan's eventual confession.

'We think it's one of the big reasons he turned himself in,' he said. 'He thought they had seen him and his car, and I think he was hedging his bets. He was expecting a knock on the door, and he decided not to wait for it. He thought he'd try to control the situation instead, by coming forward.'

No doubt cursing his ill luck at having been spotted, Colgan hoisted Layla's body out of the boot and started making his way across the rough surface of the car park. He alternated between dragging her and lifting her, dragging her and lifting her, showing no regard for the exposed skin of her body as it was scratched and ripped on the stones. Finally, after going over an embankment and forcing a path through some rough foliage, Colgan spotted a slight incline leading downwards towards a wall. He dropped Layla on the ground and rolled her body into the dip. She lay there, bloodied and bruised and entirely naked except for a shoe and sock on her right foot. Her pants were tangled around her right ankle, back to front and rolled down. Colgan turned around and walked back to the car. But he wasn't finished yet.

'This part sticks out in my mind and I'll never forget it,' says Detective Tom Doyle, shaking his head. 'When we interviewed him, I asked him to account for the cut on Layla's head, because what he had described still didn't account for that.'

Colgan told detectives how he climbed back up the side of the embankment and searched in his car until he found his wheel brace— a 12-inch heavy metal stick with a curve at the end. He then walked back to Layla's body, climbed down into the dip, raised the wheel brace high and brought it down once, twice on Layla's head.

During the post-mortem, Marie Cassidy discovered the deep wounds that had fractured Layla's skull. In her report, she noted: 'The lack of brain damage, despite the skull fracture, indicates that this was probably inflicted while her head was fixed, most likely when she was already immobile and on the ground.'

In Rathfarnham Garda Station, Detective Tom Doyle pauses and shakes his head again. 'I asked him why he did it. And he said, "I knew that she was dead, but in the event that she wasn't I couldn't bear the thought of her lying there dying, so I took the wheel brace out of the car and smacked her on top of the head with it."'

Doyle lapses into silence. 'I'll never forget when he told me that,' he says then. 'That was the sort of humanity he showed to a fellow human being. You wouldn't do it to a dog on the street. If you thought it might be dying, you'd try to get it to a vet. But that was his level of thinking. His good deed for Layla was to take a blunt instrument and hit her over the head with it. That was the kind of person he was. An animal really.'

Colgan's last 'merciful' act for Layla made no difference, in the end. The manual and ligature strangulation earlier had caused irreversible brain damage. Because Layla was young and healthy, it just took her longer to die. But eventually, as her body started to become hypothermic in the freezing vastness of the mountains, Layla's life slipped away. She breathed her last, alone and beaten and hidden in the darkness.

Colgan collected Layla's bloodstained clothes and stuffed them into a bag. Marie Cassidy would later note that the blood spatters were on the outside of the garments, in a pattern that suggested Layla was physically attacked while she was still dressed.

Colgan threw the wheel brace in the bag too, and stored it in the boot. He drove some way down the mountains before picking up his phone. At 2.20am, Mary Gleeson was woken by the phone ringing. She heard her husband at the end of the line, in a 'distressed state', asking her to come and collect him. When she went to pick him up, she wondered at the scratches and cuts on his body. He told her the gardaí had beaten him up. In an uneasy, suspicious silence, the newlywed couple drove home.

As soon as he got a moment alone, Colgan hid the bag of Layla's clothes in a bin in a shed beside his house. For three days, he kept his silence. Then he told his wife that he had been with a woman, and that he had something terrible to tell her. He confessed everything to her, believing her love for him was so strong that she would not turn him in.

Detective Sergeant Tom Doyle says that this sort of behaviour has been seen before in killers. 'A lot of these guys use an individual as their conscience, and they literally believe that person is their conscience,' he says. 'In this case, I think Philip Colgan looked on his wife as his conscience. I think he believed that because she was very close to him and loved him very much, she wouldn't expose his crime. And if he told her about what he had done, and she didn't expose him, then his conscience had effectively said that his actions were all right.'

But Gleeson didn't believe her husband's actions were all right. She convinced Colgan to write down everything that had happened, and together they went to Rathfarnham police station to make a statement.

Detective Sergeant Tom Doyle describes his impression of Colgan when he first met him. 'Normally when you look into people's eyes you see their character, their personality, emotions, charisma, thoughts,' he says. 'You can sort of see the person in them. But looking into Colgan's eyes, there's just nothing. It was like looking into pure emptiness. A black hole. He's only the second person in my entire career where I've seen nothing—nothing at all—behind his eyes.'

Colgan sat down heavily, and started to tell the detectives what had happened. He told them where Layla's body could be found. A team of gardaí set out to find her. It soon hit the news. An unidentified female had been discovered, murdered, in the Dublin Mountains.

For the Brennans, life was continuing as normal. On Friday, 5 March, Mags heard a news bulletin about a woman's body having been found in the mountains. It only barely registered with her, and she didn't give it a second thought.

That evening, she noticed her son, who was ten years old at the time, checking Teletext on the TV. He said he was checking something for school. In fact, he had heard that the woman in the mountains had a small scar on her eyebrow and had thought immediately of his big sister's scar. Worried, he read the report again on Teletext, but didn't say anything to anyone.

Early the following morning, Mags and her husband Dick were cooking a fry for breakfast, when the phone rang. 'It was my Mam, ringing to ask why Layla hadn't been in to see her for two weeks, because Layla went to see her regularly,' says Mags. 'But then she mentioned the body in the mountains. I just told her not to be silly, and that I'd ring Layla that day and tell her to visit her. I made it sound as if I wasn't worried at all. But I knew. Suddenly I just knew. It went throughout my entire body.'

In a daze, Mags walked back to the kitchen, where Dick was just putting the food on the table. She told him that her mother was worried that the woman in the mountains could be Layla.

'Dick stood up and said, "Jesus Christ, I'm going out to get her and I'm bringing her home for once and for all. She can't be worrying people like this. I'm bringing her home,"' says Mags. 'He tried to make it sound like he was annoyed. But everything just drained out of him. He went totally pale.'

For some time, Dick drove aimlessly around the area, trying to work up the courage to go into the police station, terrified at what he might hear. Finally, he went in, and told them that he hadn't spoken to his daughter in a couple of days, and that her name was Layla.

The gardaí heard the name, and knew. Dick was brought to Rathfarnham Garda Station to identify his daughter's body.

'He went without telling me, because he didn't want me to have to come with him and do it,' says Mags. 'I can't tell you how long they were. It must have been at least an hour and a half, maybe two. But it only felt like a few minutes before the gardaí pulled up outside. They said they'd identified Layla. She was the woman in the mountains.'

Mags leans back, almost detached now as she recalls this most awful of news, as if the true horror of it has yet to be fully accepted. 'That was that then,' she says, her eyes glazed. 'They said that someone had turned themselves in already. And that was that.'

In the first statement he made to gardaí, Colgan confessed to everything that had happened. But as the day progressed his story began to change and then change again, so that by the end of the day the killer had concocted an entirely different and somewhat fantastical tale about how Layla was killed.

'I think as time went by during the day he may have felt that he was betrayed by his conscience, who was his wife, so he decided to try to save himself,' says Tom Doyle.

In one of Colgan's versions of events he claimed that he went into a gay bar where he met a Scotsman called Wayne, with whom he had sex. Then Wayne suggested to Colgan that the two of them pick up a woman. They enticed Layla Brennan into the car, and Wayne had sex with her. Then he pulled out a knife, and forced Colgan to kill Layla and hide her in the mountains.

In a later rendition, Colgan said that actually he hadn't been in a gay bar at all, but had picked up a homeless person on the street. And the homeless person had made him kill Layla.

Finally, another version of events emerged. It was this last story that Colgan swore in court was true. He said he was with a homosexual homeless man, with whom he had sex. As they were driving in his car the man spotted Layla Brennan and asked Colgan to stop. Layla got in the car, and the three drove off towards Donnybrook. Layla was acquainted with the homeless man, said Colgan, and she owed him money. The debt was large enough to warrant both men having sex with her.

When they reached the rugby grounds, Colgan said he got out of the car and walked over to a canopy to shelter from the rain, waiting for his turn to have sex with Layla. Less than half an hour later, he returned to the car and found Layla face down on the back seat of the car, her bra around her neck. He said he knew she was dead. The other man was still there, and he claimed Layla had tried to rob him.

Both men then hid the dead woman's body in the mountains, and Colgan watched as the unidentified man hit her on the head with the wheel brace. He said that at this point he became nervous for his own safety, being in the mountains in the company of such a savage killer. 'I had been nervous in the first place, going any further into the mountains with him,' Colgan told the packed courtroom. 'So when he came around the back of the car, I grabbed him. I felt if I didn't I was going to end up getting hit with the wheel brace.'

The two men had a 'pretty violent' struggle, and Colgan managed to render the other man unconscious. He put him into the boot of his car and drove further into the mountains. To this day, Colgan has refused to say what happened to the man. Asked if he was alive, he replied, 'I'd rather not answer that.' Asked where he went in the mountains, he replied, 'I'd rather not answer that.' The only other detail he would supply was that he left the scene approximately fifteen minutes later. Colgan said he had a motive for killing the homeless man. He said that the man could easily have gone to the gardaí and said that Colgan had killed Layla Brennan, and because of his history, gardaí would believe the homeless man. And he, Colgan, would end up back in prison, an innocent man. So he had to kill him.

'This was his defence in court,' says Detective Sergeant Tom Doyle. 'And, you know, he was a sharp enough character, because the story he came up with in the end was just close enough to the facts to be plausible. The jury went out for hours and hours and we were left wondering if they might actually believe what Colgan was saying.'

It wasn't just the jurors who found themselves swayed by Colgan's innocent, beguiling appearance. Mags Brennan admits that she too had her doubts. 'In the stand he came across so charming and honest and straightforward,' she says, 'I actually started to worry that the wrong person would be sent to prison. Of course, I knew he was telling lies. But some part of me just believed him. If I had been on that jury, I don't think I would have convicted him. I think I would have believed he was an innocent man going about his business.'

It was only when the verdict was announced that Mags got a glimpse of the truth behind Philip Colgan. 'I've never seen anything like it,' she says. 'You might think I'm being strange, but the minute the verdict of guilty came in I just saw what he was. I saw this change come over his face.'

She sweeps both her hands in an arc from her chin to her hairline. 'It was like he took off a mask. Maybe that sounds weird, but that was my perception. And it was then that I saw him for the first time.'

The trial was over, but the damage was irreversible. During the case the Brennans heard every violent, horrific detail about the injuries inflicted on Layla. They had to force themselves not to think of the terror and pain she endured during her final moments. And they had to listen, in silence, as their daughter's killer stood on the stand and took from her one final thing: her dignity.

'The words prostitute and heroin addict were plastered over every newspaper report,' says Detective Sergeant Tom Doyle. 'When you meet Mags and Dick, you know that if you built Layla around them you would have to have a beautiful person. I think one of the toughest things that Mags had to endure in the trial was when the defence barrister was addressing the jury, and he was speaking about Layla being a girl of the night and a prostitute. He said no one cared about her, that she was in the gutter. And poor Mags just lost it. The emotions she must have felt at that time, I can't even imagine. Here was this barrister, defending the man who had killed her daughter, now standing up in front of a jury referring to her daughter as gutter trash. And there was very little she could do about it. And it was that that was printed in the paper. It was this image that stuck in the minds of many people afterwards. A heroin addict. Prostitute. Someone we're not supposed to care about.

'On the news that night we tried to claw back a little bit of her dignity. We spoke about Layla being a loving daughter and sister, who had a job and boyfriends, and loved dancing. We spoke about her as if she was a human being. There is never any dignity in murder. But there was certainly none for Layla, the way she was killed and the way she was referred to afterwards.'

Aside from the trauma of the trial, everyday life had changed for the Brennans for ever. Mags's mother had a stroke when she heard the news. Her father, to this day, has never been able to talk about the murder.

Dick found he could no longer live in the family home in Clondalkin. 'He couldn't bear to be near it,' says Mags. 'Especially her bedroom. He went to live with my mam and dad while we were looking for a new house. He took two or three months off work. He couldn't function. He was crippled with grief.'

The whole Brennan family attended counselling for six years, both as a unit and individually. Now, they don't talk about Layla being murdered. They talk about the girl they knew. The daughter. The sister. The person they loved. They don't say she was killed. They say she died.

Mags, too, has gone to counselling. She has done everything she can to cope with what has happened. But she says every time she hears that a rapist has been released from prison early, she goes through it all again.

She worries that there is a dam, holding back emotions, in the recesses of her mind. She worries about what will happen if that dam breaks down.

'Anyone I've talked to professionally about it has said that I am dealing with it because I am able to talk about her,' says Mags. 'Although there are certain things I can't talk about, or think about still. But I worry. I think it's all just pushed back somewhere,' her hand raises towards the back of her head. 'It's like I'm still waiting for it to hit me.'

Her eyes take on that glazed look again. Like a curtain falling. 'I don't think I have dealt with it yet. But hopefully I'm wrong.'

Philip Colgan was sentenced to life in prison. He has recently applied for parole. In Rathfarnham Garda Station, Detective Sergeant Tom Doyle lifts the parole application from his desk.

'The parole board ask for our opinion, and my views are very straightforward,' he says, looking at the sheet of paper. 'Philip Colgan never showed any remorse. Nothing. He is a serious risk to society.'

'There's a difference between a psychopath and a sociopath. A sociopath is a cold, calculating individual with no feelings. I reckon that's what Philip Colgan is. I don't believe the public is safe with this character on the streets. He is an entity unto himself. If he gets out he'll kill again. I have no doubt. He'll kill again.'

Chapter 11
Larry Murphy Attacks

The two hunters watched in surprise as the car sped towards them, the engine rudely intrusive in the silence of the mountains. For a brief second the driver's face was illuminated in the darkness, before the vehicle was swallowed by the forest.

It was then that they saw the woman. Naked and bloodied and tangled in barbed wire. She screamed when they walked towards her, recoiling in terror from their outstretched arms. She thought they too were going to rape her and beat her and try to kill her. She screamed again.

As the hunters wrapped the shivering woman in a jacket and guided her towards their car, they exchanged a horrified look. They had recognised the man who had sped past them. He was local to the area, a well-respected carpenter.

The men drove as quickly as they dared to the garda station in Baltinglass, where they handed over the victim and their information.

It was just before midnight on 11 February 2000. Barely a month into the new millennium. The previous two decades had been marred by the disturbingly regular pattern of women disappearing in the Leinster area. The mountains, too, had acquired a macabre reputation as the favoured burial ground for the country's killers.

That was the night the name Larry Murphy became known to the police. It was also the night that signalled the end of the unsolved series of attacks on women in the area. It is widely believed that this is no coincidence. Larry Murphy is one of the only convicted criminals in Ireland who is suspected of being a serial killer.

'I wouldn't look any further than him for some of the other cases,' said one detective. 'Murphy's a prime suspect. It's just a question of proving it.'

The eleventh of February 2000 had started normally for the young businesswoman. Based in Carlow town, she had had a busy week, and was looking forward to the promise of relaxation at the weekend.

On Friday evening she had her last scheduled appointment with a young civil servant. At around 7.30pm, while the two women were in the midst of their meeting, a local person noticed a well-built man in his mid-30s acting suspiciously, skulking around outside the building.

The meeting finished around 8pm, and the civil servant returned to the parking lot. As she clipped her way briskly across the tarmac, she noticed a man sitting on his own in a blue Fiat Punto, parked just a short distance away. 'His car was facing onto the roadway,' the woman later told gardaí. 'I would describe him as thirty-five years of age, with straight brown hair cut short, with a rounded face.'

The woman checked her watch just before she opened her car door, conscious that she needed to get home by 8.30pm. The time was exactly 8.10pm. As she sat into her car, she looked again at the man sitting on his own in the Fiat Punto. Something about his demeanour had rattled her. 'It looked to me as if he was fidgety and he kept putting his head down and raising it again for another look at me,' she said. 'For some reason I became nervous and I picked up my mobile phone to see if it was on. I started the car and drove out.'

Inside the building the 28-year-old businesswoman was collecting her belongings and locking up for the weekend. She put the day's takings of £700 into two money bags, which she then put into her black handbag. Finally ready to go home, she walked to where her car was parked a short distance away.

It was already dark outside, but the car park was not deserted as she would have expected at that late hour on a Friday evening. Instead, there was a man standing opposite her car, about twenty feet away. 'I noticed him because there seemed to be a light shining near him,' the woman said later. 'You don't usually see anybody around that area in the evenings. I think he had his hands in his pockets. He looked distracted and he was just walking over and back.'

Slightly uncomfortable at being unexpectedly placed in such a vulnerable position, the woman continued walking to her car. She couldn't have known that Larry Murphy had been spotted in the car park earlier that evening. That detectives believe he had been lying in wait for her for at least an hour.

'The type of predator this man is, he seems to plan exactly what he's doing,' said one detective. 'It looks like he was waiting specifically for the victim to emerge from the building, which would suggest that he knew that she was going to come out eventually. And if he knew that, then he must have known she worked there. So there's a good possibility this was all planned. He could have been watching her for a few days, or even longer. It doesn't appear to have been a spur-of-the-moment attack.'

As the woman got close to her car she used her keys to deactivate the central locking. Just as she was approaching the driver's door, the man started moving towards her. Within seconds he had traversed the twenty-foot distance between them and was standing beside her. The speed at which he moved ensured the woman had no time to register the rapidly increasing danger of her position. 'Even though I saw him, I was startled,' she said. 'He said something like, "Give me the money" or "Can I have the money?"'

Before the woman could react, Murphy made his next move, swift, efficient and violent. He punched her straight in the face. There was a sickening crack as the woman's nose broke and she stumbled backwards in pain and shock. One hand to her face, she threw herself towards the car door in a desperate attempt to escape. But already Larry Murphy was entirely in charge.

He used her own momentum to push her into the car, leaping in on top of her and easily containing her struggles. Putting his two hands around her neck, he forced her across the interior of the car and into the passenger seat.

'When he got me over to the passenger seat he said, "Where are the keys?" I said I didn't know. I dropped one set of keys before I was pushed in the car. I still had another set in my hand. He eventually got the keys for the car in the footwell. He was delighted that he got them.'

Murphy was disturbingly calm throughout the entire first phase of the attack. Within a matter of seconds, he had succeeded in assaulting and abducting a woman from a public car park, and no one had seen him do it. The speed and precision with which he had moved led detectives to believe he must have done it before.

'Again, it all pointed to careful planning, and even practice,' said one detective. 'Murphy had rendered this unfortunate lady completely powerless within a matter of seconds. That is not easy to do. It begs the question, how did he seem to know exactly what he was doing? Could this really have been his first time carrying out such an attack?'

Inside the car, Murphy forced the woman to lie down in such a way that her head was over the handbrake. Then he put his elbow heavily on top of her head to keep it in place. When she struggled, Murphy leaned harder on his elbow, pushing the side of the woman's face painfully into the handbrake. Once again, she was effectively helpless.

As Murphy threw the car into gear, the woman's mind raced over what had just happened, wondering what it was that her attacker intended to do. 'He moved the car a short distance and at that stage I thought he would just rob me and then drive somewhere to let me go,' she said.

However, she soon realised she had no such hope of the ordeal ending early. Murphy had only driven across the car park to get close to where his little Fiat Punto was parked. Before he attempted the risky manoeuvre of moving his victim from one vehicle to the other, Murphy calmly ensured the woman would have no chance of trying to escape.

He ordered her to take off her bra. She did so, her hands shaking as they battled with the clasp. Murphy grabbed the bra from her and then used it to bind her wrists together. He employed his considerable strength to tie the straps as tightly as he could, painfully cutting off the woman's circulation to her hands. Almost immediately her fingers started to turn blue.

'He asked me to give him the money again,' she said. 'I told him I couldn't because my hands were tied. I felt numb with shock and fear. I thought he was going to kill me there.'

Murphy reached into the back seat to where the woman's black bag rested and found the money bags inside. He pocketed the cash. Then he took a Carlow GAA headband that was hanging from the rear-view mirror and slipped it over the woman's head, using it as a gag. Finally, he told her to take off her boots. She managed to reply through the gag that she couldn't, because her hands were tied. Not to be deterred, Murphy removed the woman's boots himself and left them on the floor.

'What he did was very interesting really, and very smart,' said one detective. 'He'd managed to tie the woman up, gag her and prevent her from running away—all by using her own clothes and her own possessions against her. This meant he didn't have to carry anything with him prior to the attack, and he didn't risk leaving anything that could be traced back to him at the scene. It was very cunning.'

Murphy got out of the car then, and dragged his victim out with him. 'I thought he was going to leave me there,' she said. 'But there was another car. I was kicking and screaming. He made me walk in front of him with his hand on my back.'

Again, Murphy was moving with frightening speed. Before the victim realised what had happened, she saw the boot of the Fiat had opened in front of her. 'He caught me by the back of the neck and pushed me in head first with a lot of force,' she said. 'I kept kicking and screaming. When he put me in the boot I was facing outwards.'

Murphy slammed the boot shut and started the car. He pulled out of the car park and started driving very fast out of Carlow town. The woman was tossed around inside the boot. As she screamed she heard the car radio being turned on at full volume, drowning out her cries for help.

'I could feel small flat metal things under me,' she said. 'There was a smell of oil and a football. I could feel something behind my head. We seemed to be going very fast.'

Murphy drove with purpose. He knew exactly where he was going. He had been there before, during one of his only other documented attacks. It was a very remote area called Beaconstown, a canvas of fields and farmland, lying nine miles outside of Carlow town between the villages of Maganey and Kilkea. Murphy knew that on this cold winter night it would be completely deserted. For what he intended to do, that meant it was perfect.

He negotiated the winding roads with confidence, taking particular care during the last half mile of the journey that led him up a pot-holed dirt track. After about twenty-five minutes the woman felt the car coming to a stop. The engine was turned off and the music stopped abruptly. For a few seconds, there was a stark silence before the woman heard the creak of the car seat being rolled down. Then heavy footsteps, as Murphy approached the boot.

'I could hear the click of the boot,' said the woman. 'He pulled me out and pushed me in front of him into the driver's seat and told me to sit down. We were in a field, in a very dirty, mucky dirt track area. I couldn't see any lights.'

As the woman sat in the car she saw that the seat had been pushed back. In the back of the car, behind the passenger's seat, she saw a baby chair. She thought again of the football in the boot. She realised with horror that her attacker was a father.

Murphy casually removed the woman's clothes before undoing his trousers. He raped her then, demanding that she respond to him, demanding that she kiss him and hold him during the assault.

'I felt so numb, I couldn't move,' she said. 'I just hoped it would all end. I feared for my life the whole time. I thought "This is it."'

When it was over, the woman moved into the passenger seat, putting as much distance as she could between herself and her rapist. Murphy seemed more inclined towards conversation then. 'He asked me if I was married,' said the woman. 'I lied and said yes. I lied because it felt safer and I was so afraid.'

In what was certainly a bad sign for the victim, Murphy then told her a little bit about himself. He said he was married and that he had two young boys.

The woman then held up her hands, showing Murphy that they had turned completely blue. She told him the bra was tied so tightly that it was extremely painful, and asked him to undo the knot. To her surprise, he did so, before taking her out of the car again.

Standing on the side of the road he ordered her to put her clothes back on. But with the feeling gone from her fingers, and the trauma of the rape still searing through her mind, the woman found that she was unable to dress herself. Murphy helped her then, putting on her clothes before tying her up again.

'This time he tied my hands behind my back with the headband and tied my bra around my mouth,' said the woman. 'I pleaded with him not to put me in the boot but he said he had to because I'd start making noise.'

Murphy forced his victim back into the boot and then set off again, driving fourteen miles east, crossing the N9 route from Carlow to Naas at Castledermot and driving up into the Wicklow Mountains to a heavily forested area called Kilranelagh. Again, this region was very familiar to him, lying just three miles from his home of Woodfield outside Baltinglass. Again, the place was totally secluded, known only to locals. It was about 10.15pm when Murphy finally arrived at his destination. The journey had taken him twenty-three miles from Carlow town.

'This time we travelled for about twenty minutes,' said the woman. 'I'd say we were on a main road for a while, and then a lot of turns and crossroads. I knew at that stage I was on country roads. I knew that even after having pleaded with him, he still wasn't going to bring me home.' The car stopped again, and again the woman heard the click of the boot before she found herself looking up into the face of her attacker. Behind him she saw trees on either side. This time she could feel that the car was parked on a slope. She could hear the gurgling of water nearby, and a cold fear ran through her. 'I thought we were in front of a lake or something,' she said. 'I thought he was going to drive into a river. I felt I had no chance.'

Murphy pulled the woman out of the boot again, this time directing her towards the passenger seat of the car. In the distance, through the trees, she saw a solitary circle of light. It was a local bed and breakfast called Kilranelagh House, the only sign of life in the entire area, and much too far away to hear her screams.

'He lay down and said "Make love to me"', said the woman. 'I said "If I do, will you bring me home?" He said he would. I knew deep down he wouldn't. He was trying to make me feel guilty for him, as if he were the innocent one.'

Even through the haze of fear and pain, the victim was entirely accurate in this perception. When he was later interviewed by gardaí, Murphy admitted that he had raped the woman in Beaconstown but suggested that it was his victim who had precipitated the second sexual encounter.

He said that after raping her the first time he intended to leave her home, but didn't. 'When I stopped the car the second time I took her out and sat her in the car,' he said. 'She started talking to me. I told her I had two kids and she said she would like to have kids herself some day. She asked me to take her home and said she would do anything I wanted if I took her home. I told her I would leave her home. So she told me she would make love to me. I had sex with her but that was her own choice. We made love in the car. I didn't try to kill her at all. I had sex in two places with her but the second time was her own choice.'

This statement gives a chilling insight into Larry Murphy's ability to twist reality to suit his own version of events.

Before assaulting her again, Murphy undressed himself and once again made the woman remove her clothes. He then raped her three times, forcing her to have anal and oral sex with him. 'At one stage I asked if he had a gun, because he may as well have shot me, the pain was so bad,' said the woman.

One detective points out that the second assault was different from the first. Murphy was more frenzied and more violent now. 'He had become very aggressive at this stage,' said the detective. 'He was losing some of the control that he'd had earlier and his mood was changing.'

Murphy started telling his victim more information about his family, this time saying that he would never see his wife and children again. He told the woman that his name was Michael, that he was from Baltinglass and that he worked in Dublin. He told her that his two boys were aged two and four years, and he told her their names. The victim knew that he shouldn't be telling her these details, not if he was truly going to let her free. In the pit of her stomach the certainty grew that she was going to be killed.

Eventually, Murphy decided it was time to hit the road again. He bound the woman for the last time, using the head band around her wrists and the bra as a gag. Then he put her back in the boot.

'Larry Murphy was going to kill that woman, there is simply no doubt about it,' says one senior detective. 'Everything he had done that night indicated that he never meant to let her go. She knew too much about him, she had even seen his face very clearly at one stage when the internal light in the car went on. From the minute he abducted her in Carlow, really, he had no doubt about what he was going to do with her.'

Lying in the boot, beaten and bruised, the woman had long since come to the same conclusion. This man was never going to let her go alive. But instead of becoming paralysed with fear, the terror of this knowledge brought out all her survival instincts. With amazing fortitude the woman started planning to fight back.

While Murphy was talking to her about his family she had been subtly working at the headband around her wrists, twisting and turning it so that it had loosened considerably. By the time Murphy locked her away in the boot, she had managed to untie the bindings entirely, finally freeing her hands. She cast around on the floor of the boot, reaching blindly in the darkness for anything that might serve as a weapon. Her fingers fell on the cold cylindrical shape of an aerosol can.

She was wondering whether it might work when suddenly the boot opened again. Murphy, for some reason, had returned to ask the woman to turn around so that she would be facing towards the front of the car. Seizing the unexpected opportunity, the woman grabbed the aerosol can, pointed it at Murphy's face and pressed the nozzle.

The plastic button went down, but there was no resulting spray. The can was broken. And Murphy was furious at this display of defiance. He knocked the can out of her hand, pushed the woman further into the boot and slammed the hatch.

There was a brief silence, as Murphy seemed to ponder his next move. Evidently his plan had been to take the woman to a third location, where he would almost certainly have killed her. However, now that she had surprised him with her resilience, he seemed to decide that he would take no more risks. He returned to the back of the car with a plastic shopping bag and opened the boot one more time.

Inside, the woman lay still, knowing that she had upset him and terrified at the consequences. 'When he opened the boot I barely lifted my head,' she said. 'He put a white plastic bag over my head and I could smell some chemical. I felt light-headed and I couldn't breathe. I remember the bag had red writing on it. He was trying to stop me breathing.'

The woman fought him fiercely then, with a strength borne of desperation. She clawed and swiped at his hands as he pulled the bag down around her face. 'I kept struggling to get the bag off my head,' she said. 'He took the bag in his hand and put it on my mouth. He kept holding the bag over my mouth and I definitely felt like I was going to die.'

As she started to lose consciousness, the woman made one last-ditch effort at survival. She kicked out with her legs and to her surprise she managed to get her right foot over the edge of the boot. It was the most unevenly matched of fights, with Murphy even slamming the boot down on the woman's legs in an effort to subdue her, but she persevered. Then, through the flashes of black and white and red, the woman became conscious of lights in the background.

'I kept struggling until eventually I had my two legs over and could feel my legs on the ground,' she said. 'The next thing I remember I was crawling on the ground and he was gone.' Murphy, too, had seen the lights of an approaching vehicle. The situation had now gotten completely out of hand for the previously calm rapist. Unable to control his battling victim, he let her fall out of the boot and ran to the driver's seat.

The approaching car was driven by two hunters, Kenneth Jones and Trevor Moody, who were making their way through the forest with their headlights on full. They had set out earlier that night to go hunting foxes on the slopes of the Keadeen Mountain.

Dressed in boots and combat jackets, the hunters also carried two rifles with telescopic sights, and a powerful lamp. They were scanning the forest for possible prey when they spotted Murphy's car.

'The hunters know the area. They are the best policemen in the Wicklow Mountains,' said one detective. 'They drive up into the hills and they have their lamps and they watch every car or van moving for miles. They watch until everything is put to bed. When there is no movement they go out with the lamps.' The men slowed down as they approached the little Fiat Punto, which had its sidelights on and was parked in their path on the narrow lane between the pine forest and the ash trees. They saw a movement at the back of the car and thought at first that they had disturbed a courting couple.

Then a man quickly came from behind the car, and sat in the driver's seat. Kenneth Jones turned immediately to Trevor Moody, and said 'I know this guy, do you?' Moody replied that he did. Both hunters focused on the man's face, illuminated in their headlights, and knew him to be Larry Murphy from Stratford.

Moody had a particular reason for recognising Murphy. Four years earlier, the carpenter had groped one of his female friends in a pub in Donard. The woman had later pointed him out to Moody, and the image of the man's face had remained ingrained upon his memory.

But Moody had no time to reflect on this as Larry Murphy revved the engine and sped past the two men, his car narrowly avoiding their own vehicle as he scraped through a gap in the lane. The Fiat Punto disappeared into the forest towards the main road to Baltinglass.

It was then that they saw the woman, naked and bloodied and running away from them towards a ditch.

When Murphy had finally let her go she had fallen on the ground with the plastic bag still over her head. The relief she felt when her attacker had driven away was then replaced by disbelief and terror at the sight of yet another vehicle, containing two men, parked in the near distance. Convinced that yet more rape and torture awaited her, she ran for her life in the opposite direction. But in the darkness of the mountains, she didn't see the barbed wire fence in front of her. She screamed in pain and despair and she became coiled in the sharp metal prongs.

The hunters leapt out of their car and went over to the woman. She screamed hysterically as they approached, desperately trying to free herself from the fence. As the men got closer she screamed again, saying 'Are you with him?'

Trevor Moody assured the woman that he was not as Kenneth Jones ran back to the car to get a torch. The woman nodded at Jones as he ran away, and said, 'Is he with him?' Again, Moody assured her that neither of them was affiliated with her attacker. They would help her, he said, and take her wherever she wanted to go. She was safe with them, he said.

And finally, the woman gave up the struggle. Her shoulders drooped and her body went almost limp as she allowed the men to untangle her from the fence and lift her clear of the barbs. They stood her between them, wrapped a big jacket around her shoulders and walked her carefully back to their jeep. As she sank into the car seat, she told the men that Murphy was trying to kill her. She told them how he had raped her repeatedly before putting the plastic bag over her head.

The men exchanged glances, trying not to let their horror show. Moody said that they had recognised the man and that they should go to the garda station in Baltinglass to report him. The woman complied, happy to let someone else do the fighting at last.

There were three gardaí on duty in Baltinglass station. They were prepared for the usual rumblings of a Friday night shift, but none of them expected such a violent, significant case to land in their laps.

Garda Peter Cassin was sitting at the hatch when the two men and woman came in the door. Cassin could see immediately that the woman was injured and deeply distraught. He saw that there was dried blood around her nose and mouth, and blood all over her teeth. A bra hung around her neck, tied at the ends in a crude knot.

The gardaí immediately called for medical help, and made the woman as comfortable as they could while they waited for an ambulance to take her to Carlow hospital. Cassin sat with the woman as she cried and shivered with shock. He tried to assure her that she was safe, and that no one could hurt her.

Meanwhile, Garda Seamus Murphy put a call into his senior officers to alert them to the fact that a serious crime had been committed.

When the woman was taken to hospital for treatment, the two hunters quietly informed the gardaí of what they knew. As the night stretched into the early hours of the next day, gardaí began to form a ring of road checks around the area, and made discreet inquiries about Larry Murphy's whereabouts. By the following morning, they had a team of officers prepped and ready for the arrest.

After Murphy had fled the scene of his crime he had driven directly to his home town of Stratford, and gone into the comforting familiarity of the local pub. It was the last stop in a distinct pattern that Murphy had established throughout the night—he gravitated towards places that he knew. This was to become significant during a subsequent investigation into his past, which sought to establish whether he had any links to other serious crimes.

In the Stratford Arms pub Murphy bought a bottle of whiskey, some of which he drank straight from the bottle as he drove slowly to his house in Woodfield.

He left the whiskey in the car and made a beeline for his bedroom, barely acknowledging his wife, who was in the kitchen. His two small children were already fast asleep.

He peeled off his clothes and threw them on the floor, before throwing himself naked onto the bed. He didn't feel the need to wash. His sleep was restless, as he replayed in his mind the final few minutes of his time on the mountain and the shocked faces of the two hunters as he sped past them into the night. He had recognised the men and he suspected they may have known him too. He later admitted that he was expecting the gardaí to call the following morning.

Sure enough, at 8.20am the doorbell rang. Murphy answered the door to a team of seven gardaí, led by Detective Sergeant James Ryan from Carlow. He nodded at their request to come inside, not bothering to feign surprise at their appearance. He led the way towards the living room, and cradled his head in his hands as Ryan told him he was being arrested for the rape of the young businesswoman.

He shook his head, saying he didn't know why he had done what he did. 'Why did I do it? I didn't need to do it,' he said, his voice barely audible.

Before he went to the station, Murphy had the deeply unpalatable task of breaking the news to his wife, Margaret. She was still in her pyjamas when he brought her from the bedroom into the living room full of gardaí. Murphy kept it brutally simple. 'I raped a girl last night,' he said.

Margaret stared at him in shock, tears welling in her eyes. It seemed she too had been fooled by her husband's public persona of a good, honest man.

A short time later, Murphy was brought to Baltinglass station and asked to empty his pockets. He had put back on the same clothes he was wearing the previous night, and was still carrying the £700 he had stolen from the woman. He produced it for gardaí, and casually identified it as 'the girl's money'. In his other pocket he had £444 of his own cash.

After consulting with a solicitor, Murphy agreed to make a statement. His portrayal of events was carefully crafted to suggest that there was no element of premeditation in what he had done.

He said that he had spent the day working in Greystones before driving down to Baltinglass to settle a payment with a solicitor. After that he continued on to Bennekerry near Friarstown, to visit his brother. Instead of going home then, he drove west into Carlow town, where he wanted to get some chips. He told gardaí that he parked down a side street, and was walking down the path when he saw the young businesswoman coming towards him.

Despite having been seen by witnesses in the car park almost an hour before the attack, Murphy did not make any reference to having been in the area for any length of time. He said he had never seen the woman before in his life, and that he didn't know what came over him when he approached her. 'I just flipped,' he said. 'I said to her "Give me your money." She said "Fuck off." I hit her then. I hit her with my hand on the side of the face. She stumbled back onto the seat in the car.'

Murphy went on to describe how he moved the woman's car across to where his Fiat Punto was parked. He said that the woman was sitting beside him 'with her head on my knee'.

He then explained how he'd asked her to remove her bra, before using it to bind her arms. 'At that stage I took her out of her car,' he said. 'She walked out. I told her to get in the boot of my car and she sat in. At this stage I took off up the road. I don't know why I did. I stopped at a lane. I raped her. I put her in the seat of the car. I removed her trousers. I just raped her.'

Murphy gave all the details of the sexual assaults and pinpointed on a map the locations to which he had taken his victim. As he was describing his violent, brutal actions his voice remained at a monotone, and he showed no semblance of regret or shame at what he had done.

The detectives were baffled and frustrated by his lack of remorse. In an effort to force him to confront the consequences of his attack they told him about the physical injuries and psychological trauma he had caused his victim. He barely looked up as he mumbled his reply. 'Well, she is alive, isn't she?'

That signalled the end of an exhausting, upsetting day. At 8.05pm Murphy was charged with rape and abduction, and an application was made to the Director of Public Prosecutions to also have him charged with attempted murder. In the file to the DPP, the gardaí said they did not believe that Murphy ever had any intention of releasing his victim.

Despite having a confession from Murphy, detectives felt distinctly uneasy. They considered the calm, calculated way in which he had perpetrated his crime and the ease with which he had abducted the woman. The attacks bore all the hallmarks of someone who had done it before. Yet somehow this brutally violent man had never come to their attention. The detectives wondered what else Larry Murphy was hiding in his past.

A casual look at his life revealed nothing more than was to be expected from a hard-working family man. Having grown up in the village of Stratford, on the outskirts of Baltinglass in Wicklow, Murphy never really ventured far from home. His entire life was centred on the Wicklow, Kildare, Carlow and Dublin region, and he possessed an intimate knowledge of the area.

One of seven children—five sisters and one brother—Murphy was educated in Scoil Chonglais vocational school in Baltinglass, where he impressed his fellow pupils with his skills on the football field.

While he had no significant interest or ability in academic learning, Murphy excelled at woodwork in school and early on it was clear that he had a promising career in carpentry ahead of him.

When he was 16, his father retired from the construction industry with a disability, and Murphy decided to leave school. The former vice-principal of Scoil Chonglais had also been Murphy's woodwork teacher, and he took the young man under his wing.

For six years, Murphy worked alongside his former teacher, making salad bowls and other wooden tableware items, and developing a particular talent for wood cutting and finishing.

When he wasn't working, Murphy spent much of his time hunting, a hobby through which he became familiar with the hinterland around Baltinglass and beyond to the Wicklow Mountains. He owned a twelve-gauge shotgun, and used his status as a local to gain access to farmland to shoot pheasants and foxes. He was later to use this geographical knowledge of secluded areas during the brutal attack on his victim in 2000.

In the nineties Murphy branched out from woodwork and went to work on various building sites as a freelance carpenter and roofer. This work took him all over the Midlands and into the East. As he was usually working on two or three jobs at one time, his livelihood meant he was constantly travelling, constantly on the road. Detectives noted that this type of unregulated working arrangement was very suitable for someone who might want to stalk or attack women.

In 1994, Murphy met his future wife Margaret at a disco in the Kilkea Castle Hotel. The couple married soon afterwards and from then on Murphy became a dedicated family man. He earned a good wage, he didn't drink too much, he provided well for his wife and children. Locally he was regarded as reliable and hard-working. Contrary to being a dangerous rapist, many of Murphy's neighbours actually thought of him as a perfect husband.

But there were some very strong indicators in his past that hinted at the simmering savagery underneath. As journalist Stephen Rae points out in his book *Guilty*, the first incident—or at least the first incident known to gardaí—shows that Murphy really was capable of anything.

It was the summer of 1996, four years before Murphy would be caught in the midst of his brutal attack in the mountains. He and Margaret were at that time living in a house in Ballinacarrig, Castledermot, in Co. Kildare.

It was a Sunday, and Murphy had spent the day relaxing and having a few drinks, before returning home. He found Margaret in the kitchen with one of her close friends, a young woman in her mid-twenties who was a regular visitor to the house.

Murphy asked Margaret if she would like to go out for a drink, but she declined. He said that he was going to go out anyway, and offered a lift to his wife's friend, who had mentioned that she had no way of getting home.

The arrangement suited everyone, and at about 8pm that evening Murphy and the young woman set off for Castleroe. The atmosphere in the car was relaxed, as Murphy told the young woman that he had bought a present for his wife, reaffirming again his image of a caring husband.

They approached the left turn for the young woman's house, but Murphy didn't slow down or put on his indicator. The young woman pointed out that he had passed the junction, and asked him where he was going. But Murphy said nothing as he continued on a few hundred yards down the road, before suddenly turning the car right into a lane at the back entrance to a farm.

At some time since leaving the house, Larry Murphy had suddenly decided he was going to attack the woman. Whether this was in his mind when he offered her a lift, or if the impulse overcame him as he was driving her home, is known only to himself. What seems clear is that once the idea formed in his head, he seemed unable to control the urge to follow it through.

Growing uneasy now, the woman asked Murphy again where he was going and what he was doing. Again, he was silent. As they approached a fork in the lane, he finally brought his car to a stop. At this stage the woman was extremely scared. She stared at Murphy, demanding to know what he was doing.

'Without saying anything he put his left arm around my shoulder,' she said later. 'I cannot remember exactly, but he may have put his right hand on my leg.'

This was a particularly intrusive gesture as the woman was wearing shorts. She pushed out at Murphy, trying to throw him off her, screaming at him to stop. Suddenly he put both his hands around her throat and pushed her down towards the front of the car seat. Throughout the attack he remained totally silent.

'He said nothing,' said the woman. 'His expression had totally changed on his face. It was a side of him I had never seen before. I got my hand on the door handle beside me and broke his grip on my neck. I jumped out of the car and ran back along the lane towards the main road.'

The woman ran as fast as she could, but Murphy soon caught up with her and grabbed her again. This time, however, there was panic—not intention—in his face. The urge to attack the woman appeared to have gone, leaving him with the stunning realisation of what he had just done. He pleaded with the woman not to say anything to his wife.

She stared at him. It was still broad daylight. He was her close friend's husband. She knew him well, certainly well enough to identify him and ruin his marriage. The temerity of the attack was astonishing.

However, she was somewhat reassured by Murphy's evident distress, and eventually she agreed to get back in the car and allow him to drive her home. For the entirety of the journey, he pleaded with her not to say anything to his wife.

When they reached her house, the woman ran inside and went straight into the bathroom, where she locked the door. 'I was very frightened and upset by what had happened,' she said. 'He came after me and banged on the bathroom door. He asked me to let him in, that he wanted to talk to me.'

The woman ignored Murphy's pleas, her mind racing as she tried to decide what to do. Then she heard the sound of a car on the driveway. Margaret Murphy had changed her mind and decided that she would join her husband for a drink after all. She had driven to her friend's house to meet him.

Murphy left his post outside the bathroom and went into the kitchen. The young woman followed him, her face streaked with tears. When Margaret walked in, she saw immediately that something very bad had happened. She asked her friend what was wrong. The young woman didn't reply.

Instead, perhaps aware that there was now no way of covering it up, it was Murphy himself who told his wife what had happened. He said he had grabbed the woman while he was driving her home.

The young woman never reported the incident to the police. She remained on friendly terms with Margaret, but kept her distance from Larry Murphy, quietly regarding him with fear and hatred.

It was the first known indication of Murphy's tendency towards extreme violence.

That same summer, there was one other incident that prompted a few other local people to change their view of Larry Murphy. One evening in the Glen Lounge pub in Donard, Murphy lunged at a woman in the bar, grabbing her inappropriately. His actions caused a row in the pub, but it was decided that the assault did not merit being reported to the police.

However, the woman remained shocked and upset by the episode, and she too started keeping her distance from Murphy. Some time later she was in the company of her brother's friend, the hunter Trevor Moody, when she spotted Murphy a short distance away. She nudged Moody and pointed in the direction of the carpenter before telling Moody what had happened in the pub. The hunter took in Murphy's cold blue eyes and square shoulders, and never forgot his face. Four years later, even in the darkness of the mountains, he recognised him immediately.

Having uncovered this history of attacks on women, detectives began seriously looking at Larry Murphy in relation to a number of ongoing investigations into missing and murdered women in the area.

They were conscious that he had lived very close to where Jo Jo Dullard was last seen in 1995, and he was also working in the area where a teenage girl disappeared in broad daylight in 1998. There was even a possibility that he could be linked with the disappearance of Annie McCarrick in Glencullen.

Murphy's name was referred to the officers in charge of Operation Trace—a special garda unit set up to investigate whether there was a link between some or all of the missing women cases in the Leinster area.

What they discovered—or didn't discover—is discussed in Chapter 13.

While detectives set to work trying to establish if there was a link between Murphy and the other unsolved crimes, the 35-year-old carpenter's case finally came to court.

On 11 May 2001 he pleaded guilty to four charges of rape and one charge each of kidnapping and the attempted murder of the young businesswoman. In an appeal for leniency, Murphy's solicitor said that before the attack he had been 'a completely ordinary, respectable human being' with no previous convictions.

Judge Paul Carney sentenced him to fifteen years in prison for his crime. As the court session came to an end, Larry Murphy fainted and fell to the ground. The barristers stepped over his inert body and left the courtroom. Two prison officers lifted him off the floor, and escorted him to Arbour Hill.

Chapter 12

Five Hours of Terror at the Hands of Robert Quigley

She is scared, now, to go anywhere alone. Scared to be at home. Scared to go outside. Suspicious of strangers. Frightened, even, of sleep. But most of all, since the night of Saturday, 18 November 2006, the woman is terrified of getting taxis.

Sometimes there is no choice, no other way to get home. So she signals for a cab, and sits where she can see the driver, and clutches the handle of the door. Ready every moment to flee. As each second stretches interminably, she tries to block the images that flood her mind. The face of her attacker, leering at her with sickening confidence. The rasp of plastic cable ties cutting into her bound wrists. The flashes of red she sees every time he hits her with the baton. The blackness of the mountains. The fear that she is going to be raped. The certainty that she is going to be killed.

In Tralee Circuit Court she sits now, on 8 October 2007, one year since it happened. She is dressed all in black, as if for a funeral, flanked by her friends and a concerned-looking blonde garda. Her mid-length blonde hair curls slightly on her shoulders, her make-up is perfectly applied. Only a slight enclave around her lower jaw hints at her injuries. She is, undoubtedly, a very striking young woman. But her eyes betray her. Even as she smiles and talks quietly to her companions, with every lapse in conversation her eyes lose all animation. The woman is brave. But she is haunted.

Sentencing was meant to be handed down at 10am. It's now 2.45pm. A clerical error resulted in copies of vital documents being sent to the wrong courthouse. Not a long delay, in legal terms, but on this day it seems cruel. As each hour ticks by, the woman sits straighter on the hard wooden bench, her palms clasping more tightly on her lap.

Then, with very little ceremony, a door opens and Robert Quigley is escorted into the court. Heads strain towards the dock, people morbidly eager to see the monster that has inflicted such pain. And then their shoulders relax and they look again towards the judge. Because Robert Quigley isn't the sort of man you look at for long.

He's of average height, somewhat overweight. His black hair is short and thinning prematurely for his 27 years. Under his long-sleeved black polo jumper his belly protrudes in a bloated circle, a product of beer and inaction.

He sits down immediately, gazing straight ahead. His eyes speak of a sort of confused bewilderment. There is no air of menace from this man who has committed such a brutal attack. No hint of the controlling fantasist who had taken to prowling the streets at night, looking for vulnerable female victims. Rather, he seems like the type of man that would be 'the quiet one' in the group, a man who might often be the butt of jokes he does not understand. Worthy of mild sympathy, if anything at all.

But at the back of the courtroom, his victim knows differently. Gone is the haunted look from her light brown eyes, replaced now with a burning fury. She stares directly at Quigley, the ferocity of her gaze scorching through the air. She seems to be willing him, daring him, to look at her. But Quigley keeps perfectly still. He doesn't risk even the most perfunctory of glances around the courtroom.

And then, finally, the judge is ready. A clerk calls for order. The judge taps his fingers on the bench, frowning at the paperwork in front of him. What sentence do you give to a man who has not killed, but has destroyed a life forever?

One year previously, the future was looking bright and promising for the young woman. Born in the West of Ireland, she had moved to Dublin to complete a master's degree in college.

She had been living in the city for just one year, but was already involved in a wide and active social scene. She was only 22 years old, but the woman had already grieved the loss of her father, and her perspective on life was maybe a little more measured than her peers. She didn't allow herself to worry too much about life's difficulties, thinking of herself as a 'happy-go-lucky' person. Her open, friendly attitude won her many friends. She trusted, this young woman. She expected people to be good.

That Saturday, 18 November, was a particularly cheerful day in her life. She was graduating from her master's course, and was proud of her achievement. Her mother had travelled up from home to celebrate, and her brother—with whom she was very close—was also with her for the day.

At around 6pm, after the ceremony, the woman and her brother brought their mother in a taxi to Heuston Station. They waved good-bye as she took the train home, and then the siblings hailed another taxi back into the city centre to continue their celebrations.

It had been a big day, and promised to be a big night. The young woman had dressed carefully for the occasion. She wore a knee-length black skirt, a white blouse with a black ribbon on it and black sandals, all complemented by a knee-length white coat. In her black designer DKNY bag she carried her mobile phone, keys and driver's licence.

The first stop was the Odeon pub on Harcourt Street, which turned out to be disappointingly quiet. The woman and her brother left after a short time, and walked down the road to Dicey Reilly's pub, where they met with one of the young woman's flatmates. Soon a large gang of friends had joined them, everyone joking and laughing and in excellent humour after the day. The young woman sipped at bottles of Bulmer's Light, and glowed happily in the friendly atmosphere.

Sometime after midnight, the group left Dicey Reilly's and stood in the queue for the newly opened club in town, Krystal. However, the venue was operating a guest-list-only policy, so the group made a diversion to the adjacent nightclub, Copper Face Jacks.

The woman ordered another bottle of Bulmer's Light, and contin-ued joking with her brother. But it had been a long day, and she was starting to feel tired. She was due to start work on Monday, along with ten other new graduates, and she wanted to be in top form. She was looking forward to starting her new job, and the opportunity of meet-ing a whole new set of friends. It was after 2am now. Getting late. The woman starting thinking about getting a taxi home.

Robert Quigley was sitting outside the club in his car. He was parked in the taxi rank. His metallic purple Vauxhall Cavalier had a specially fitted aerial on the roof, giving the vehicle the appearance of a hackney. On the floor in front of the passenger seat lay a pair of 10 x 25 mini-binoculars. In the back seat was a black baton, similar to that used by gardaí, alongside a bunch of black plastic cable ties.

Quigley sat quietly, with purpose. His eyes scanned the crowds of people spilling out of the various clubs, his attention focused on the women. Particularly the women who were on their own.

'He had it planned, we're sure enough about that,' says one detective, smiling grimly. 'He had installed aerials on the roof of his car, radio aerials, you know? The aerials had no use, but they gave the impression that the car was a hackney. That part of it would almost have been enough to point us towards what this guy was at. But we came across other evidence in the course of the investigation.'

The detective tells me about an interview with a bouncer who worked in a popular nightclub in south Dublin City. The bouncer knew Quigley, having noticed him engage in a curious pattern of behaviour at the club. He told detectives that Quigley would arrive at the club at around 2am, just before it closed. And he'd sit at the bar, having one drink, his eyes sweeping the crowd. He always seemed to focus on the girls, especially girls who seemed to be drunk.

'There were a number of incidences involving women that happened around that club,' says the detective. 'But nothing that we could tie with certainty back to Quigley. However, taking it all into account, we're pretty clear on what his objective was when he set out that night.'

Even if detectives hadn't been certain that Quigley planned his actions that night, a few enquiries into his recent past would have been enough to convince them. It wasn't the first time he had attacked a woman. Robert Quigley had form.

Originally from Seskin View Road in Tallaght, Robert Patrick Quigley was born on 18 March 1980. He achieved almost 500 points in his Leaving Cert, displaying an intelligence belied by his appearance. He got a diploma in electronics and spent some time using his skills to work with cars.

Apart from a road traffic offence, Robert Quigley had managed to avoid getting any previous convictions. This did not mean, however, that he hadn't committed any crimes. In his early twenties he began a serious relationship with a young woman, with whom he fathered a child. However, after the baby was born, Quigley's behaviour became increasingly violent and bizarre. He began physically abusing his girlfriend.

One evening he used an imitation firearm to threaten her and her family. The girl and her parents thought the gun was real. They were petrified. It was the first hint of Quigley's obsession with control, a real manifestation of his fantasy about being part of a powerful organisation—whether a criminal gang or the Garda Síochána.

'He attacked her and threatened to kill her, but it wasn't prosecuted because of insufficient evidence at the time,' says one detective. 'There's no contact between them at all now. She's terrified of him.'

After that relationship ended, Quigley moved to Tralee in Co. Kerry, where he found a job working as a bouncer. In December 2005 he met a 21-year-old shop assistant called Bridget Donegan, and by early the next year they were officially a couple.

Then, on 20 August 2006, just a few weeks before he carried out the most vicious assault of his life, Quigley turned on his girlfriend. They were driving in his car on the main road from Limerick to Castleisland, when he suddenly, inexplicably, began arguing with Donegan, claiming that she had been unfaithful to him.

Ignoring her protests, he swerved suddenly off the main road and took the much more remote route leading into Dooneen Woods. At this point, Quigley was shouting in earnest at Donegan, saying that he was going to 'get rid of her' for what she had done. He claimed he had links to the late Dublin gangster, Martin Cahill, and that these contacts would help him to make her pay for being unfaithful. He also told her he had a gun.

As they pulled into the car park in the wood, Bridget Donegan noticed two other vehicles were already there. Perhaps in an attempt to stop her trying to raise the alarm, Quigley told her that the men in the cars were associates of his from Dublin, and that they were there as 'back-up', in case he needed help in punishing her.

Terrified and crying, Donegan continued pleading with Quigley to believe her, that she had not been unfaithful. Without any warning, he punched her in the face, and wrapped his hand around her neck, restricting her air supply. Reaching into the back seat he grabbed a black baton and waved it menacingly at her.

Then he produced pictures of her family and said they would not be harmed if she did everything he asked. He told her that he wanted a large sum of money, punctuating his request by hitting her hands and arms with the baton. Deeply distressed by the threatened involvement of her family, Donegan agreed to do anything he asked. With relative ease, Quigley had gained complete control of another person. It is this sense of power that detectives believe Quigley craves most. In silence, he drove his girlfriend home.

A few weeks later he told Donegan that he needed the money immediately, or his associates from Dublin would come to Tralee to hurt her and her family. Donegan didn't doubt Quigley for a second. She knew that he was watching her in case she made any attempt to contact the authorities. She later said she was 'really afraid there were people coming to hurt me and my family'.

He watched contentedly as she approached both the Tralee Credit Union and Bank of Ireland for loans. The first establishment agreed to lend her €4,000. The second gave her €8,000. Donegan handed almost all the money in cash to Quigley in early September. He also took her bank card from her so that he could withdraw the remainder of the loan at his leisure. Having used and abused her, and confident that she would be too frightened to alert the police, Quigley ended the relationship.

Donegan didn't alert the Gardaí. But she told her family. They debated what was best to do. Eventually, they contacted the authorities. But not before Quigley had done much more damage to another innocent woman.

Despite having manipulated €12,000 from Donegan, the next few weeks didn't go awfully well for Robert Quigley. He had been a witness to a murder in Tralee and had given a statement to gardaí about what he saw. He claims this had led to him being assaulted twice a week, having his car regularly vandalised and all his money taken from him. Given his propensity for lying, it's difficult to know whether there is any truth in these allegations. There is evidence, however, that he had stopped paying rent on his apartment in Tralee, and as mid-November approached he came under increasing pressure to leave the premises. He had nowhere else to go.

On the morning of Saturday, 18 November Robert Quigley travelled to Dublin. Perhaps he came to the capital knowing exactly what he intended to do that night. Maybe he just wanted a break from what appears to have become a disturbed existence in Tralee. Quigley's story to detectives was that he planned on visiting an old friend from a FÁS course he had attended in Baldoyle. He also said he was considering applying for a job in Dublin.

At 8pm on Saturday evening, tired after his day, Quigley drove his car to Killiney beach in South Dublin. There he made himself as comfortable as possible and fell asleep. He told detectives that he didn't stay in his parents' house in Tallaght because he didn't want them to know he was in town.

At around 1.45am, Quigley woke up, stiff and cold. He put the keys in the ignition, and headed straight for Harcourt Street in the city centre. He claims that this was a normal thing for him to do, that he often bumped into friends from the bar trade in town. While he was unable to provide the names of anyone specifically, he insisted that he would regularly bring the car into town in the early hours of the morning and meet people he knew.

Shortly after 2am, he parked his car on the left-hand side of the road, in between Harcourt Street Garda Station and Copper Face Jacks. He says he didn't know that this was a well-recognised taxi rank in the city. He pulled his baseball cap low over his forehead and sat there quietly. Waiting.

It was just after 2.20am when the young woman decided to call it a night. Her image was clearly captured on CCTV footage at 2.22am, her blonde hair and white coat shining brightly as she walked down Harcourt Street trying to find a taxi. The road was flooded with people, all pouring out of the numerous nightclubs in the area, all trying to get home. Most of the cars that drove by were already full. The chances of finding an available cab seemed slim.

Then the woman spotted a purple hackney parked in the taxi rank. She walked over to the driver's window and asked if he was free. Behind her, a garda walked slowly down the footpath, her eyes alert for trouble. The driver looked out from under his baseball cap, taking in the striking blonde woman standing there, on her own.

Within a few minutes, the woman was sitting in the back of the car, behind Quigley. As he started the ignition, the young woman rested her head against the window, watching people waving futilely at taxis that were already full of passengers. The warmth of the car combined with a happy fatigue. The woman closed her eyes. Just for a few moments, she thought. She fell asleep.

Robert Quigley claims he genuinely intended taking the woman home. He told detectives that he felt sorry for her, because he saw that she was having problems getting a taxi. He claims that he tried to wake her up, but couldn't and therefore he couldn't find out where she lived. So he drove about mindlessly, not sure what to do. It's an implausible excuse, and certainly does not explain why he took the sleeping woman straight out of the city, into the darkness of the mountains.

The purple car didn't attract any attention from late-night revellers as it sped quietly through the dimly lit streets of Rathmines, Dundrum, Sandyford and Rathfarnham. There was virtually no traffic, and within fifteen minutes he was out of the city. When he reached the Dublin Mountains, Quigley slowed down at an area informally known as the Viewing Point, a natural plateau in the mountains from which the entire city can be seen. He parked the car, and began methodically smoking his way through a packet of Benson and Hedges cigarettes. It was then that the woman woke up.

She quickly took in her surroundings, alarm building in her chest. She rubbed her eyes, trying to clear the images of the thin winding road behind her, the remote countryside plunging down in front of her, and the strange man sitting calmly in the driver's seat. She looked at his plump face, clean-shaven and pale, staring expectantly at her. Her heart beating faster, she bombarded him with questions, asking him who he was and how had they ended up here, in the mountains.

'The first thing I remember is the man saying to me that he was a cop, and that I was in big trouble,' the woman said. '[He said] that there was a hundred grams of cocaine found in my bag, and that people I had been hanging around with had planted it on me. He said, "I know you're a nice girl and I know that you wouldn't do anything like this." He knew I didn't know anything about such things. He was explaining to me that a hundred grams of raw cocaine had been found in my bag. He started saying that his boss was going to raid my friend's house and that he had to keep me out of the way in the Dublin Mountains while this raid was going on. I knew in my heart and soul that something bad was going to happen to me, so I kept asking him questions and talking to him.'

The woman struggled against a cloud of confusion. While on one level she believed Quigley was a member of the gardaí, all her instincts were warning her that he was also a very dangerous individual. Something about his demeanour, the satisfaction he seemed to be getting out of her predicament, suggested he was just barely keeping his real impulses under check.

'I thought the man was going to rape me,' said the woman. 'All during the night he kept saying he "didn't want to have to do this". That's how I knew he was going to do something. All I was thinking was that if he was going to rape me there was nothing I could do, only put my head in another place. I was terrified. I asked him continuously could he not just take me to the garda station or to see my brother. He said "We can't go back to the garda station, we have to wait until my boss calls." He kept telling me to look at him and saying "Why are your eyes dilated if you're not doing drugs?" I just kept saying "I'm not, I'm not." All I wanted to do was to cry, but I couldn't even let myself do that because I knew it would be giving into him and then he could do what he wanted to me.'

Quigley kept up his harassment, feeding his fantasy of being in a position of total authority over another person. As he grew increasingly insistent that she was taking drugs, the woman decided that her best hope might be to agree with him. Then, she thought, he might bring her to a garda station—to safety.

But as soon as she admitted to using narcotics, Quigley's eyes widened with pleasure. Unexpectedly for him, the woman was playing along perfectly with his game. His voice took on a scolding tone as he told her of how much trouble she was in. He warned her that she was going to end up in prison, locked in a cell alongside murderers and rapists. Now that she had admitted to her crime, he said that he had to officially arrest her. He reached for the cable ties to use as handcuffs.

'He then reached into the back of the car and grabbed a black piece of plastic wire,' said the woman. 'He told me to put my hands behind my back and he tied them together using the plastic wire. I was really scared. He said the police knew everything about me because they had been watching me for the past two weeks. I kept saying I wanted to go to see my brother, and he said, "You'll get one phone call when you go back to the station, and you'll need that for your solicitor."'

No one knows what prompted Quigley to make up such a bizarre tale. Detectives say that at no stage during the investigation did he give any plausible reason for his actions. 'It certainly wasn't a spur-of-the-moment thing,' says one detective. 'He did a lot of driving; he had her in that car for over five and a half hours in the end. So he had a lot of time to think, to let her go or assault her or kill her or do whatever he wanted to do. We don't know why he took so long, but it seems that he was just playing with her. We think it was a control thing. It gave him this sense of control to be able to say that he was a garda, to have her helpless in the car. We think that's why he just kept driving around. He enjoyed that feeling of power.'

Shortly after he had handcuffed her, Quigley moved the woman out of the back seat and brought her to sit alongside him in the front. He continued smoking, and talked to her about his life, his ex-girlfriend, his son. She stayed quiet, soaking in the details of her surroundings. She noticed he wore a chunky silver bracelet on his right hand, that he had no obvious tattoos, and that he was speaking with a slight American twang. She saw that the upholstery of the car was dark, and that there was a digital clock in the centre of the dash. She listened in a daze as the man kept talking, telling her that his father was a cop from Dublin.

Then suddenly he grabbed her by the hair and pulled her head back, leaning in close to her face. 'What are we going to say?' he said. Shocked at how fast he had moved, the woman managed to gasp that she would say whatever he wanted her to say. He let her go abruptly. Then his phone rang.

'He picked it up and got out and walked to the back of the car,' the woman said. 'I couldn't hear him talking, but I could see him talking. I remember thinking "How am I going to get out of here?" I started looking for the door handle. It was silver, close to the dashboard. It was too far away for me to reach because my hands were tied.'

Quigley got back into the car and told the woman that the phone call had been from his boss. He said that the gardaí were preparing to carry out the raid, and that they should be ready in about twenty minutes. He started driving again. To the east of the mountains a sliver of light ran over the horizon. The sun was starting to rise.

Quigley drove to a small clearing in the middle of the mountains on Military Road, Glassamucky. He stopped the car again. Then, in an eerie repeat of his actions just a few weeks earlier, he became very angry, very quickly.

'I thought if he was going to do something he would obviously do it somewhere quieter,' said the woman. 'That was when he tried to kill me.'

Quigley wrapped his two hands around the woman's throat and began squeezing hard. His two thumbs pressed down together on her windpipe, cutting off her air supply. As the woman struggled against him, Quigley reached into the back seat and grabbed the cover of his wheel brace—a strong strip of leather, shaped like a belt.

'He took each end of it in each hand and pushed it against my throat,' said the woman. 'My head at this point was pushed back against the headrest. I couldn't breathe. I couldn't get any air. I really thought every second I was going to die because there was no way I could go any longer without breathing. All that was going through my head was I was ok, because I was going to heaven with dad. I just wanted to die. I wanted it to be over. I remember thinking, would the next gulp be the last one. But what about my mother, brothers and sisters? They wouldn't be able to cope.'

As Quigley watched the woman gasping for breath, he quietly whispered to her that he had come close to killing someone before. Then, suddenly, he released the pressure on her neck. The woman sobbed violently, her lungs drawing in oxygen. As she struggled to recover, Quigley put his hand on her leg. 'I don't want to have to do this but I have to,' he said.

'He reached inside my skirt and started to pull down my knickers,' said the woman. 'I pleaded and pleaded with him not to do it. I said, "You don't have to." He said, "No I do, I have to do it." I would have rather he kill me than rape me. I couldn't bear to think of him on top of me. Even thinking of it now is really upsetting. He got them down as far as my knees.'

Suddenly, providentially, a silver car came rumbling down the road towards them, containing two men who had arrived early in the mountains to set up an orienteering course for that day.

It was the woman's first glimpse of other people, her first hope of rescue. She lashed out at Quigley, struggling desperately against him and screaming at the car, pleading with the driver for help. The car came within a couple of yards of them, and the two men saw the woman's mouth open in a scream, but they presumed they were just seeing a couple having an argument. They drove on.

Unable to control her desperate struggles, Quigley abandoned his attempt to sexually assault the woman and slammed the car into gear, speeding off in the other direction. The woman continued screaming and shouting at Quigley to let her go. She managed to get her feet up and started kicking his head over and over again. Quigley punched her away, before parking the car just a short distance away. He reached again into the back seat, this time grabbing a black bat which looked to the woman very similar to the batons carried by gardaí.

'All he had to do at this point was open the door and let her out,' says one detective. 'That was all he had to do. But instead he pulls out this old bat and gave her a serious beating with it. He said it was a stick that he used for working on electronics, and that was why it was in the car. That explanation doesn't make much sense to us.'

With a sickening crack, the first blow landed on the woman's head. 'I thought again I was going to die,' she said. 'I could feel each punch and hit over the head doing damage. I'm not sure if he hit me in the face, but he seemed to be aiming for my head.'

The force with which Quigley attacked the woman left her with gaping wounds in her face. As one blow landed, she felt her nose fracture and the bone breaking in her cheek. Another swing knocked out three of her teeth. Blood poured from her nose, her mouth, her forehead, soaking deep red into her white blouse and coat. Quigley later said that it was only after he hit her that he saw all the blood.

'He went to pull something from the back of the car and I thought it would be a gun,' said the woman. 'I was hoping it would be, because it would be a quick end to the pain and I wouldn't have to suffer any more. To think now I was wishing he was going to pull a gun out is awful.'

Through the pain, the woman kept fighting, screaming to be let go. Then somehow, in the confusion of the struggle, the passenger door swung open behind her. The woman half fell, half jumped out of the car. And she started trying to escape.

'I was so scared he was going to come back after me and finish me off,' she said. 'It was like it was never going to end. All I could think of is if he came after me I would have to run off the road and onto the grass because it would take time for him to get out of the car and run after me. I remember thinking, "Run", but I couldn't run. I kept walking up the road. That's when I saw the two cars in the distance. I just kept screaming when I saw the cars. I wanted to get their attention. I didn't want them to drive away.'

As he watched the woman making her way back up the mountain, Quigley decided he had better make a quick escape. He sped down the mountain towards Rathfarnham, throwing the black bat out of the car as he drove.

Her attacker gone, the woman finally made it to the safety of the men. 'When I finally got to them I really got upset,' she said. 'I knew I was safe but I think the realisation of it all came to me and I couldn't stop crying. At one point in the car I remember thinking "There's so much blood on me." My hands were still tied behind my back. In the hospital I didn't care what they did to me because I knew I was safe. The only thing I wanted was to see my brother. When I did hear his voice I was so happy, beyond words.'

Robert Quigley drove away, his mind racing. He went down Pine Forest Road, straight through Rathfarnham and into Rathmines and then Ranelagh. It was then that he noticed the woman had broken the indicator switch lever during her attempts to kick the horn. He parked the car and went to Spar. The nearby CCTV cameras captured him as he walked into the shop and came out carrying a bag containing cigarettes, a J-cloth, cleaning fluid and superglue. Quigley used the glue to try to fix the damage to the car, and the cloth to try to clean away the blood stains. He stayed in Dublin until about 8pm on Sunday evening, before leaving for Kerry.

At 3am he arrived in Tralee, the journey having taken him longer because of the damage to his indicator. He drove to Banna Beach, parked, and slept for a few hours. He woke up at seven o'clock on Monday morning, and stayed sitting in the car until 6pm that evening, the events of Saturday night playing over and over in his head. Eventually, he left the beach. It was time for him to return to work. To real life.

As the woman was being tended to in hospital, where it emerged she needed reconstructive surgery on her face, gardaí were alerted and immediately sprang into action.

Led by Detective Sergeant Joe O'Hara, an incident room was set up at Shankill Station, and both Shankill and Tallaght detectives launched a major investigation into the case.

Within a few hours the details of the attack were circulated to the media, along with an appeal for information from anyone who might have seen anything suspicious in Harcourt Street or in the Dublin Mountains. To the frustration of detectives, no one seemed to have seen anything.

'There were loads of people up in the mountains, people driving up and down that road all night,' said one detective. 'You'd think maybe that hour of the morning, someone would take note of a car parked up there, or at least have noticed Quigley speeding away. But they didn't. No one saw anything.'

However, during an interview with the two men who had disturbed Quigley during the attack, detectives got a lucky break. One of the men was a car importer, and through force of habit he had taken in very specific details about the purple Vauxhall as they passed it on the mountains in the early morning.

'It was one of the very important aspects of the case, the statements made by these two men on the first day,' says one detective. 'This man was certain and adamant about the exact make of the car and the registration. Normally the description we would get would be, say, a green Toyota. But this guy could tell us it was an English-registered car, purple, he knew the make and he had noted two letters from the number plate—P and O. And he turned out to be spot on about all of it.'

The information about the car was immediately entered into the PULSE system, which sent out a nationwide alert to every garda station in the country.

Detectives then set about trying to trace the attacker's movements after he drove down the mountains. During brief, extremely difficult interviews with the victim, they had managed to establish that she no longer had her bag, containing her driver's licence and mobile phone. Gardaí tracked the phone, and to their astonishment saw that it was still powered on, and appeared to be heading south.

'We tracked it all the way to Naas, and then the battery went dead on the phone,' says one detective. 'But at least it gave us a sense of where the car was heading. We couldn't understand why he had kept her phone, with all that people know now about how easily a phone can be traced. But when you look at the profile of these guys, there's a certain amount of trophy-keeping involved. When we eventually caught him, he still had her shoes and driver's licence too. It seems like he intended to keep something of the victim to remind him of the attack.'

Again, detectives interviewed the victim. Initially, the trauma of the attack had caused a blank in her memory. She could only focus on the fear that her attacker was still out there, and that he had her driver's license, complete with her home address. She worried that he would come looking for her. But as the hours went by, she began remembering more details about the attack. She told detectives about the material of the car, the digital clock, the pale, clean-shaven face, and the bracelet with a criss-cross design.

As the investigation gained pace in Dublin, in Tralee Garda Station Detective Garda Martin Riordan arrived into work and did a routine check of the computer system. He saw the alert for the suspect vehicle. He remembered that a man living in the area, Robert Quigley, had had his purple English-registered car brought into the station recently for non-payment under the Finance Act. Quigley had failed to register his car with customs, in an attempt to avoid paying tax. His vehicle had been taken off him for two days while the situation was rectified. Detective Garda Martin Riordan picked up the phone and called Shankill Garda Station in Dublin. He told them he might have some interesting news.

On 22 November 2006, a team of gardaí led by Detective Sergeant Joe O'Hara travelled to Tralee. At around 3pm they arrived at the garage where Quigley had found a job as a mechanic. He looked up, shocked, as the gardaí approached. Standing well over six feet, and formidably built, Detective Sergeant Joe O'Hara loomed over the man who, just days before, had felt invincible power.

Quigley initially said he had no idea why the detectives would want to speak with him. When he was told it was concerning an incident in Dublin, he capitulated and said he had given a lift to a girl in Dublin recently. The last time he saw her, he said, she was getting into a car with two men. At 3.10pm, Robert Quigley was arrested, and taken to Tralee Garda Station for questioning.

'He gave an excuse for everything, right down to the assault and sexual assault,' says one detective. 'Actually, he totally denied the sexual assault. And he said that the only reason he hit her was because she was hitting him. It was a case of self-defence, he said. We still don't know if he intended to kill this woman. But he came very close to it, put it like that. We don't know if he would have stopped, if those men hadn't come along when they did.'

The case against Quigley was watertight. A forensic examination of the car found the victim's blood was all over the interior. Her shoes and phone and driver's licence were found in the boot. Eventually Quigley abandoned his excuses of self-defence and pleaded guilty to charges of assault causing harm, false imprisonment and—after much denial—sexual assault.

It was now up to Judge Carroll Moran to decide what sentence to give to a man who had caused such wanton, unnecessary pain. To help him in his decision, the victim tried to describe the effect the attack had had on her life.

For two weeks afterwards, she couldn't eat or speak properly because of the way her teeth had been pushed back in her mouth and her lip had been deeply cut. In the hospital, everyone stared and asked her what happened. She found this deeply embarrassing and upsetting, as each time it reminded her of the assault.

'When I walked down the street, everyone was looking and staring at me,' she said. 'Some people asked what happened. Others weren't so nice and laughed in my face, made fun of it, said I had two nice shiners and I deserved it. My relationship with my friends has suffered, as they do not know what to say to me or if they should mention the attack. I always wonder what people will think of me, and if they think how stupid I was to get into the situation.'

The woman couldn't start her new job until her injuries had healed. On Monday, while she was undergoing reconstructive surgery on her teeth, the rest of the graduates from her class started work. 'I felt like I was missing out on so much,' she said. 'During those two weeks they were able to get to know each other and bond and make friends. Because I was late starting I felt left out. Even still, six months on, I feel I missed so much of the social side of getting to know my work colleagues. When I did start, I still had bruises on my face and my teeth. It was hard trying to explain why.'

However, the ramifications of the attack stretched far beyond the woman's working life. She found that she now needed someone with her at all times. 'Even if it's walking to work, I need someone,' she said. 'Travelling on a train home, I would have to make sure there are plenty of people in the carriage with me. I cannot trust people. I am a lot more nervous going out. I am always on guard, looking around. I cannot stay by myself in the apartment or at home. I am in constant fear that something could happen. At night I always have to have the [bedroom] door open and make sure someone in the house has their door open too. I sometimes have nightmares about the attack which can be very upsetting and scary. Sleeping is meant to be relaxing, but now I go to bed hoping I don't have a bad dream.

'I hate getting a taxi by myself. I feel nervous, scared and uneasy. Not knowing what this person could do to me. If they lock the door, I ask them to unlock it. I have my hand on the door handle all the way home and feel like every second in the car is an hour. All the time I am thinking what I will do if he does something to me.'

Having reviewed the details of the case, the judge continued to flounder. He said that he still had no explanation and no understanding as to why 'this man did what he did' and if he was likely to do it again. 'There doesn't appear to be a rational explanation,' he said. To aid him further in deciding on the sentence, he ordered a psychiatric evaluation of Robert Quigley.

The psychiatrist came to perhaps the most disturbing of conclusions. There was really nothing wrong with Robert Quigley. He suffered no mental illness. He had a history of 'fantasising and fabricating stories', but that was all. Judge Carroll Moran was no closer to finding the answer that everyone wanted to know: Why did he do it?

It's 2.45pm in Tralee Circuit Criminal Court on 8 October 2007. The woman stares at Quigley. Quigley stares at the judge. The judge stares at the psychiatric report in front of him, tapping his fingers on the bench.

Finally he raises his head and sentences Robert Quigley to twelve years in prison, four years of which are to be suspended.

A murmur ripples around the courtroom. Twelve years is a heavy decision relative to jail terms handed down for similar crimes. It seems like quite a victory for the prosecuting team, the investigating gardaí, the victim. But in reality, Robert Quigley won't serve twelve years. He won't even serve eight. Possibly, probably, he'll be free again within six years. His victim, on the other hand, can never escape her sentence.

'I think about the attack all the time,' she says. 'I thought at this stage I wouldn't think about it so much, but I do. It's awful to think that there are such people out there. My mother lives by herself at home and I know she feels a lot more nervous now. Because we now know that awful things can happen to us, and not "other people". Reading stories about other girls that have been attacked and killed. It is upsetting and lonely to think that could have been me.'

Chapter 13

Unsolved Cases, Operation Trace and the Cold Case Unit

After two decades of assaults, murders and disappearances of women in the Leinster area, there was a serious and genuine fear among the public that a serial killer was at work. Senior officers finally admitted that this chilling theory had to be considered. Too many women had been taken. The geographical area was too small. The coincidence too great.

As well as the horrific unsolved cases already documented in this book, there were two more tragic incidences of women going missing in Leinster, both high-profile, both of which detectives strongly suspect may be linked.

The first was that of 21-year-old Jo Jo Dullard, who vanished from a dark country road in Moone, Co. Kildare, on the night of 9 November 1995.

Jo Jo had spent the day in Dublin with her friends, and had missed the last direct bus to her home in Callan in Co. Kilkenny. She decided to get a bus to Naas and hitch the rest of the way home. By 1995, people were becoming sharply aware of the dangers of getting into a car with a stranger, but on this dark winter's night Jo Jo felt she had no other option.

After getting off the bus in Naas, the young woman stood at the side of the busy road, her upturned thumb stuck out by her side. A short time later, a man stopped and offered her a lift. He was going to Kilcullen. It was just five miles down the road, but it was still a step closer to her ultimate destination. Jo Jo got in the car, grateful for the brief respite from the cold night.

It was after 11pm when she was dropped off in Kilcullen, still forty-five miles from home. After a few minutes, another motorist pulled up beside her. He told her he was going to Moone. Jo Jo knew that this would bring her to within ten miles of Carlow town, where she had a friend who would put her up for the night. Relieved to be getting closer to a warm bed, Jo Jo got in the car.

It was 11.35pm when the car arrived in Moone. Jo Jo thanked the driver and got out. She spotted a phone box at the side of the road and decided to call her friend, Mary Cullinane, before starting to hitch again. At 11.37pm, she made the call. She explained to Mary that she had missed the bus but that she'd managed to hitch as far as Moone. As she talked, she kept her eyes on the road, watching for approaching headlights that could signal her ticket home. About three minutes into the conversation, she suddenly said 'Hold on'.

Mary was left in silence for a moment, until Jo Jo abruptly returned to the other end of the line. 'I have a lift,' she said. 'See you, Mary.' Jo Jo put the phone back in the receiver. She was never seen again.

In the immediate aftermath of her disappearance, gardaí received a huge public response to their appeals for information. From all over the country, people contacted detectives with possible sightings of Jo Jo. The most promising sightings were made by four people who independently saw a woman matching Jo Jo's description in Castledermot on the night she disappeared.

The witnesses told gardaí about seeing a young woman wearing a black cotton jacket, blue jeans and boots, standing at the side of the road at around 11.55pm. The timing of these sightings, the accuracy of the descriptions and the fact that Castledermot is only five miles from Moone, has led gardaí to believe that there is a strong possibility that this woman was Jo Jo Dullard.

However, despite numerous appeals, the person who drove Jo Jo to Castledermot has never come forward, even though he apparently dropped her off safely. Did he impulsively decide to turn the car around and offer to drive her the rest of the journey home, before abducting and killing her? Or is he just reluctant to become involved in the investigation?

As well as searching for evidence to prove that it was Jo Jo who was seen in Castledermot, detectives were also dealing with a number of other possible leads.

A year after Jo Jo disappeared, a taxi driver came forward to say that he had been driving just outside Waterford at 1.20am on the morning of 10 November 1995 when he saw a red car with English registration plates parked at the side of the road. One man was standing on the roadside, urinating. As he drove past, he saw a young woman running barefoot from the back of the car. A second man appeared behind her, grabbed her by the hair and dragged her back into the vehicle.

Gardaí believed they knew the identity of these men. They investigated the possibility that the woman in the car was Jo Jo Dullard, but the lead came to nothing. A number of other promising lines of enquiry also ran cold.

Eventually, reluctantly, the investigation into Jo Jo Dullard's disappearance was wound down. Her name became a permanent fixture on the missing person's list.

Three years later, another young woman effectively vanished into thin air. The teenage girl was originally from Co. Kildare but had moved to the UK to attend college.

In the summer of 1998 she was back home in Ireland for the summer holidays. On the day that she disappeared, the young woman appeared to have been preparing for the future. At around 2.20pm she was captured on CCTV camera visiting her local bank branch. There, she purchased a bank draft to the value of £180 to pay for her new academic year.

Ten minutes later, she walked down the road to the local post office, where she sent the bank draft to her college. When she emerged, she chatted to a number of local people on the street before setting off in the direction of home, a route that brought her down a narrow, tree-lined country road and past the local evangelical church.

The last sighting of the young woman was at 3pm, when she was spotted walking down the road just 300 yards from home. From there, she vanished.

When her mother arrived back to the house early that evening, she was immediately worried to find that her daughter wasn't home. It was out of character for her not to leave a note or somehow let her parents know if she was going out. Within hours, the gardaí had been contacted and a search began.

Incredibly, despite the early involvement of the gardaí and despite an intensive investigation, no trace of the young woman was ever found. Detectives combed the area where she was last seen, but there was no evidence of any struggle. None of her belongings or clothes were ever discovered, her bank account was never touched, she never again made contact with any of her friends and family. The young woman had simply, terribly, just disappeared.

It was this case, on top of so many other unsolved missing women cases, that finally led the Garda Commissioner, Pat Byrne, to take action. He ordered the establishment of a special detective unit, charged with re-examining the cases of a number of missing and murdered women in an effort to see if there was any common link between the crimes. They called it Operation Trace.

Initially, the detectives in Operation Trace were focusing on six specific cases: Annie McCarrick, who went missing in the Dublin mountains; Jo Jo Dullard, who was last seen in Moone; Fiona Pender, who was seven months pregnant when she disappeared from Tullamore in 1996; Ciara Breen, who was only 17 when she went missing in Dundalk; Fiona Sinnott, who was never seen again after leaving a pub in Wexford in 1998; and the teenage girl who disappeared in Kildare.

However, as time progressed, the unit included the unsolved murders of Antoinette Smith and Patricia Doherty in their investigation. They also unofficially looked at the case of missing woman Eva Brennan.

When Operation Trace was set up, the then Garda Commissioner Pat Byrne warned people not to expect any miraculous results. 'We have no bodies, which means we have no crime scene,' he pointed out. 'And that itself is a tremendous disadvantage. This is not about raising hope for the relations of these girls.'

Asked if the Gardaí suspected that a serial killer might be responsible for the crimes, Byrne replied: 'It is an aspect that is being considered. We have to find out whether two or three of these murders are related.'

In order to do this effectively, everything that was known about each victim and each suspect had to be compared. This, in itself, was a mammoth task.

The detectives in Operation Trace adopted a serial killer profile system that was already in use in the National Crime Faculty in Bramshill College in England. Called the Violent Crime Linkage Analysis System (VCLAS), the programme was used to collect and compare information on all known sexual and violent offenders, all known victims of such attacks, and all known violent incidents. The system was then able to build a database containing profiles of offenders, victims and violent incidents.

Detectives also used 'geographic profiling', a relatively new investigative tool that was developed in the 1990s by former Canadian detective inspector Kim Rossmo.

The system is based on research showing that the hunting methods used by African lions matched almost perfectly the predatory movements of a serial killer. Lions look for weaker prey—very young animals, or old or injured animals. They wait at a watering hole, because they know that other animals will come there to drink. 'We see that all the time with criminal offenders,' said Kim Rossmo. 'They go to target-rich environments to do their hunting. Spatial patterns are produced by serial killers as they search and attack.'

The profiling system has had some notable successes in Canada and the us, even tracing one serial killer to within half a mile of his home. It works on the basis that most serial criminals operate fairly close to home. 'Criminals are like any other human beings in that they develop a pattern,' said Rossmo. 'The activity in people's lives tends to be around their home or their work. For example, if you're in your office, you're likely to buy your coffee and your newspaper in the same places all the time. You don't go halfway across town to get a cup of coffee, because that's inconvenient. Criminals and serial killers are no different. They have patterns.'

However, neither the vclas system nor the application of geographic profiling succeeded in throwing up any clue as to the identity of the killer—or killers—of the women.

The Operation Trace Unit also applied 'victimology' to the victims. This involved a microscopic investigation of the women's lives in an effort to see if there was any common link between them.

'We looked at what schools they went to, dance classes, music classes, sports clubs, distant relatives, everything,' said Detective Sergeant Alan Bailey, who spent many years working with Operation Trace. 'But there was nothing to link them. It was almost strange that we didn't find a link, because Ireland is so small and people tend to know each other. But there was nothing there.'

It was noted by Professor Max Taylor from the Applied Psychology Department of ucc that the women tended to disappear at certain common times of the year, particularly November to December, February to March, and July. He also noted that the number of disappearances were 'accelerating' in that there had been only one every couple of years, and now they were occurring at about two a year.

The detectives looked at the timing and dates of the disappearances in an effort to establish if there was any pattern to the crimes.

They checked the phases of the moon against the days the women disappeared, to see if any link might be established.

Every possibility was explored by detectives, but to their frustration none of it produced any concrete results. However, they did succeed in determining that the disappearances of Fiona Sinnott, Ciara Breen and Fiona Pender appeared to be entirely independent incidents.

'We have prime suspects for each of those cases, and we're pretty much satisfied that they had no link to each other or any of the other disappearances,' said one detective. 'But with the other cases, we just couldn't seem to get a break.'

Then, two years after Operation Trace was established, one of the most violent rapists in Ireland finally came to the attention of the Gardaí—35-year-old carpenter Larry Murphy was caught in the midst of his violent assault on a young woman in the Wicklow Mountains.

As soon as the officers at Baltinglass Garda Station heard the full details of the attack, they immediately contacted the Trace Unit, informing them that they had just arrested a brutally violent man with a very interesting modus operandi.

The detectives reviewed the details of Murphy's crime with a terrible, growing excitement. It seemed clear from the calm, organised way in which he had carried out the attack that Murphy must have offended before. 'It bore all the hallmarks of someone who had experience,' said one detective. 'Very few people would be capable of carrying out an attack like that without ever having committed a similar offence before.'

However, an investigation into his past found that Murphy had no previous convictions, although detectives noted with interest the unreported incident involving his wife's friend, and the inappropriate behaviour towards the local woman in the pub. The more they learnt about Murphy, the more he seemed to fit the profile of a potential serial killer.

'Certainly, a person who committed a crime like that which Larry Murphy committed, you'd have to look at him,' said Detective Sergeant Alan Bailey. 'We know he was a loner and that he was not very popular in his community. We know that women found him intimidating, but not physically. And we know that he was capable of very effectively abducting a woman.'

In the course of their enquiries, the investigation team from Operation Trace then discovered some very significant information.

Just days before the teenage girl went missing in Kildare, Larry Murphy had been working as a roofing contractor on a house in the area.

'We could put him there before she went missing, but there was no work being done on the house on the day she went missing,' said one detective. 'Having said that, Larry Murphy was that type of a predator that he could easily have gone back there on his own.'

Conscious that they now had a tenuous link between Murphy and at least one of the Trace cases, the detectives began casting the net wider. Rumours abounded that Murphy had also been doing building work on Johnny Fox's pub around the time Annie McCarrick disappeared, but after extensive investigation the detectives are now satisfied that this was definitely not the case.

They turned then to the disappearance of Jo Jo Dullard. They knew that Larry Murphy was living very close to where Jo Jo had disappeared on that fateful November night in 1995. Was it he who had picked her up outside the phone box in Moone? Or did he come across her in Castledermot, and find himself unable to pass such a vulnerable target?

'We tried in every possible way to find out if he had been driving around the area the night Jo Jo Dullard went missing,' said one detective who worked closely with the Trace unit. 'We did house-to-house enquiries and we went back to see if we could put him in any place on that road on that particular night. We checked every pub to see if he might have dropped in for a pint. But we just could not definitively place him in the area.'

Finding a link between Murphy and the other Trace cases seemed even less likely, although there was one obvious similarity between the murder of Antoinette Smith and Murphy's attack on the business-woman—the use of the plastic bag to cause suffocation.

'There was a plastic bag used in the Antoinette Smith case, but it might have just presented itself as an opportunistic weapon, rather than have been a pre-chosen device to kill,' said Detective Sergeant Alan Bailey. 'It's not strong enough to prove anything, certainly.'

With the recent success of the Phyllis Murphy case still fresh in their minds, detectives then hoped that science might help them to tie Murphy to any of the missing women. They located and confiscated all the cars Murphy had ever owned and sent them for forensic examination. Each vehicle was stripped down and thoroughly examined for any trace of forensic evidence, but none was found.

Officers then requested permission to visit Murphy in Arbour Hill prison, to ask him directly if he had any involvement with any of the missing women.

'He didn't say a word,' said one senior detective. 'Unfortunately for us, he was just very smart. He went into that courtroom and pleaded guilty to his crime and never said another word about his activities to anyone. I hate to say it, but I think if he is linked to anything else it seems the only way we're going to find out is if he confesses. And he's simply not going to do that.'

While the failure to tie Murphy to any of the other crimes was a set-back, some officers took a pragmatic view of the situation. 'You know, it's quite possible that the only reason we haven't found a link is because there is no link,' said one detective. 'There was a lot of talk and specu-lation about Larry Murphy being "the man", but we have looked at hun-dreds of suspects for these crimes, and it's entirely possible that any one of them could be our guy. Murphy was certainly not the only suspect.'

Indeed, some of the most violent and notorious criminals in Ireland have been investigated by Operation Trace.

Among them is John Crerar, whom many detectives believe would not have been able to control his murderous impulses following his attack on Phyllis Murphy. 'Crerar was walking around a free man for twenty years before we caught him,' said one detective. 'And in that time he thought that he had got away with committing murder. That would have made him confident. We haven't found anything concrete to link him to any other attacks, but he's still of interest to us.'

It has been suggested that in fact John Crerar and Larry Murphy may have worked together, feeding off each other's appetite for violence. However, this has been considered and rejected by Trace detectives. 'I doubt very much that they ever worked as a team,' said one detective who used to work with the unit. 'Murphy was an excel-lent carpenter, Crerar was a former solider. There was a big age gap between the two. I don't think they would ever have been in the same circles, to facilitate a meeting between them.'

When Michael Bambrick was arrested for the murder and dis-memberment of two women in Ronanstown in Dublin, he was considered by the Operation Trace unit, but the fact that he didn't own a car made him an unlikely suspect.

When Robert Quigley was arrested for his attack on the young woman in the Dublin Mountains in 2006, he too was added to the list of possible offenders. However, his age was his alibi—he would have been only 13 when Annie McCarrick went missing and just 15 when Jo Jo Dullard disappeared.

The Trace detectives also looked very closely at one of the most prolific rapists ever to roam Irish shores—Robert Howard.

Born in Wolfhill in Co. Laois, Howard had committed a horrific litany of rapes, sexual assaults and murder over his lifetime. The 63-year-old is currently serving a life sentence in Frankland Prison in Durham for the rape and murder of a 14-year-old schoolgirl, Hannah Williams, in 2001. He is also the only suspect for the murder of 15-year-old Arlene Arkinson in 1994. He is known to have attempted to rape a six-year-old child in 1965, a young woman in 1969 and an older woman in 1973. In 1991 he held a 22-year-old woman captive in his caravan in Co. Tyrone for several weeks, raping her repeatedly, and in 1993 he abused a 16-year-old girl at his flat in Castlederg.

Howard appears to have been beset by violent impulses since his youth. When he was 16 his father threw him out of the family home and the young man spent some time living rough. One local man later discovered some cans and blankets in his father's hayshed, suggesting Howard had slept there. Among the debris, the man found Howard's diary, in which he had made entries about his fantasy of breaking into women's houses while they were in the bath and attacking them.

Howard was arrested for many of his crimes. Every time, he went to prison and was eventually released. And every time he was set free, he attacked again. He moved easily between the Republic of Ireland, the North and Great Britain. Despite his violent past, his movements were rarely monitored and liaison between the police forces in the different countries was minimal. For most of his adult life, Robert Howard has prowled both Irish and British countryside, attacking, raping, and sometimes killing women.

While he has finally been given a life sentence for one of his crimes, detectives are now extremely interested in finding out more about his past. Shortly after his most recent arrest, police from Northern Ireland, England and the Republic of Ireland held a one-day conference in Dublin to discuss other crimes with which he might be connected.

For the investigation team at Operation Trace, their interest lay in whether Howard could be linked to the disappearance of any of the women in the Leinster region. However, because of his habit of constantly moving around, unnoticed by authorities, it has proven difficult to determine whether he was in the area when any of the women went missing.

There is also the fact that Howard generally seemed to ingratiate himself into the lives of his victims before launching his attack, a modus operandi which does not fit with the apparent random nature of the Trace cases.

'His MO was somewhat different to what seems to have happened in the cases of the women we were looking at,' said Detective Sergeant Alan Bailey. 'He befriended his victims or his victim's families before attacking them. Having said that, we are certainly continuing to look at him. He has persistently offended against women, and given his proclivities he would have to be a suspect for us.'

While the team at Operation Trace was actively looking for suspects, at one point a well-known child serial killer came looking for them.

Clifford Robert Olsen rang Baltinglass Garda Station from his prison cell in Quebec in Canada, claiming to have vital information for the Operation Trace detectives. He said that a friend of his, who had since died, had murdered five of the missing women and that he, Olsen, knew where they were buried.

Olsen is one of the most notorious serial killers in Canada, and is currently serving a life sentence for killing eleven children during the seventies and eighties. Initially, given his gruesome reputation, detectives treated his claims seriously. However, after some investigation it emerged that Olsen had gathered information about Operation Trace from the Internet, and was simply indulging his own fantasy of being involved in the crimes. Another possible lead ended in nothing.

The Operation Trace Unit is still active, but to date the investigating team has failed to find any link between the cases of Annie McCarrick, Antoinette Smith, Patricia Doherty, Eva Brennan, Jo Jo Dullard or the teenage girl from Kildare.

'Commonality is what we need, and so far we've found none,' said Detective Superintendent John McMahon, who is currently heading up the unit. 'There is no evidence at all to link the cases. But we'll keep trying, obviously. We just need that one break, and that could do it.'

While the Operation Trace unit continues to search for that elusive link, in the adjoining office at Harcourt Terrace a relatively new unit has been established to look at unsolved cases from the last twenty-five years. It's officially called the Serious Crime Review Unit, but is more commonly known as the Cold Case Unit.

Having been set up in 2007, the cold case team of eight detectives has been charged with reviewing over 200 serious unsolved crimes dating back to the 1980s. Each member of the team has vast experience with murder cases, and has attended a training course in the UK on the specific techniques required when reviewing cases.

Recently the unit has re-opened the case of Antoinette Smith in the hope of finding something new in the files that might point to her killers.

'We'll completely review the case, take our time with it, and hopefully something will emerge,' said Detective Superintendent Christy Mangan, who is leading the team. 'There is still a very good chance of solving cases now, even those which are twenty years old. It depends entirely on the case in question. We're working on a number at the moment which will hopefully yield results and already it looks like we will unearth new evidence in some of the cases.'

The team assigns a deadline of two to three months to each case. In that time, they thoroughly review all the documents in the file, ranging from witness statements to forensic reports to exhibits. If physical evidence has been retained in a case, and if it's in good condition, that case is given priority on the grounds that new DNA technology might help to substantially advance the investigation.

The statements of witnesses are also very important, according to Mangan.

'It's amazing how people have moved on from their old circle of friends over the last fifteen to twenty years, and this has proven very helpful to us,' he said. 'In some of the cases we've found people are much more willing to talk now because they don't have a personal involvement in the case. We're hoping that we'll find people who had important knowledge at the time, but who, for whatever reason, didn't come forward. There are always people out there who know something.'

With 200 unsolved cases awaiting their attention, and many more on the sidelines, the Cold Case Unit has a mammoth task ahead. However, Detective Superintendent Christy Mangan is confident that through perseverance and hard work they will succeed in solving some of these crimes. Killers will be caught. 'Every crime leaves a trace,' he says. 'It's our job to find it.'

Both Operation Trace and the Cold Case Unit will continue their investigations. If they get that vital break, maybe one or more of the murderers will be caught.

But for the families who are left behind, the damage cannot be repaired. Of those family members who spoke bravely to me about the loss of their loved one, a common, heartbreaking theme emerged. The pain does not go away.

In cases where the murderer has been arrested, the family has to deal with the horror of knowing the gruesome truth about what happened to their sister or daughter or mother or wife. Where the killer has not yet been caught, the family is left with the ache of wanting to see him brought to justice. Where a woman has simply vanished, the family must battle with the devastating images of what might have happened to her. But in all the cases, whatever the outcome, the common theme is pain.

And through it all, the Dublin/Wicklow Mountains, which have been host to so much violence and horror and death, loom large over the people of Leinster. Honor Bright's murder is marked by a plaque near where she was killed, and fresh flowers are regularly left there in her memory. But for the other women, those who have been found and those who are still hidden, there are no fresh flowers, there is no plaque. Just the bog, and the forest, and the silence. Where no one heard them scream.